Ryan T. Pugh lives in North writing Christmas books.

His plans for retirement involve sitting next to a window all day, shaking his fist at passers-by and knocking angrily on the glass.

He is unmarried but has a bit of a thing for Cate Blanchett.

What the critics say:

'The funniest part was the price - he must think we're made of money'
Bill Gates

'The literary equivalent of *Stay Another Day*'
Marina Hyde

'Ergo, errare humanum est, if you'll permit the jest'
Jacob Rees-Mogg

'Tonight, thank God it's him, instead of you'
Bono

'Not if I was the last woman on Middle Earth'
Cate Blanchett

Also available

Semi-Professional Writer
Kismet Quick - A Norfolk Odyssey
Amusements

Find out more at ryantpugh.co.uk

Stocking Filler

Ryan T. Pugh

To,

Coral & Co.

Something for your
Christmas 'Cravings'

Love,

Ryan T. Pugh x

Boo-Boo-Books

The moral right of Ryan T. Pugh has been asserted. First published in Great Britain in 2019 by Boo-Boo-Books.

ISBN:
- 9781093608663 -

Contact: ryantpugh@outlook.com

Cover by Sarah Ann Corlett

For Dan & Joanna Harvey - on their interdependence day

Contents

'You know something, sweetheart? Christmas is, well, it's about the best time of the whole year. You walk down the streets, even for weeks before Christmas comes, and there's lights hanging up, green ones and red ones. Sometimes there's snow, and everybody's hustling someplace. But they don't hustle around Christmastime like they usually do. You know, they're a little more friendly. They bump into you, they laugh and they say "Pardon me" and "Merry Christmas". Especially when it gets real close to Christmas night. Everybody's walking home, you can hardly hear a sound. Bells are ringing, kids are singing, snow is coming down.

And, boy, what a pleasure it is to think that you got some place to go to. And the place that you're going to has somebody in it that you really love. Someone you're nuts about.

Merry Christmas.'

Jackie Gleeson, *The Honeymooners*, ''Twas The Night Before Christmas', 1955

'Like all intelligent people, I greatly dislike Christmas.'

George Bernard Shaw, 1893

introduction

Well, now. Fancy seeing *you* here. I never knew *you* loved Christmas, too.

Embarrassing, isn't it? Not very hip. You might just as well say you're infatuated with curtain rails or announce that you're chairperson of the Savage Garden fanclub. You'll probably have to hide this book come the new year, tucking it discreetly behind the row of internationally revered literary fiction on your IKEA bookshelf.

Anything to stop people from knowing your shame.

The reason why it's humiliating to admit you love Christmas is this: by doing so, you're effectively declaring that you're a bit soft in the head. You're admitting that you either believe in things like fairy-dust and the nativity story (as I do), or that you're a sucker for capitalism (as I am). Such confessions are unlikely to draw much approval. Neither mental negligence nor consumerism shall ever be in vogue. Except on ITV2 reality shows set in and around Essex.

Not that virgin births and till-receipts are the only causes of a yuletide obsession. More often than not, we festive fruitcakes are so darned fruitcakingly festive because we had the sumptuous flavours of Christmas kneaded into our doughy brains during childhood. I don't know about you, but my Christmases were a toy-laden dream in otherwise barren years. It was the only time we had an excess of food in the house, the only time I ever saw a pineapple that didn't come from a tin.[1] It was the only time my family all sat around the same table to eat (and, by default, the only time we'd use the one table big enough *to* seat us all). Nothing else in the calendar compared to Christmas. Birthdays were its closest rival, but they belonged to the individual. After the initial present opening, the rest of your birthday was a hard-sell, having to inform adults that today was *your* special day:

'Oh, is it?' they'd reply, betraying a look which suggested they weren't wholly sold on the date's significance. 'How lovely for you.'

Christmas, meanwhile, was a communal celebration. The whole world rejoiced.

OK, maybe not the whole world. Far from it, in truth. In 1984, a heavenly throng of drugged-up haircuts famously posed the question 'Do they know it's Christmas time?' The answer was, and is, on the whole, *no*. Around half of the global population generally neglect to celebrate Christ's birth on the valid basis that most of them have never heard of him. Even in ostensibly Christian countries such as ours, things are far from clear-cut. Not everybody who *knows it's Christmas time* is fully on-board

---

[1] The pineapple invariably remained uneaten on the basis that nobody quite knew how best to approach it. It lay in the fruit-bowl like a hand-grenade.

with the idea of setting aside each December 25th to *let in light*, *banish shade* and what-have-you.

The cliché would be to liken Christmas to Marmite, but perhaps it's more apt to liken it to the Coffee Cream found in tins of Cadbury's Roses during the 1990s. You either love it, or it makes the linings of your stomach quiver.[1] This is my fourth book and I don't think I've ever had such a polarised reaction to a project. It has easily garnered the highest number of pre-orders, with some merry individuals requesting multiple copies to give as gifts:

'Put me down for twelve!'

Yet it's also elicited the most frequent statements of savage *un*intent:

'Yes, well, I won't be buying *that* one.'

Just as you can see a Christmas lover's smile broaden at mere mention of the season, so you can also see a fiery grimace brew on its detractors. Their eyes almost cave into their soul when you cheerily remind them that there are just ninety-six shopping days left. Despite this, the fact remains that from the dippiest of festive fairies to the most gnarled of grinches, nearly everybody has an idea of how Christmas should be done *just so*. And one thing almost universally agreed on between fairies and grinches is that Christmas has lost its meaning, whatever we think that meaning is/was.

Getting to the bottom of what it is people expect from Christmas is tricky. As you'll see in these pages, the idea that Christmas was once a passionately observed religious celebration, or a time of communities peacefully coming together in a spirit of goodwill, is largely codswallop. No such Eden has ever existed. By the time Jesus himself got to his first birthday, the Nazarene locals were already complaining that

---

[1] The Coffee Cream has made a comeback in recent years. It's been reshaped and given the wonderfully grandiose name 'Coffee Escape'.

Christmas wasn't what it was and that Quality Street tins weren't as big as they used to be. The oldest Christmas tradition of them all is the tradition of believing that Christmas has lost its sense of tradition.

As far as I can tell - and, believe me, I've read reams of dreary conjecture on the subject - the idea of a family-centred, publicly-celebrated Christmas truly came to life at some point in the 1960s, possibly as a result of the growing popularity of that small box of tricks called the television. Never before had such a vast audience been shown, rather than told, how Christmas could be done. Decades on, television has left people with a hazy perception of Christmas as a time of family, gifts, roasted poultry, carols, little donkeys, and lonely old pensioners who stare at one-bar electric fires. Fittingly, it is telly addict Abed from the American sitcom *Community* who, for my money, gives the best summary of the season:

'The meaning of Christmas is the idea that Christmas *has* meaning - and it can mean whatever we want.'

Seventeen centuries on from the Roman invention of Christmas,[1] that's what we've been left with. An empty meaning to fill as we see fit.

With all this in mind, you might be wondering just what angle this book intends to approach Christmas from. And why it's so bloody big, considering the pithiness suggested in its title. I'll come to the second point in a minute, but regarding the first, this is a book, by and large, about the *British* Christmas experience, its traditions and its quirks. There are chapters about Christmas songs and Christmas films, as well as a diary which I kept in the run-up to last year's big day. There is also an alphabet of Christmas in which I cover as much festive trivia as possible. Not very original? No. The world doesn't need another potted festive history, yet here I am presenting it with one,

---

[1] Yeah! How's *that* for a teaser?

expecting my offering to draw surprise upon being unwrapped. If this book *does* have a new angle, it's that it swoons over modern Christmas in a way that's likely to do its author no favours in terms of finding a wife.[1]

 Perhaps, then, it might help clear things up to state what this book *isn't*. It *isn't* aspirational or twee. It *doesn't* contain a traveller's guide to kooky continental Christmas markets. It *doesn't* have tips for how to make snowman-shaped bunting, nor offer up any recipes for stollen or a coeliac-friendly panettone. You *won't* hear me suggesting ways to spruce up the home come December, recommending you leave a sprinkling of dried orange zest in your hallway to give your house that inviting Christmas tang. What you'll be getting is bountiful pub quiz fodder and jokes about yule logs.

 The bountiful pub quiz fodder, by the way, is why the book is so bloody big. I meant it to be half the size, but I couldn't stop finding ridiculous facts. It could easily have been *twice* as thick still. I urge you not to be put off by its length, however. This book is there to be dipped into. I don't expect anyone will read it from beginning to end (although I have included a number of long-running gags for those foolhardy enough to attempt such a feat). In hindsight, I should've offered a promotional deal of the kind you see in yankee roadside diners, where the bill is negated if the customer can eat all of their 8lb steak without bursting the wall of their stomach. Anybody bold enough to read every page of *Stocking Filler* ought to get their money back.[2]

---

[1] As you shall see, however, there are plenty of things about the modern Christmas that I feel decidedly grumpy about.

[2] Let me make it quite clear that they *won't*, however.

Before we start, a quick word about the music chapters.

My aim was to discuss Christmas songs which were either deserving of a wider audience or had back-stories worth recounting. Some Christmas songs - and their origins - are so well known, due to the outpouring of attention they get each year,[1] that to add further discourse seemed a fool's errand. I'm talking about the mega-hits here: Slade, Mariah Carey, Nat King Cole, Bing Crosby, Wham![2] et al. Songs that have been so drained of nourishment they struggle to bear festive fruit. That's not to say the twelve songs I *have* written about are rare and artsy fartsy. Most people will know most of them (although I'd like to think I may alert a few readers to the existence of some). Nor, might I stress, are they necessarily my twelve favourites. They are, instead, twelve *of* my favourites - and are listed in no particular order.

I'd have loved to have included a bit more about Christmas movies, but, and this may be a controversial statement, there aren't many good ones out there. Once you've reeled off the obvious classics - *Elf*, *Home Alone*, *White Christmas*, *It's A Wonderful Life* - the selection thins. This is why I've written about Christmas films *and* Christmas TV, and, in some instances, films and TV which aren't strictly Christmas-themed but which exude the spirit of the season.

Oh, goodness, my friend, you'll be a walking yuletide trivia machine by the end of it all. (Well, until January, when you

---

[1] Mainly on Channel 5 documentaries called *'The Greatest Christmas Songs Ever!!'*, which feature talking heads of a calibre even local radio would sneer at.

[2] I love that Wham! have an exclamation mark in their name. P!nk has one, too. Then there's Therapy? with their hideous question mark. I'd like to start a band with a semi-colon after our name, and an unclosed quotation mark. It would drive the pedants crazy: 'Grammar Boyz;

forget everything.) You'll never look at Christmas the same way again. You may never look at me the same way again, either. Because, as always, there's plenty of me on show betwixt these covers. That wasn't my intention. I can't help it, though. Hand me a pen and watch my ego swell. As ever, my hope is that by holding a mirror to myself, other people might catch their equally silly festive reflections in it, too.

Right. Less of this metaphysical cobblers. Let's get the bauble rolling. As the jolly old Ghost of Christmas Present hollered to Scrooge whilst surrounded by choice meats in one of the upper rooms, 'Come in! Come in! And know me better, man!'

Ryan, October, 2019

Note On The Text

This book contains a lot of 'facts'. The reason for the inverted commas is that, where Christmas is concerned, nobody can agree on anything. Even the church can't get its story straight, which, considering they've had about two millennia to do so, is quite an achievement. Almost every book, documentary, article or essay addressing the *history of the season* has a different take on events. Particularly troublesome are the more recent surveys of our contemporary Christmas habits and tastes; they have a tendency to offer wildly conflicting views of just what Christmas means to the modern Briton. As a result, any such findings are best taken with a pinch of icing sugar. I've done my best to sift through the numbers and, where appropriate, generally use statistics or facts that I believe most likely to reflect reality.

 Like all authors of Christmas books before me – those giants on whose shoulders I loiter – I'll do my best to challenge the myths and to realign the wonky narrative.

 No promises, though.

 I've also been incredibly loose with how I've alphabetised my, well, alphabet. This was purely an attempt to divvy things up satisfactorily.

The Christmas Alphabet

A is for...

Advent Calendars

Those 17th century Lutherans, eh? Absolute party animals. When they weren't busy depicting Christ's ascension in tapestry form, or learning key passages from Paul's dispatches to the Corinthians by rote, they were doing even crazier things, such as silently contemplating the meaning of predestination and inventing advent calendars.

The nutters.

Rather than making the sort of multicoloured, chocolate-packed advent calendars we're familiar with today, however, the Lutherans took a more sober approach. Being altogether easier to please, the children of Lutheran households would mark the arrival of each day in advent by scratching a fresh line of chalk onto a doorframe. The excitement was such that they required sedating shortly afterwards.

The earliest known *physical* advent calendars, of a style somewhat more recognisable to the modern reader, were made of wood and are thought to date back to the 1850s. As with a great number of entrants in this laugh-a-minute alphabet, though, the historical details are sketchy. The first *professionally* produced advent calendar, however, was almost certainly that designed by a Munich printmaker - who, I'd like to think, managed to wangle a hefty staff discount on cardboard - at the remarkably late date of 1908.[1] He based the idea on the paper calendars his mother used to make for him as a child, complete with little windows and hidden sweets. Germany went wild for his innovation, buying advent calendars by the tonne and hastily wiping all traces of chalk from their doorframes. As well we know, a few decades on from 1908, the people of Germany went wilder still, the upshot of which being World War Two. During the conflict, it was decided that precious resources such as cardboard couldn't be wasted on frivolities, temporarily halting the mass-production of advent calendars in the Fatherland.[2]

Just as a portrait of Queen Victoria larking around her Christmas tree had once sent sales of firs sky-rocketing,[3] so a photograph of US president, Dwight D. Eisenhower, opening an advent calendar with his grandchildren would provide a similar commercial spike. Such was the General's popularity by Christmas, 1953 - and in spite of the photographs in question

---

[1] Although some even argue about this, claiming that the first calendar was made in Hamburg in 1902. The argument has never been satisfactorily settled, largely on account of no one caring. What *is* agreed, though, is that these commercial calendars enforced the misconception that advent begins on December 1st, when, technically, it begins on whichever Sunday happens to be closest to Nov 30th (i.e. St Andrew's Day).

[2] This didn't stop the Nazis making a small selection of their very own propaganda advent calendars, though. Instead of reindeer and snowscapes, theirs featured pictures of torpedoed Allied ships and exploding Russian tanks. It was all part of their plan to replace Christianity with secularism, which, I'm happy to report, went about as well as all their other plans.

[3] Which you'll read about later. There's just so much to look forward to!

revealing that his grandchildren were distinctly underwhelmed by the calendar (one of the poor mites, in particular, looks as though she's reading her own obituary rather than partaking in a gleeful Christmas tradition) - the images sparked a mad rush for the product Stateside. It wouldn't be long before the rest of the western world muscled in on the craze.

The first chocolate advent calendars came along in post-ration-book bonanza of the late 1950s, but our own dear Cadbury's didn't enter the fray until 1971. Surprisingly, from that point on, Cadbury's still only made chocolate calendars intermittently, missing many years out altogether. Only as late as 1993 did they stub out their fags, roll up their sleeves, and commit to producing a new chocolate effort every December.[1]

Strictly speaking, from a Christian point of view, the period of advent is supposed to focus just as much on Jesus' glorious return as it is his birth (although this tradition has largely fallen by the wayside). As if to prove my point, the very word 'advent' originates from the Latin *adventus*, meaning 'arrival' or 'coming'.[2]

I told you this would be fun, didn't I?

Annuals

What childhood Christmas stocking would be complete without an annual of some sort? The Victorians had coal and

---

[1] Cadbury's now ensure that the last few windows on their calendars - 22nd, 23rd, 24th, 25th - are placed over their logo, leaving their brand name displayed for as long as possible throughout December. It's what the Lutherans would've wanted.

[2] Please try and remember this fact. I plan to use it in a joke later on.

oranges as a yuletide staple, we have selection boxes and *The Beano Book*.

The archetypal annual is hard-backed, A4-size and full of comic strips, posters (that are almost impossible to remove), and coaster-sized wordsearches that even the most bird-brained child can complete without throwing a festive paddy. Although usually focusing on big hitters such as *Paw Patrol* and *Barbie*, all sorts of niche tastes have been satiated by these publications over the years, from *The Paul Daniels Magic Annual* to 1981's *Master The Rubik Cube Easily*. The genre arguably peaked with the outstandingly specialist tome *Rick Astley vs Jason Donovan 1989* (which, sadly, contained a lot less bloodshed that its title promised).

When new annuals hit bookstore shelves each autumn, they appear with a glossy freshness, a positive promise of the year to come. In the run-up to Christmas, their popularity soars. Then, as the year on their cover comes into being, they get lumped into a lowly basket by the shop door - 'Wow! All Annuals 99p!' - and lie there through January, outcasts from the publishing world.

It's the dates that age them so:

'*Dandy Annual 2019*[1]*... David Cassidy 1976... Repressed Schoolgirl 1958...*'

Imagine if it were customary to attach the year of our birth to our own names. We'd sound equally ancient:

'Hi. Nice to meet you. I'm Ryan Pugh 1983.'

---

[1] *The Dandy* ceased to be a weekly publication in 2012 - as a result of sales dropping to around 7,500 a fortnight from their once gargantuan *weekly* reach of two million in the 1950s - but there *is* still a hardback annual produced every year.

(Quick fun fact: why was *The Dandy* called '*The Dandy*'? Because it was made in Dundee.)

We wouldn't stand a chance. Youngsters would stick us in nursing homes by the age of forty, force-feeding us mashed roughage and loudly enquiring whether we've taken our morning dose of levothyroxine yet.

Usually if a book is popular, it stays popular, for at least a while.[1] The quick death of annuals bucks that trend. And yet, they *can* get a second wind. Within thirty years or so of publication, annuals develop a tongue-in-cheek, retro charm, turning up in those bizarre upmarket charity shops which specialise in over-charging. Some annuals are so revered they get put up at auction, sold to the man with the twitch for £2,000.[2] There's hope for *The Paul Daniels Magic Annual* yet.

If you're wondering whether the rest of the world partakes in this annual purchasing of annuals, the answer is no. Like mince pies and the voice of Noddy Holder, their appeal is yet to leave the island. Although how long until annuals disappear altogether is a matter of concern. Sales have halved in the last decade alone. With Britain's current international relations, we may be back on coal and orange stocking-fillers in the not-too-distant future anyway.

At least it'll be retro.

---

[1] One exception is when the author falls out of public favour, generally as the result of some scandal or other, and sees their sales plummet. The best example of this has to be Lance Armstrong's autobiography, *It's Not About The Bike*, which, we have since discovered, could arguably have been renamed, *It's Primarily About The Drugs*.

[2] Two of the biggest such auctions have taken place in the last year (in the market town of Aylsham - in your hero's home county, Norfolk, no less). An original 1938 *Dandy* annual sold for £1,250 in 2019, just one year after a copy of the first ever *Beano* annual went for £2,700.

Artificial Trees

'Buying an artificial tree is like buying junk food.'
Roger Hay, British Christmas Tree Growers Association

Considering most things in this alphabet originate in either Germany or the 19th century, it should come as little surprise that artificial trees stem from both Germany *and* the 19th century.

The original artificial trees, of a 19th century German vintage, were produced to quell deforestation. Oddly, they were made out of wood and covered in goose feathers. Regardless of the fact that making an artificial tree out of wood is a bit like making a vegan sausage out of a pig, the trees' popularity meant that they were soon being sold in the United States, where their commercial fate was sealed. They didn't, however, take off in the UK until as late as the 1930s. With a gorgeously British lack of pizazz, our first mass produced artificial trees were made by a company who specialised in toilet brushes. The company used their inside knowledge of bristles to create faux pine needles that were both frightfully unrealistic *and* sturdy enough to give your loo a good post-season-of-plenty going over.[1]

Around two million artificial trees are now sold in the UK each year. According to a 2018 survey conducted by Admiral Insurance - yep, weird - three times more people purchase artificial trees than real ones. Yet, regardless of their popularity,

---

[1] The company's name is Addis and they're still going strong. Your current bog brush was probably made by them. Their proudest contribution to British history, according to their website, is to have made popular the notion of owning a toothbrush in the early 1900s. No mean feat considering how, at that time, the interior of the average British mouth looked worse than that of the average British water-closet.

6

mention to somebody that you have a fake tree and, unless the person you're talking to also has one, the response tends to be along these lines:

'Oh, you hateful, pathetic waste of flesh. You disgust me. I actually feel a little sick just talking to you.'

With nature very much the order of the day, we're now only permitted to like artificial things on the condition that we do so ironically, as a guilty pleasure. As the above quote from the chap at the British Christmas Tree Growers Association[1] testifies, artificial trees are the McDonald's Big Mac Meal of the Christmas world. Junk food for the soul. Well, to hell with those sneering cabbage-munchers. Let me say it now: *I* have a big fake Christmas tree and I adore it. I love its perfect shape, height and sturdiness. I even love the way it sheds the occasional papery pine needle onto the carpet. Granted, it doesn't smell the same as a real tree, but it does have an equally beautiful festive scent, a cross between tinsel and the Christmas section of a garden centre. And, unlike real trees, it never reeks of cat wee at the base.[2]

Ultimately, any 'real vs fake' debate is irrelevant. When a tree is up and decorated, when the room is dark and when the string of electric lights is flicked on at the wall, it doesn't matter whether the tree was grown on a Hampshire farm or factory-packed in the Guangdong Province. The duel between pure and artificial, like the duel between Rick Astley and Jason Donovan, is lost to time. All that matters is that, for the next few weeks, your home will be in Christmas mode.

---

[1] Just imagine what their meetings are like.

[2] The argument over whether artificial trees are worse for the environment than real ones is ongoing. It's thought you'd need to use a fake tree ten times for it to become environmentally sound. A not unreasonable goal, given you don't buy it from Argos.

B is for...

Bad Jumpers

Go make an angel layin' out in the snow
You know it keeps you warm wherever you go
You waited all year long
To put your ugly Christmas sweater on

Wengie, *Ugly Christmas Sweater*, 2018

Not all traditions have yawn-inducing origins in Germany or the 19th century, mind. Some are bold and bright and fresh as a holly sprig.[1] The tongue-in-cheek wearing of wacky jumpers is one such example of a new festive trend.[2] Already something of a standard for those in the know, sales of the things were sent due north in 2012 when Save The Children created an official fundraising Christmas Jumper Day.

The proliferation of 'bad jumpers' has reached such an extent that you can now purchase them at most major clothing retailers. Go into any branch of Debenhams or Next and you'll see them there, with their knowingly over-snazzy weaves and pictures of *Star Wars* characters wearing Santa hats. The children in the Bangladeshi sweatshops can barely keep up with demand – it's no wonder they need saving. Not that UK children get away scot-free. Figures reported by *Tes* in 2019 suggested that children from poorer backgrounds were

---

[1] The festive association of which *did* have its origins in Germany, I regret to announce. Damn those sprigs.

[2] The jumpers were once known affectionately, Stateside, as 'Cosby sweaters', after Bill Cosby's sitcom knitwear. However, after recent events involving Dr Cosby, the jumpers are now known by the less pithy name, 'Inmate Number NN7687 sweaters'.

8

overwhelmingly absent from school on Christmas Jumper Day due, most likely, to the shame of not being able to afford sarcastic items of clothing to complement their non-sarcastic ones.

How did this tradition start? Hard to tell. *Bridget Jones's Diary* played a part, specifically the scene with Colin Firth wearing a bright green jumper with Rudolph on the front.[1] The rise of social media and, with it, the ability to share photographic evidence of oneself dressed as the 'life and soul' of the office must have helped, too. Such are the jumpers' ubiquity, vlogging pop sensation Wengie[2] released a song about them in 2018.[3]

The joke - if we're feeling agreeable enough to call it that - of bad festive jumpers abruptly ends on one's first visit to the post-Christmas retail sales. For in most clothes stores at the turn of the year, it isn't long before you'll find the very same jumper you bought way back in November. Except, this time, instead of taking up a well-lit position by the entrance and costing £29, it's on a lonesome rail, abused by the scavenging hands of many, with a red tag on its shoulder quoting an all-new price of £4.

Box, Christmas Eve

Concerning the modern Christmas, two things are generally agreed upon. The first is that children simply don't get enough presents. The second is that the season isn't sufficiently costly

---

[1] A joke that got a *huge* laugh in cinemas at the time but which now, like the rest of that film, looks as distant and aged as those surviving discoloured flickers of soundless footage from Victoria's jubilee.

[2] Google her. Actually, don't.

[3] Google it. Actually, don't.

for parents.[1] As a way to address these vital issues, a recent addition to the childhood Christmas experience has been conjured up: the Christmas Eve Box.

A typical Christmas Eve Box is supposed to contain, in the words of one *Daily Mirror* feature, 'small things' such as pyjamas and books, DVDs and games. Things that *I* myself would consider quite considerable gifts. The idea is that the boxes are homemade and lovingly crafted, although, as an article in *The Sun* assures us, Matalan also offer a 'gorgeous selection' of ready-made ones.

'To do the boxes on a budget,' continues *The Sun*, 'plenty of mums just grab cardboard boxes and cover them in festive wrapping paper.'

Well done, mums.[2]

This soon-to-be UK tradition is already a tradition in the USA. The idea mysteriously took hold here in 2016 and has become progressively popular each year since. But, for all its ostensibly yankee traits, scratch below the surface and you'll see that its roots grew in a more familiar patch of turf. The Christmas Eve Box is, says one *Daily Telegraph* piece, 'understood to be borne of the *German* tradition of opening presents on Christmas Eve'.

---

[1] If only. Generally, people spend around a *quarter* of their annual outlay in December. Figures from early 2019 suggest that just over one in *ten* people in Britain took out payday loans for at least some of their 2018 Christmas shopping (more than double the rate of people who did so in the USA, for comparison). The real problems start in January, however, when most workers have gone five weeks without an income and are expected to pay off their loans at a rate of around 6000% APR.

[2] Dads, meanwhile, are too busy for such frivolities, what with their hard day's graft at t'mill. The poor saps don't get home til late on Christmas Eve, and even then they just want to sup a pint o' best in their favourite chair, slipping the wife half a crown for her troubles.

Of course it is.

A likely reason that the Christmas Eve Box has become popular is that, rather than being a diplomatic attempt to honour the customs of our good friends from Germania, it instead satiates a child's noisy impatience at the thought of having to wait one whole night to open their 'main' presents. I'm not sure how good an idea all this is. Then again, maybe we do owe the kids something extra at this time of year. After all, the telly's crap now.

It might also serve us well to note these words from an essay in *Vanity Fair* magazine:

'In the good old days it was possible to give a child practically anything, and receive in return a gratitude which has now gone completely out of fashion. But for the modern child you have got to do better. You have got to dig down a bit.'

The article was written by a P. Brooke-Haven. It was one of the many pseudonyms used by the young P.G. Wodehouse. But that's not the important thing. The important thing is that it was written in 1915. Even in the good old days they were talking about 'the good old days' and how unsullied its youth were.

Oh, sod it. Let the children have their boxes.

Eat, drink and be merry.

And put a silly jumper on while you're at it.

Boxing Day

'By the lord Harry, I shall be undone here with Christmas boxes.'
Jonathan Swift, *Journal To Stella*, 1766

Although a day of torture for children, as they realise that it's another 364 sleeps until Christmas, Boxing Day is generally something of a joy for most adults. The pressure is off and the day is empty, but the riches of the season are still at hand. None more so than at the dinner table where the year's second finest meal is concocted. Christmas dinner gets all the glory, but the Boxing Day lunch is an unsung hero, loaded with gouty fodder: pickled onions, cold ham, cold turkey, beetroot, stilton, piccalilli, cold sausages, pork pies, tomatoes, breadsticks, coleslaw, lettuce (for show), fancy crisps, tiger bread, brie, cucumber, everything, *every* thing. And all stacked so high onto the plate that it would cause even the orphan Oliver himself to tentatively enquire, 'Please, Sir, could I not have quite so much?'

The name 'Boxing Day' is yet another of Victorian Britain's contributions to this alphabet, coming from the then-tradition of wealthy, cane-swinging citizens giving their knuckle-dragging inferiors alms boxes containing sweets, fruits and other gifts every December 26th. Likewise, in churches, cash collections at Christmas Day services were put into small boxes and handed out the following day to those who could affect the most convincing limp.[1]

The day's official title is, as we all know, St Stephen's Day (when Good King Wenceslas[2] 'first looked out') and remains primarily known as such by most Catholic-leaning countries. For those who don't have their copy of Eusebius' *History Of The Church* to hand, permit me to remind you that St Stephen was the first - and, in my opinion, best - Christian martyr. Stoned to death in AD34 for giving the Jerusalem townsfolk too much lip, it's believed that Stephen was an orator of such gift that his public talks enticed vast numbers to follow the teachings of another chap who'd recently met a sticky end in Jerusalem on account of having given the townsfolk too much lip. By the time

---

[1] These alms boxes get a mention in a range of literary classics, including *Cider With Rosie* and *Wuthering Heights*.

[2] Real name: Vaclav, Duke of Bohemia. But that doesn't scan as neatly.

Stephen was whipping up the masses, his beloved Jesus had only been dead just over a year, and whatever curious magic he'd performed was still causing very real political and spiritual unrest in the Holy City. Singing the Nazarene's praises could land you in trouble. Seeing as Nazarene-praise-singing happened to be one of Stephen's primary pastimes, it was inevitable the locals give him the opportunity to be with his mate Jesus on a more permanent basis.[1]

Quite suitably, given the method of his demise, Stephen was officially named the patron saint of headaches. It's equally apt for those who awake on his annual day of remembrance having over-done it with the port the night before.

---

[1] One 15th century English poem stated that they 'stoneth him with a stone'. Probably the best way to do it, though, to be fair.

The 12 Songs Of Christmas

#1

2000 Miles - The Pretenders

If ever a song didn't deserve to be piped through an overheated shopping centre on a boisterous November afternoon, it's *2000 Miles*. Even people who don't know the story behind The Pretenders' 1985 Christmas hit must struggle to fritter money away in a chainstore when it's playing, feeling it tug at the sleeve of their conscience. From the song's creeping fade-in jangle to its strummed final chord, *2000 Miles* has a sad undertow unbefitting a typical Christmas hit. Chrissie Hynde's wailing top line doesn't help matters:

He's go-horr-horr-horr-horr-hah-horn, two thousand mi-hi-hi-hi-hiles
It's very far

Once you *do* know the meaning behind her words, the curious melody and restless guitar line[1] acquire an additional doleful weight. On the face of it, the lyrics tell a classic boy-girl story of separation. The truth is more melancholy still.

The Pretenders are a rare beast: a 1970s British group with an American singer. And a female one at that. Riders of the new-

---

[1] Which is eerily similar to that on The Smiths' sublime b-side, *Back To The Old House*, written, equally eerily, at around the same time.

wave rock scene, they were formed by Chrissie Hynde,[1] and featured Brits Pete Farndon and James Honeyman-Scott (and a succession of drummers). Following a rush of early hits, including what would be their only UK number 1, *Brass In Pocket*, Pete Farndon was fired from the band in 1982 for excessive drug use. He wasn't the only band member partaking of the fruits of society's ills. Two days after kicking out Farndon for drug addiction, James Honeyman-Scott himself died of a cocaine-induced heart-attack, aged just twenty-five. (Pete Farndon would eventually die of unnatural causes, too, just a year later, in his bathtub.) With the band's original trio whittled down to one, Hynde soldiered on. She relied, as she would do continuously from that point, on session musicians (literal pretenders), re-jigging the line-up when needed.

'Don't feel sorry for Chrissie Hynde,' wrote *Rolling Stone* in 1984. 'There's a new band now, another hit album, a seven-month world tour - even a baby daughter. Somehow, Chrissie Hynde just keeps on going.'

As you'd expect, Chrissie Hynde isn't one for retrospection. She hates discussing her work, once claiming that she doesn't even know *how* she writes songs:

'People talk about songwriting clinics and how to construct a song and I'm sitting there thinking, "I didn't know that". I listen to some of my early songs and think, "I didn't even have a f-ing chorus in it".'

Her views on *2000 Miles* are almost non-existent, short of once dismissing its lyrics as 'stupid'. On paper, you could argue she's

---

[1] Hynde had moved to London from Ohio and was part of the King's Road scene of the 1970s (a scene which BBC4 manage to shoehorn mention of into *every* documentary they broadcast, even ones about Tudor England or yeast), hobnobbing with Malcolm McLaren and gigging with The Clash. Her previous band were called The Moors Murderers. They'd have never got a gig on *Tiswas*.

right. It has numerous blink-and-you'll-miss-it Christmas clichés:

The snow is falling down
Gets colder day by day
I miss you

But, for all Hynde's silence, one thing we *do* know is that the song is about the death of her young bandmate, James Honeyman-Scott. It was written quickly and, allegedly, without much conscious thought. Given its subject matter, and its author's staunch disassociation, it's no wonder it feels so instinctively abstract, so unlike all other Christmas songs.

2000 Miles is filled with the most beguiling turns of phrase. Why two-thousand miles? What's the significance of that number? Chrissie Hynde doesn't know. Or, if she does, has never revealed her secret. My feeling is that she was borrowing from the aura that the number two-thousand had in the run up to the millennium. Before the 20th century ended, there was a baseless association of the upcoming year 2000 with the arrival of Christ.[1] It wasn't just Christians who were at it. Hippies and *Fortean Times* subscribers were chipping in, suggesting millennial realignments of ley lines and the subsequent arrival of our Saturnalian overlords. Predictably, when the evening of December 31st, 1999, passed with little more incident than a few beery debates about the validity of the Millennium Dome as a taxpayer's expense, the number lost its power to bewitch. Way back in 1983, though, I wonder if Chrissie Hynde - whilst

---

[1] For another Christmassy example of this, see Chris de Burgh's wailer, *A Spaceman Came Travelling*, in which he sings, '*When 2000 years of your time has gone by, this song will begin once again to a baby's cry*'. Oddly, the song was inspired by de Burgh's interest in both the poetry of W.B. Yeats and Erich von Daniken's long-forgotten bible for wind-chime owners, *Chariots Of The Gods?* (a book so loose with facts that its own author felt compelled to give its title a question mark).

inadvertently perched on a ley line – subconsciously picked up on the two-thousand mystique, and, by doing so, was ascribing a spiritual, godly quality to her former bandmate and friend. It's the following line that makes me think it:

The children will sing
He'll be back at Christmas time

The middle-eight is just as ethereal:

Two-thousand miles
Is very far through the snow
I'll think of you
Wherever you go

She sings about thinking of him wherever *he* ('you') goes, as though the boy is still on a journey, still alive. It is one of the most alluring lines I have ever heard. At the start of the piece, I said the song's message added a 'doleful weight'. I should have said that it also somehow makes everything buoyant and light. It is a juxtaposition that I can't quite put into words. How can something be heavy and sad, yet airy and spiritual? How does that happen – and in a Christmas song, of all places?

Despite bad-mouthing her own 'stupid' lyrics for *2000 Miles*, Hynde was, at least, full of praise for her then-new guitarist's beauteous performance on that record. The instrument, remember, vacated by James Honeyman-Scott.

Chrissie Hynde re-recorded *2000 Miles* in Sweden in 2014. I'm taken by a quote she gave to a music magazine at the time:

'I think it [*2000 Miles*] captures the mood of the season perfectly as it gets cold in Sweden, reindeer wander the streets freely and the snow was coming down! Happy Christmas!'

Decades on, she is still keeping herself distant from the lyrics, suggesting the song is inspired by reindeer and snow, before quickly ending the statement with an unanswerable 'Happy Christmas!' This can be read two ways. Either she does truly think *2000 Miles* is 'stupid' and is keen to dismiss further discussion, or she still can't bring herself to talk about the person central to its story.'[1]

Sometimes in a dream you appear
Outside under the purple sky

Hynde's 2015 autobiography, *Reckless*, wraps up her life story before it truly gets going, detailing very little post-1983. Her reason, given in a magazine interview, is that once she 'got to where Pete and Jimmy died, I thought, "This feels wrong."'

Whatever it is Chrissie Hynde is truly singing about on *2000 Miles*, she sings it like she means it.[2] And she doesn't strike me as the sort to sing about reindeer.

2000 Miles exudes the spirit of absent friends and hovers gently in the background of our Christmas consciousness. It sings at you in the shopping centre, while other festive standards yell. It's an 'Oh, yeah - I forgot about that one' sort of song. Of all the Christmas tunes, it's the one I feel most sad to lose when January comes around, and is the first I rush to greet in December. It exists both outside of Christmas and wholly within it.

I can hear people singing
It must be Christmas time

In a 1984 album review, the *New York Times* flippantly referred to *2000 Miles* as 'a song about missing a man at Christmas-time'. They were right.

---

[1] The video certainly *is* stupid, by the way, with Hynde loafing between snowy trees whilst wearing Salvation Army regalia.

[2] If you ever needed firm evidence of the importance of sincerity in pop music, listen to Tom Chaplin's (former Keane lead singer) version of *2000 Miles*. It's got less heart than Dorothy's Tin-man.

#2

Driving Home For Christmas - Chris Rea

One of many seasonal classics that has taken a while to be fully adored, *Driving Home For Christmas* took a while to be released, too. Although re-recorded and successfully re-packaged as a single in 1988, the song had been knocking around for years. The lyrics were already a decade old by the time the record hit the charts.

 Having just been ditched by his record label and, subsequently, his manager, the young, bearded Chris was well and truly out on his Rea by early December '78. He called his wife to tell her the bad news, that the exciting young pop star she'd married was probably going to be doing dishes in the family restaurant from here on in. Resisting the temptation to flee, she instead drove down from Middlesbrough in her Austin Mini to pick her husband up from Abbey Road studios.[1]

 Whilst driving home for Christmas - and possibly for the rest of his life - Chris held the last of his show-business funds tightly in his hands: £220. Snow fell, clogging the motorway in grey mush and further slowing their journey. Inspired by the gloomy drivers around him, Chris[2] began jokingly singing the words, 'I'm driving home for Christmas' to his wife. Although he knew it was silly, he wondered whether there might be a song in it.

---

[1] Becoming, in the process, one of two people to have ever made the journey between those two particular destinations. The other person being Chris Rea.

[2] I normally refer to people by their surnames, but it doesn't feel right constantly referring to someone as 'Rea'.

He picked up a scrap of paper from the Mini's footwell. Being too dark to write the lyrics in one go, he had to wait for passing cars to illuminate his lap before quickly penning snippets of ideas:

Top to toe in tailbacks...
I take a look at the driver next to me...
I got red lights all around...
I'm moving down that line...

Upon arriving home - 'at the house we were about to lose our mortgage on' - at 3am, frozen and dejected, they found a letter on the doormat. Expecting it to be a bill from the milkman or a telegram from Abbey Road saying he'd left his brolly in reception, Chris was intrigued to discover it was actually from the PRS. His single, *Fool (If You Think It's Over)*, hadn't charted in the United Kingdom but had, he'd heard, made gentle rumblings in the United States. The couple read the cheque over and over. The sum took their breath away. Combined with the cash in his pocket, Chris Rea's show-business funds now came in at a grand total of £15,220.

With the music career back on, the scrawled Christmas lyrics were hastily put in an 'old tin full of unfinished stuff' and weren't dug out again until the mid-80s when, fooling around with a jaunty piano line in rehearsal, Chris realised that his Christmas lyrics fit the tune perfectly. The band knocked up a slow, jazzy accompaniment and slapped it on a b-side to the 1986 single, *Hello Friend*.[1] It was even mooted that *Driving Home For Christmas* be given to Van Morrison (who, presumably, would be additionally appreciative of its lyrics on account of his name being a mode of transport). Luckily, for all concerned, the offer was never made.

---

[1] Which crashed into the charts at number 79, before losing momentum.

A couple of years later, in the hope of providing himself with a hit, Chris Rea re-recorded the song with a snazzier intro and slightly slicker pace. As with a number of festive favourites, the new, up-tempo *Driving Home For Christmas* performed abysmally in the charts, cruising into the public consciousness at a similar pace to the car which Chris Rea and his wife had driven home on that snowy night ten years previous. It stalled at number 53 but - and this is often key where Christmas hits are concerned - it performed well on the radio. Sales were low but it had reached an audience, thus making further airplay likely the following December. And the December after that. And so on.[1]

Despite Chris Rea's reputation as something of a grandparents' favourite, *Driving Home For Christmas* has lately proven popular with a younger audience. My guess is that the lyrics pop into their minds as they themselves drive home for Christmas from university or their city-slicking lives. Anyone who's ever had the pleasure of hearing the song whilst in the process of driving home for Christmas will know how sweet an accompaniment it is. Such has been the song's enduring quality with those young enough to know how to use streaming services, *Driving Home For Christmas* re-enters the charts almost every year and, in 2017, achieved its highest ever UK chart placing of number 14.[2]

The archetypal slow-burner, even Chris Rea took time to appreciate the song's merits. Referring to it as 'a car version of a

---

[1] Today, each time the radio plays it, the songwriter, one Chris Rea, receives around £20-£40.

[2] For all its re-releases, it has only ever reached number 1 in Slovenia, where it shifted somewhere in the region of sixty-three copies.

carol',[1] he near-enough refused to perform it live.[2] He now has warmer feelings toward it:

'If I'm ever stuck on the M25, I'll wind the window down and start singing "I'm driving home for Christmas" at people in cars alongside. They love it. It's like giving them a present.'

Isn't that grand? Particularly so for those fortunate enough to experience it. Imagine being gridlocked and winding down your window to see Chris Rea belting out *Driving Home For Christmas* from the next car along. Nobody would believe your story:

'Oh yeah?' they'd reply. 'And MC Hammer just told me not to touch his windscreen.'

A little known fact, and one Mr Rea may be keen to keep to one side, is that for all his claims that releasing a Christmas song was a bit corny and uncool, he'd already tried, and failed, to have a Christmas hit in 1987 with the guitar driven *Joys of Christmas* (which reached a royalty-avoiding number 67). And he released yet another, *Winter Song*, in 1991. Both are perfectly acceptable yuletide songs, but neither have the allure of *Driving Home For Christmas*. Nor would you expect them to. It is a once in a lifetime Christmas song. It captures everything about the pull of home, that joy of getting your 'feet on holy ground', and of singing aloud to someone though they're miles away:

So I sing for you
Though you can't hear me

Most importantly, due to the origins of its lyrics on that snowy night, *Driving Home For Christmas* has an unmistakable ring of

---

[1] A car-ol?

[2] When he finally did relent, he said 'If I'm going to sing this f-ing song, we're gonna do it properly.' He had twelve cannons firing out fake snow onto his unsuspecting audience. It cost him £12,000 to clear up the mess.

truth and none of the forced together-forever, time-of-remembrance nonsense of many other festive musical offerings.

I take look at the driver next to me
He's just the same

The ring of truth. It's the one thing a songwriter can never manufacture. And, more often than not, it's one thing us much-maligned philistines of the general public are rather good at detecting. We know a true story when we hear one. Even if we do need to give it a few years to settle.

The Yule Log

AUGUST

Mon 20th -

It was my birthday yesterday. Thirty-five-years. And counting.

I have a 'No Christmas' policy until the day after my birthday. To even think about Christmas out of season is gauche, but, clearly, any time after August 19th, i.e. today, is absolutely fine and not at all weird. So, on a dripping hot summer's afternoon, I dipped my toe in the cool festive water: I checked a website about Christmas TV. It gives the latest scoop on terrestrial TV Christmas scheduling, saying things like:

'POINTLESS' XMAS SPECIAL FILMED TODAY - JULY 26TH

BBC TO SCREEN JUDI DENCH DOCUMENTARY (CHANNEL TO BE CONFIRMED) OVER CHRISTMAS PERIOD - JUNE 22ND

ITV HAD A BUSY WEEK FILMING THE CELEBRITY 'CHASE' AND 'CATCHPHRASE' XMAS SPECIALS - JUNE 1ST

It's not often I pity celebrities, but to have to sit in a TV studio for six hours wearing a Santa hat in June - as the world around them melts - must be deeply discombobulating. ('Deeply Discombobulating' sounds like an afternoon gameshow, presented by Sandi Toksvig.) Why these Christmas specials can't be filmed a little later in the year, perhaps during the semi-festive dark autumn evenings, I don't know. Daily gameshows are depressing enough as it is. The very thought of a 'Catchphrase Christmas Special', filmed in summer, is enough to make me reach for an upper.

But now here I am, in August, getting my own deeply discombobulating taste of the festivities. Writing about Christmas. Thinking about Christmas. Humming the classics:

'I really can't stay

But, baby, it's cold outside...'

Well, about twenty-four degrees in the shade.

Although it can't move, speak, or see, Christmas has been born unto us (me) this day.

Thurs 23rd -

Saw an advert on telly for a 'luxurious Christmas hamper'. The contents looked like they'd been hastily cobbled together during a mad rush to get into an Anderson Shelter. Processed food galore. The Spirit of the Blitz, in the form of canned meats.

The tins in the hamper were the sort you'd expect to find bending the shelves of your elderly neighbour's larder: meatballs, Fray Bentos pies, mushy peas, new potatoes. Luxurious. Their best-before dates probably clocked in at around the April 2048 mark (although I suspect the poor animals within were slaughtered pre-

Brexit, somewhere west of Buenos Aries, before being slopped into their tinned coffins).

I do feel sorry for those old folk who <u>still</u> don't understand the internet and are, therefore, only exposed to 'special offers' they see on television adverts or on flyers that fall out of weekend newspaper supplements. Their houses must be full of hampers, special pillows, special shoes and commemorative royal plates. All paid for in eye-watering monthly instalments.

Fri 24th -

There's been a re-jig of the frozen aisle in Tesco. The ice creams and lollies have been 'Reduced To Clear' or, in some cases, turfed out altogether. The freezers were half empty. Winter is coming.

Whenever I see the yellow 'Reduced To Clear' sticker it makes me think of the phrase 'reduced to tears'. I end up buying stuff out of sympathy. I couldn't stand to see a packet of Penguins reduced to tears.

In one corner of the shop, sans fanfare, were tubs of Quality Street and Roses.

Things are getting serious.

Mon 27th -

The years pass and still 'University Challenge' remains king of the quiz shows (although 'Only Connect' deserves mention as the king's first offspring and natural heir).

I love these first round matches in autumn, mainly because I know some of the answers. The later rounds, aired in the spring, are too alienating, especially when the maths questions go on so long that you could re-grout the bath tiles by the time they're done:

'Derived from the plutal route of nine-sevenths, the base cortex of which emblem recreates the denominator, as a theory first expressed by Klimp in a theses on rotational properties in 1779?'

It's not great for morale when you don't even understand the question yet have to witness what is effectively a tall, pale child - 'Harrington, Balliol' - pipe up with the answer. But, ah, how these early rounds give you a chance, an illusion, that, with a firmer hand from your parents, you might've once been on the show yourself.

I got six answers tonight. I was proud. Although three of them were in a bonus round about film posters. I'm not sure if knowledge acquired whilst walking past cinemas holds the same intellectual currency as knowledge acquired from those ashen, haunted libraries of Oxbridge.

Paxman was on form, doing his 'Come on!' bit whenever one of the contestants dithered on their answer for more than a second. I like it when he does this because I'm forever shouting it at the telly myself. 'Hurry up, you idiot,' I'll bark at the tall, pale children who have already scaled heights of intellect I'll never reach.

My one and only gripe with 'University Challenge' is how some of the teams are comprised entirely of post-graduates. Thus, you get beige-cardiganned 57-year-olds smugly sipping water, having battered a gaggle of teenagers in a bonus round concerning the works of Steve Harley & The Cockney Rebel.

It's not exactly an even playing field.

Fri 31st -

Plenty of 'Back To School' stuff in the shops. This was so painful when you were younger. Woolworths used to be hard at it from day one of the holidays, giving you no time to feel liberated. I can remember the posters even now: 'Back 2 Skool', written as though in chalk. Going back wasn't all bad. Aside from the anxiety of new teachers and new forms, it was fun to see your friends again and ridicule any slightly pretentious changes they'd made to their appearance since July. The two biggest thrills, though, were seeing - and ignoring - girls you loved, and inhaling a sweet waft of that spongy layer of foam that lined your new pencil case.

The 12 Things To Watch Of Christmas[1]

#1

The Lion, The Witch & The Wardrobe

The biggest victim in this digital age of viewing is the late Sunday afternoon slot. The space now occupied by *Escape To The Country* and repeats of the previous week's *A Question Of Sport* was once home to a wealth of family-friendly fayre.[2] The BBC's *The Lion, The Witch & The Wardrobe* was one of them and the one I'll talk about here, but others include *The Borrowers* and *The Tailor Of Gloucester.* Even on the heathen wasteland of ITV, they had things like *The Darling Buds Of May* and *Mr Majeika*.[3]

The programmes listed above were certainly too lavish to be tucked away midweek on children's television. Many were made with international appeal in mind. Yet, for all their period

---

[1] I know, I know. Rubbish heading.

[2] That's not to say *A Question Of Sport* isn't family-friendly, it's just you wouldn't exactly gather your kids around the telly to watch it. Unless you hated your kids.

[3] In earlier decades, the Sunday afternoon slot was reserved for equally appealing content: Dickens adaptations, *The Forsyte Saga*, *Anne of Green Gables* and so on.

costumes and spectacular sets, half the joy was in their scheduling. Sunday afternoons. In winter. Usually in the run-up to Christmas. Week by week, episode by episode, you could feel the season drawing near. You could measure it by the ever-darkening days. By the final Sunday episode, deep into December, the afternoon would be lit only by the television's glow and Christmas tree lights.[1]

The Lion, The Witch & The Wardrobe began on Sunday 13th November, 1988, and ended on Sunday 18th December. Everything about it held me spellbound: the children with their evacuee knitwear, plummy accents and unerring confidence around adults; the country house, complete with obligatory stern mistress, dotty uncle and kindly, plump scullery maid; then, the wardrobe itself, inviting the children in through its forest of fur coats, deep into the dark trees, towards the solitary gas lamp of Narnia's snowy idyll.

'How funny,' says Lucy, upon first opening that portal to another world.

How funny.

Narnia was cold, mysterious: 'Always winter but never Christmas'. Gripped by an evil force but coloured with kindly characters, it was so enchanting that I was repeatedly disappointed by the presence of hardboard whenever I attempted to push my own way through the black foliage of my parents' wardrobe. I couldn't work it out; everything else in there was the same as on the telly: the impossible darkness; the hanging clothes brushing down against my ears; the shoes and

---

[1] By which point, excitement had reached fever pitch. You knew that the upcoming week at school would be even more slack than the last, as teachers and dinnerladies entered that intoxicated state of 'almost finished'.

belt buckles digging up into my bare feet. But *my* journey always ended with the hardwood. No Narnia, however hard I pushed.

How funny.

Although it was supposed to be comely, *The Lion, The Witch & The Wardrobe* scared me witless at time. The big, furry characters of Narnia were all so lifelike, yet so uncanny, that even the friendly ones were a little frightening.[1] The White Witch was completely terrifying, in the deepest Freudian sense.[2] The way she flitted between her come-hither voice and Medusa stare.[3] The mother-figure gone wrong. It was enough to taint the sleep of my five-year-old self. But it didn't stop me from watching every week. Why would it? Fear is thrilling.

During a 2018 ITV screening of *The Witches*, somebody wrote this on Twitter:

'Watching the witches [sic] and it's been cut to within an inch of its life! Loved it when I was a kid, kids these days too soft.'

But who edited *The Witches* for broadcast that day? Not a child, I expect (unless ITV are breaking all kinds of employment laws in an attempt to claw back lost advertising revenue). It's adults-these-days, not kids-these-days, who are the softies, sanitising anything they can get their mitts on.

---

[1] Some of the costumes were sufficiently impractical to ensure that the actors inside them spent most of the film-shoot slipping on the ice and having to be picked up by aides. How I would have *loved* to have seen that on *It'll Be Alright On The Night* (rather than the endless clips of various small-town American weather presenters getting splashed by a big wave).

[2] Come to think of it, the big furry beavers were quite Freudian, too.

[3] She was played by Barbara Kellerman, who was only 38 at the time. I thought she was about 250.

31

Those Sunday afternoon adaptations instilled a suspicion which I carried with me through the later years of my childhood: that books might be worth bothering with and that I should probably try and read some.

 What is clear to adults, and what we neither cared about nor understood as children, was that the C.S. Lewis' Narnia stories are near enough a retelling of the New Testament: the evil White Witch versus the brave kingly lion, Aslan, who dies for Edmund's sins (before coming back to life). I can't help but wonder if the BBC's *Lion, Witch & The Wardrobe* affected my adult suspicions, too, in something beyond the MFI hardwood at the back of life's wardrobe.[1]

You might assume I regularly re-watch *The Lion, The Witch & The Wardrobe*. Not exactly. Not at all, in truth. Other than looking at snippets of it for this piece, I haven't seen it in full since its last BBC repeat in 1991. I don't want to. I want to leave the memory alone.

 It's hard to put a precise date on when these literary adaptations came to an end, but the late 90s is as good a shout as any.[2] Whatever the reason for their absence, and whomever we blame,[3] by the turn of the millennium, the BBC and ITV

---

[1] During the Second World War, C.S. Lewis (no relation to C.J.), as a respected scholar, was asked by the BBC to deliver a defence of Christianity in what was a time of great doubt. The transcripts of these broadcasts were later published in *Mere Christianity*, and it was his writings on faith, not Narnia, which made him a household name.

[2] Which means, technically, we can blame Tony Blair. Not sure why, but it may as well be his fault.

[3] Tony Blair.

had largely knocked the Sunday afternoon family drama on the head.

Whilst scooting around message-board discussions about old television, I saw this comment:

'*Tea* [in the 1970s] *was a picnic table in front of the fire with salmon sandwiches and homemade cake.*[1] *Teapot on the hearth and whole family watching the TV.*'

The second biggest victim of this digital age of viewing, if you're interested, is shared experience. Once was a time when children's television was a part of the daily schedule of BBC One and ITV. There were no offshoot children's channels. As a result, children's television reached a wider audience. Whether they regularly watched it or not, most adults knew the current *Blue Peter* presenters, what Scrappy Doo's catchphrase was, and who was in the broom cupboard.[2] Today, references to children's television are an in-joke between parents, a distant secret. Something is lost by this disconnect. It's as if the children have been stuck in a backroom to play quietly amongst themselves.

'TV sets have been the focal point in a lot of homes for many years,' said a 2018 report on child viewing habits, 'but they are falling out of favour amongst children.'

This may partly be down to very few children enjoying *Homes Under The Hammer*. They like it so little, in fact, that they'd rather watch YouTube videos on their parent's cracked iPhone screen.

---

[1] This is near-enough the same meal that the fawn invites Lucy back to his cosy underground home for. He gives her tea, sardines and cake by his fireside before sending her to sleep with his flute, so to speak.

[2] In 1983, a single episode of *Dangermouse* picked up 21 million viewers; England's 2018 World Cup semi-final against Croatia, for which the nation stopped, was seen by 20.7m.

If I could change one thing about terrestrial television it would be to restore the ninety-minute weekday window where children's programming is there for all to see.[1] Oh, and to find a little spot on Sunday afternoons, at about tea time. Long enough, let's say, for an adaptation of a children's classic.

#2

Top Of The Pops Christmas Special

If you need a barometer for how out of touch you are with modern music, there's no more accurate measuring device than the festive edition of *Top Of The Pops*. Usually screened just before her majesty reminds of us those less fortunate than we, the *TOTP Christmas Special* is as reliable a feature of the TV schedule as the annual message from the ol' gal herself.

For those who have never seen it, the Christmas special is a pre-recorded episode stuffed with live studio performances of the year's biggest hits.[2] Hosted by Fearne Cotton and whoever

---

[1] At the time of writing, CBBC spend around £55m a year on producing original content. Its audience reach is around 4% of the population. Just 300,000 children a day tune in across various devices. (BBC4, for comparison, spend just £31m but reach 13%). If the BBC want value for their money, or, rather, *our* money, they might do well to stick their costly children's programming back where it belongs; doing so may also help lower the average age of their flagship channel from its shameful current age of 61.

[2] Plus a handful of videos phoned-in from stars who, if you can believe such a thing, possibly had better places to be on the day of filming than the BBC's studios in Elstree.

34

else happens to be around that week, each song is introduced to us as having been that year's 'soundtrack to the summer' or 'global smash'. Then the artist performs their global smash – with tinsel around their neck – and you realise that not only was this hit *not* the soundtrack to your summer, but that you're not sure if *any* song was the soundtrack to it. Wasn't summer just a succession of warmer than average weeks that otherwise felt quite similar to all others?

The *Top Of The Pops Christmas Special* offers a stark reminder that your once-soft skin is hardening, and that the power of pop music to soundtrack things in your life – kisses, night walks, parties, *summers* – has waned. Now your life is soundtracked by your fan-assisted oven and the buzz of the fridge. None of these new *TOTP* acts – Jenny & The Pritt-Sticks, Ezra Johnson, The Heartattax et al – play any part in your year.[1]

The real killer is that *Top Of The Pops* is itself out of touch. No matter how hard the BBC try, the cool kids refuse to watch it. So, what you're left with is an out of touch show that leaves *you* feeling out of touch. Musically speaking, *TOTP* dumps you somewhere around the outskirts of Neptune.[2] And yet, for all that, I'll still merrily give it the time of (Christmas) day.

Top Of The Pops was everything once. A vital fixture in the TV week, around which an unshakeable routine formed:

Thursday night: watch *Top Of The Pops*.

Friday morning: talk about *Top Of The Pops* at school.

---

[1] Don't worry, I made those acts up.

[2] The only thing that can rival *Top Of The Pops* for this is skim-reading the tracklisting on the back of the latest *Now* album in Tesco. It may as well be written in hieroglyphics.

In the days before freeview, round-the-clock music channels and YouTube, *TOTP* provided near-enough the only window through which we heathens could peer into the glitzy world of the music industry.[1] Its influence must be hard to appreciate for those who never had to rely on it. As author David Mitchell put it, 'To millennials, *Top Of The Pops* may sound as quaint as 1950s radio does to my generation'. Effectively, until the late-1990s, music performance was rationed by the governing bodies of the BBC, ITV and Channel 4. Yes, a black market existed in the form of MTV and physical VHS releases, but those luxuries were generally only afforded to those with cash.

Although many early *TOTP* performances from pop's golden age were wiped by the BBC,[2] by the time *I* began regularly

---

[1] Other musical vantage points included the *National Lottery* and Sunday morning stuff like *Fully Booked* and *The O-Zone*. Honourable mention must also go to ITV's *The Chart Show*, which, despite its obsession with the B52s, was an equally valuable source of music videos each Saturday lunchtime. None of these alternatives, though, compared to *TOTP*.

[2] In the 1960s and early 70s, there was cynicism from on high at the BBC that people would still be interested in pop music in years to come. The shows were considered a waste of costly videotape. Thus, lots of performances were taped over with, more often than not, sporting events. The *only* surviving clip of The Beatles on *TOTP* is, of all places, in a 1965 episode of *Dr Who*. In it, the Doctor looks back into centuries past and sees a clip of the Fab Four singing *Ticket To Ride* on *TOTP* (his sidekick calls them 'classical music'). Countless performances by other big hitters of the age - Rolling Stones, Dylan - have also been wiped. It wasn't just music which faced the axe. *Dr Who* itself has more than a few missing episodes. The entire first series of *Monty Python's Flying Circus* was destined for the scrapheap until Terry Gilliam privately bought the reels to make copies. Luckily, though, the 1967 World Championship Snooker Quarter Finals *can* be seen in all their glory...

contributing to the viewing figures in the early 90s, popular music was treated with mighty reverence. My era of *Top Of The Pops* was more savvy than in its former days of bearded, middle-aged Radio One DJs putting their arms around thirteen-year-old girls.[1] Nineties *TOTP* involved fewer dentally-suspect female dance troupes and a lot more dry ice. The sets went from tiered platforms packed with knockabout 80s partygoers to resembling a steelwork factory on the outskirts of Düsseldorf. The episodes were presented by a rolling cast of urbane socialites, including Jayne Middlemiss, Chris Evans, Jarvis Cocker, and, er, Chris Eubank. The music was treated seriously. Bands played live. Miming was out. 'Real music' was in. And, somehow, it wasn't as fun.

Like millions of others, when digital TV arrived with its wealth of 24-hour music channels - The Box, UK Play, MTV Extra - I switched *TOTP* off. It didn't help the programme's cause when record companies got wise to the efficacy of getting their songs played on radio and satellite *before* they were released, rather than afterwards. Whereas, in the past, *Top Of The Pops* promoted tracks we'd never heard, by the early noughties, it was playing 'new' chart entries that were already dead in the water, having been doing the rounds on radio playlists and digital channels for months.

The music world flashed along at a pace with which BBC One primetime couldn't keep up. They tried moving the show to

---

[1] Too gruesome a subject to go into fully, but a thorough 2016 investigation revealed the programme's dark past, leading the *Independent* newspaper to call *TOTP* 'a breeding ground for abusers'. The show has a number of other skeletons in its closet, too. Perhaps its most eye-watering is presenter Gary Davies introducing his black co-presenter Dixie Peach as 'the only man at Radio One who has got a better sun-tan than me!'. I won't even go into Mike Read's 2014 song, *UKIP Calypso* (sung, of course, in a Jamaican accent).

Friday nights.[1] They tried calling it 'All New' *Top Of The Pops* (always a surefire way to make something sound old). Then they moved it to BBC Two, sandwiching it between a couple of perennially popular youth-oriented shows: *Top Gear* and *Natural World*. Its end was officially nigh. The last episode aired on 30th July, 2006, with a poignant closing scene in which *Sir* Jimmy Saville, in a golden tracksuit, switched off the studio lights one last time before popping out to do some 'charity work'.

But, as with *Sir* Jimmy, the *Top Of The Pops* ghost lived on in the form of Christmas specials. In 2012, after years of watching, *I* got tickets to the recording. I'd entered an online ballot and come up trumps. I was going to the *Top Of The Pops Christmas Special*! As if my festive poinsettias weren't sufficiently in bloom, it was to be the last one filmed at BBC Television Centre, too.

If you've ever 'won' a ballot for a BBC show, you'll know that your ticket doesn't guarantee entry. It just means they *may* let you in. There's a vetting process on the day. They have demographic quotas to fill. My ticket said to arrive at eleven to avoid disappointment. I got there for nine. About fifty other people had had an even better idea, though: they'd got there for

---

[1] Putting it up against *Coronation Street*, an act which quickly stripped it of a further five million viewers. When confronted with a choice between Fred Elliot's butcher shenanigans or hearing One True Voice butcher their latest single, the British public would only go one way. (About right, too. One True Voice actually had a song called *Shakespeare's Way With Words*. It featured the following lyric: *If I had Shakespeare's way with words, I would write a sonnet, put your name upon it.* It was written by Rick Astley. Or, as Fred Elliot would call him, 'I say, Astley.')

eight. I joined the back of their lengthy line along the fencing of Television Centre.

Whilst queuing on that bright December morning, I couldn't take my eyes off the iconic building. It had played such a significant role in my life. They'd filmed *Fawlty Towers* there, *Monty Python*, *Hancock's Half Hour*, *Morecambe & Wise*. It was where Andi Peters sat in the broom cupboard, where the *Blue Peter* cast welcomed in a choir of carol-singing schoolchildren each year, and where the big bouncy ball zipped about in the opening credits of *Live & Kicking*. Most importantly, it was where near enough every *Top Of The Pops* I'd ever watched had taken place. To think that I was going in there. *Me*. In there. In *there*. My lovestruck stare was interrupted when comedian Hugh Dennis walked past our queue, probably on his way to rehearse his ad-libs for the latest *Mock The Week*. With briefcase in hand, he raised his eyebrows to his public by way of saying 'Hey there'.

I'd reached the promised land.

You know you *really* want to go somewhere when, having acquired a ticket, you spend every moment before the event convincing yourself that your ticket will, for some vague reason, be rejected at the door. I was so desperate to get inside Television Centre, to touch its walls, that I was certain some burly security man would refuse me entry:

'Sorry, mate. Summink vaguely wrong with your ticket. Can't let you in. Strict security policy here, pal. Ah, good morning, Sir Jimmy. Come on through...'

We had to have our tickets scanned at the entrance gate. Mine made the machine beep. I panicked, thinking the BBC had filled its audience demographic quota of balding, overweight nobodies. But the beep was good. It meant I was waved through.

To the other side.

The inside of Television Centre was a white, concrete maze. It smelt of new carpet and old paint, or vice versa. Everywhere you looked you saw self-assured, snooty media types with rolled-up shirt sleeves and lanyards, busily walking around with pursed lips, desperately pretending they weren't particularly fussed about the glamour of the day job. It was all so quiet and staid. Thrillingly so. Thrillingly professional. Every sign made for enthralling reading:

'Studio 4 - Vacant'

'Studio 6 - Recording - Do Not Enter'

'Editing Suite'

'Writers' Room'

I drooled down my jumper. Full-on saliva. I wanted to walk, to crawl, to stop and lick the doorhandles, to savour it all, but we were whisked, whisked, along a sequence of corridors to a studio door with the words *Top Of The Pops Xmas* typed onto an A4 sheet and blu-tacked to it.

Razzle dazzle 'em.

The studio was narrow and tall, but no bigger than your average village hall.[1] Cameras and scaffolding were hidden in darkness behind black drapes. We only saw what we needed to: the lights, the platforms, the pizazz. There were four stages and we were told to stand in the middle of the room and face each appropriate stage as and when.[2] The producer told us how to cheer and how to dance and when to be quiet and when to go bananas. Already ninety percent banana, I looked up dreamily at the rafters, at the illuminated *Top Of The Pops* logos hanging

---

[1] An odd choice of comparison, I know, but I couldn't think of a better one. I tried.

[2] On the telly, it looks like each act is being cheered on by a new crowd in a new studio, and not, as is the case, the same old motley crew from a different angle.

there, and couldn't believe where I was. I'd climbed into the TV set and become part of its world. Everything was fascinating. My wandering eyes led me to peek down a darkened passage where I saw Fearne Cotton waiting, alone. Heavily pregnant, her expression resembled that of a bus driver at the start of a ten-hour shift when his first passenger tries to buy a one-way ticket with a Scottish £50 note. Her nostrils flared. Swallowing hard, flushed, she gave the impression she was seconds from vomiting over her shiny dress.

'And now,' yelled the producer, 'give it up for your hosts: Fearne Cotton and Reggie Yeates!'

Mad applause. Fearne Cotton strolled out, beaming, glowing with happiness. This was the best day of her life. She high-fived audience members, waved to us, blew kisses, rubbed her big pregnant belly and hugged Reggie, before telling us we were in for a classic show.

That's a pro for yer.

We didn't know which acts were going to be on. It was all a mystery. I couldn't help but think big: McCartney, Madonna, Beyonce. In all honesty, the line-up was underwhelming. It was hard to summon up enthusiasm for Ellie Goulding when you'd spent the morning fantasising about Kate Bush making a surprise appearance.[1]

Tainting the whole experience was a young woman in the crowd who smelt so much of unwashed areas that getting within ten feet of her was enough to make you choke on your tongue. She wore a grey tracksuit with a bumbag around her waist. Maybe the bag was actually made out of bum, because that's what it smelt like. Wherever she went she cleared a path, Moses-like. You'd never know, watching the show as it aired,

---

[1] The show was filmed over two days. I only had a ticket for the first. The second day was just as uninspired, with the then-reunited Boyzone being the year's big surprise act.

that half of the audience (the half closest to her) may have been dancing, but their nostrils were aflame. I wondered what other *Top Of The Pops* performances have been spoilt by a smelly person in the audience. Perhaps there was a rotter in there the night John & Yoko did *Instant Karma* or during Frankie Goes To Hollywood's *Relax*.

The first artist we saw was Rita Ora. I made a point of getting right to the front of the crowd.[1] I did likewise for some indie band or other who sang what is possibly the most underwhelming song I have ever heard.[2] As the day wore on, the novelty of *TOTP* faded. The mind is a queer beast. A lifetime of desire and it gets bored within a couple of hours of receiving what it always wanted. Yes, there was a lot of standing involved, a lot of waiting, and some of the acts performed the same song three or four times, but, jeez, what more could I want?

If you go on YouTube, you can see me there, at the 2012 *Top Of The Pops Christmas Special*, standing at the front, dancing like a bell-end to Rita Ora. I'd hoped to be on screen more. God knows I tried. I even shimmied myself into the foreground of every link Reggie and Fearne recorded. I can only imagine the conversations in the editing suite:

'Hold fire, guys. We've got an egghead in shot. Cut to someone better looking, stat. I don't know. *Anyone.* Her with the bumbag...'

---

[1] Crowd is a bit of an exaggeration; there were probably about 150 of us. Again, on the TV, they somehow made us look like the Kop celebrating a last-minute winner.

[2] And bear in mind I've heard *Shakespeare's Way With Words*. (I just Googled who the band were. It was The Maccabees. The song was called *Pelican*.)

The Christmas Alphabet

C is for...

Cards

The first Christmas card was produced in the UK in 1843 by an employee of the then-primitive Post Office, Sir Henry Cole.[1] The card was devised as an attempt to spike interest in Britain's exciting new postal service.[2] With the proliferation of train lines and, indeed, the invention of trains themselves, it became much cheaper and quicker to send things by post.[3] The Post Office just needed more people to do it and Christmas cards were considered a way to possibly drive traffic. The cards were also designed as an easy way for Sir Henry himself to complete his correspondence without the mind-numbing drudgery of

[1] Whose other claim to fame is to have founded the Victoria & Albert Museum.

[2] A bit like when Netflix grab your attention by making a brand new series of your favourite old show (and then ruin it).

[3] Incredibly, before train timetables existed, there was no unified agreement on what the precise time was. The towns and cities of Britain each had their own kooky timezones. As you can imagine, this created merry hell for long distance rail journeys. So, in 1847, all the railway companies agreed to use Greenwich Mean Time as their guide. The rest of the country didn't fully follow suit until 1880. What has this got to do with anything, I hear you ask. Nothing much. But there you go.

writing hundreds of letters. Rather than the classic Christmas card design of today, where we open them like a book,[1] Sir Henry's prototype resembled a postcard.

For the card's image, Sir Henry hired an artist called John Horsley to drum up a painting of a typical Christmas. The painting, which Mr Horsley upwardly drummed, depicted a middle-class family tucking into a feast whilst, around its border, sketches showed wealthy people helping the low and needy.[2] Horsley's picture caused some controversy as it also featured a toddler chugging on a glass of claret at a rate which suggested he didn't have to be up for playgroup in the morning. The sight of a drunken baby was shocking enough, but what really caught the eye was that the wine glass was being held to the little cherub's mouth by its loving mother.[3] This minor

---

[1] To reveal, more often than not, a terrible poem within: 'Christmas Time so full of cheer/With deepest love, a happy new year' etc. Sir Henry Cole's card said, 'A Merry Christmas and a Happy New Year to You', in an alarmingly un-Victorian cut to the chase.

[2] Having already spent the year kindly helping them improve their stamina on the workhouse treadmill.

[3] It's perhaps a little surprising that the drunken toddler caused such a stir. Youngsters were regularly on the sauce back then. The introduction of a legal drinking age was only introduced in 1839, four years before Sir Henry's card. Until then, it was far from unusual to find drunken children roaming the streets. And that's when they weren't off their nuts on smack. Any number of child medicines of the age - from sleeping aids to teething powders - were loaded with opiates, laudanum, cocaine and morphine. One contemporary estimated that three-quarters of all opiate-related deaths occurred in children under the age of five. These days, you can't find so much as a whiff of heroin in *any* children's medicines. It's health and safety gone mad, right?

discrepancy aside, the general public were inspired by Sir Henry Cole's idea of sending one another cards at Christmas.

As well as pictures of bunnies and dancing frogs,[1] Victorian Christmas cards often featured scenes from the sensationally snowy winter of 1836.[2] Pictures of knickerbockered tykes sledging down hillsides and fair ladies skating in pairs across frozen lakes were all the rage. They remain so today. The popular idea of the typical Victorian citizen is of a thunderously forward-looking empire builder dressed in starched cottons. This was true of some, but many of them, like many of us, appear to have been locked in a melancholy yearning for the past, for the Great Victorian Christmas of old. It's easy to forget that a Briton born in 1890 must have felt little in common with a Briton born in 1836 (just as a Briton born in 1990 will feel distinctly different from one of a 1936 vintage). The 1890 Briton may have looked at depictions of the 1836 Christmas and seen - and desired - a distant, unimaginably simpler time, a time before photography and electricity and recorded sound. A time of snowy winters.

As the decades rolled along, printing costs declined and Christmas card sales increased until, by the early 20th century,

---

[1] Victorians were fond of depicting well-dressed animals, but especially, for no discernible reason, frogs. Some animal-themed Christmas cards avoided a festive lilt altogether and merely depicted the exquisite creatures in fine detail (so as to satiate the nation's 'zeal for instruction' at that time, to quote R.G. Holloway's *Compliments Of The Season*).

[2] Technically, as her majesty didn't plonk herself on the throne until 1837, the snowy winter of 1836 wasn't a *Victorian* affair. But, you know, whatever.

the United States and most of Europe were in on the act.[1] The typical modern-day Christmas card - 4x6 inches approx. and sealed in an envelope - was developed by an American called Joyce Hall and his brothers in 1915. Hall's new cards were folded in half and opened up, allowing them to stand of their own accord (which is more than can be said of the wine-addled sprog on Sir Henry Cole's card of 1843). This new design allowed customers to write more than they could on a postcard and less than they'd have to in a letter. Perfect. Joyce Hall and his brothers called their little company Hallmark. And the rest is blah blah blah...

Today, the future of the Christmas card is up in the air. Sales remain strong but there has been a not unpredictable drop in the numbers of under-35s buying them, which may give a clue as to their ultimate fate.[2]

Whether you view Christmas cards as an innocent pick-me-up or as a flagrant waste of cardboard that would've made the advent-calendar-banning Nazis weep, the fact is they're still here. We Brits send around 900m a year (and receive, on average, around fourteen each). They generate about £50m for UK charities, smash £400m into the economy and create jobs for around 100,000 elves, I mean, people. To be fair, and it's not often I see eye-to-eye with a Nazi, the waste of cardboard *is* pretty shocking. Each year, approximately one *billion* British Christmas cards are not recycled. Their packaging is just as wasteful, requiring around 300,000 tonnes of cardboard. I'm

---

[1] The first American Christmas card was, predictably, an advert - for a shop...

[2] If you want the numbers: only 46% of under-35s bought cards in 2017, compared to 75% of over-65s. Mind you, I suppose you *can* afford to faff about writing cards when you're sat at home all day watching *Victoria Derbyshire* and laughing about how cheap it was to buy your house.

expecting to watch an episode of an Attenborough-narrated wildlife show soon in which Christmas cards are seen choking the neck of the Amazon or some such former Babylon. It's disconcerting. Sir Henry Cole's baby had the right idea. Neck the vino.

Carols

'Christmas carols? Oozy, squeezy, treacly, middle-class propaganda crap.'
Ian Pattison, *Rab C. Nesbitt*, 1988

Christmas carols have been around for hundreds and hundreds of years. A quick scan of your local church's hymn book will tell you that. Believe me, it will be loaded with the buggers. Not just the popular classics, but carols neither you, the vicar, the verger, nor the choirmaster will have ever heard in your collective lives. Carols with names like *How True Hast Thou Appealed To Mine Kin* and *Sang I Among Thee Riches*[1] all written by the ever-prolific *'Trad.'* on some vague date in the run-up to Agincourt.

In medieval times, however, carols weren't exclusive to Christmas. They were performed at nigh-on every public day of celebration, from May Day to All Saints.[2] Not just in church, either, but in pubs and taverns and on sunlit village greens.[3] It wasn't until the - wait for it, wait for it - 19th century that the songs became intrinsically linked with Christmas and,

---

[1] I made those up, but you get the idea.

[2] All Saints Day: when the locals would sing *I Know Where It's At* and *Never Ever* until their hearts were content.

[3] The word 'carol' originally meant 'to dance in a ring' (like a prick).

eventually, the church.[1] Whereas *we* think of the 1800s as being England's halcyon days, the Victorians themselves largely viewed medieval times in a similar light. Ignoring its plagues and famines, they focused on the era's positives. To them, it was an age of Romance with a capital R: the days of knights and castles and deadly escapades through the Holy Lands.

And carols. Albeit with a lower-case c.

The only problem with the medieval carols, as far as the Victorians could deduce, was that they had a tendency to be a bit bawdy. Being the sort of people to blush at the sight of a moist aubergine, such vulgarity simply would not do. Ever-industrious, their solution was to write their very own non-bawdy carols. The new Victorian lyrics would feature a lot *more* in the way of lowing cattle, hosanna in excelsis (or anywhere close to it) and bells in heav'n ringing, and a lot *less* in the way of allusions to girthy genitals and the general slagging off of the merry king's ability to govern.

Some of the medieval tunes were stolen outright, others merely had their aged style imitated. The success of these 19th century carols was lasting. From *Once In Royal David's City* to *O Holy Night*, the songs are rightly loved to this day.[2] The original

---

[1] This is possibly because the populace were running out of other festivals to sing carols at. Although we often think of the distant past as being bereft on the fun-front, they certainly knew how to let their hair down. There were thirty-three public holidays in the UK at one point. This was brutally slashed to four in 1834. The number has slightly increased since but, when it comes to public holidays, the UK still has the second fewest in the world.

[2] One enduring 19th century carol, *Jingle Bells*, was actually written for Thanksgiving and makes no mention of Christmas. It's just one of a number of American compositions that finds its way into British carol services. Others include *Away In A Manger*, *We Three Kings* and *O Little Town Of Bethlehem*.

medieval tunes, although many still linger in the hymn books, now tend to take a back-pew.

The classic church carol service, as we know it today, is said to have been the brainchild of a vicar from Cornwall by the name of E.W. Benson. Benson, so the legend goes, was so sick of his parishioners getting tanked-up every Christmas Eve that he created a carol service, in 1880, as a way to drive them from the pub and towards the church. As neat as this little story is, there is little evidence to support it. That's not to say Benson didn't leave his mark. He rose to the position of Archbishop of Canterbury and had two sons. One wrote *Mapp & Lucia*, the other wrote the words to *Land Of Hope & Glory*. Both were gay. As was their mother, who, while her husband was hastily knocking together an appealing setlist for his soused congregation, was busily conducting any one of her *thirty-nine* lesbian affairs.

Tell you what, I bet you never expected this book to be so damned sexy, did you? Even after seeing the front cover.

Carolling

In the fore-court, lit by the dim rays of a horn lantern, some eight or ten little field-mice stood in a semi-circle, red worsted comforters round their throats, their fore-paws thrust deep into their pockets, their feet jigging for warmth.

Kenneth Grahame, *The Wind In The Willows*, 1908

The act of carolling also has roots in the Victorians' love affair with the medieval. The tradition of door-to-door singing goes back as far as the days when Chaucer wasn't old enough to grow

49

a convincing moustache.[1] And what was good for the Chaucer-not-being-able-to-grow-a-convincing-moustache set was good for the Victorian set. Soon, anyone who was anyone was out there, on the post-Industrial Revolution's smog-clogged streets, belting out a tune or two from God's back-catalogue. It was known as 'wassailing', named after the hearty drink once offered to singers by way of payment.[2] There was a carol written about it:

Love and joy come to you
And to you your wassail, too

It's likely the drink's alcoholic content was the only thing keeping the poor wretches warm. Sadly, the following lyric amendment never caught on:

Love and joy come to you
I'm rat-arsed and turning blue

Other than on TV and in films, carolling is a largely forgotten art. I have still never seen a group of doorstep carollers in the mould of the above-quoted *Wind In The Willows* extract.[3] Or in any mould, to be precise.

Here's the eternal optimist, Virginia Woolf, breaking character to voice complaint about carollers in a letter sent from a Cornwall hotel on Christmas Eve, 1909:

'No one seems to have any wish to go to bed. They circle aimlessly. Is this going on in all the villages of England now?'

Critics often comment on how Woolf seemed to belong to a different age. Well, she'd have definitely preferred this one

---

[1] 'Latterly didst theyr hallow'd doorsteppe syngyng get on myne tyts,' he wrote in *The Pardoner's Tale*. (He didn't.)

[2] The singers carried a 'wassail bucket' around with them, which was filled with alcoholic nourishment.

[3] By which, I mean, young and earnest. Not field-mice.

when it comes to carol singers. Their *aimless circling* seldom occurs in the villages of England now.

Church

'...it was worth observing how far they are come from taking the Reprehensions of a Bishop seriously, that they all laugh in the chapel when he reflected on their ill actions and courses.'
Samuel Pepys, Dec 25th, 1662

It was once sneeringly said of Catholics that they'd spend their days boozing, floozing, fornicating and fighting, then nip into the confession booth of a Sunday morn, give the soul a quick rinse, and be good to go for a repeat performance in the upcoming week. The same could arguably said about today's floating devotees of the Church of England, such as myself, who, when the Christmas tree goes up and the candles get jammed into oranges,[1] arrive en masse, purely for the hoopla. All year the church pews sit largely unoccupied, except for the drippy-nosed stalwarts plonked on the end. Come Christmas, however, the place transforms into a steamy bazaar of incense, upmarket cologne and winter coats. The pews crack and bend into a merry smile with the angelic crush of bottoms.

Church isn't a tradition for everybody, but December is still the key month in the vicar's calendar, the time for him to pull up his 100% pure-wool socks and dust off his sermon about the *true* meaning of Christmas.

A 2017 poll by Sky News suggested that one in four people visit church over the festive period, and that 10% do so on Christmas Day itself. Impressive numbers. So impressive, might I tentatively suggest, that they bring into question the

---

[1] To signify Jesus' pithiness.

reliability of the Sky News team to accurately canvass opinion. Nowhere near one in ten of the people *I* know go to church on Christmas Day. One village church near me has had to *cancel* its Christmas Day services as the numbers were so low that even the family of mice who reside in the vestry skirting board were regularly concocting elaborate excuses as to why they couldn't make it. In the end, the vicar got so annoyed by nobody coming to hear his sermon about the *true* meaning of Christmas, that he knocked it on the head altogether, possibly expecting an outcry that never materialised.[1]

Conversely, it is those slate-hearted socialites from London who are most likely to wrap a designer scarf around their neck and dash off to their nearest intertwining 'twixt heaven and earth.[2] Sky News' pollsters found that as many as 14% of Londoners visit their church each December 25th to politely listen to their own vicar's take on Christmas's *true* meaning. Even if Sky *have* got their figures wrong - even if it's by as much as 50% - the number of London churchgoers might give the average swaggering Nietzschean pause. If God is dead, there are still a hell of a lot of people pretending he isn't.

That said, a separate survey of festive churchgoers found that, of church's casual visitors (i.e. those who only go at Christmas), 94% said their motivation was the music.[3] Tellingly, only half

---

[1] An urban myth exists that because the Holy Days & Fasting Act of 1551 - which required every citizen to walk to church on Dec 25th - has never *officially* been repealed, people who don't go on Christmas Day are technically breaking the law. As much as I'd *love* this to be true, the Act *was* repealed in 1969, in one of the permissive society's less daring amendments.

[2] Church.

[3] Oddly, 75% said they go to be 'reminded of the Christmas story'. Have they forgotten it?

said they went in order 'to feel close to God'. Now, of course, in response, a Christian might argue that to enjoy music *is* to enjoy God.[1] But, alas, the messages of Christianity have been muddled, argued to the point of polite withdrawal, and made all too Homo sapien. And we're left, as the poll suggests, with people who are in tune with the music and traditions of the church, but who feel alienated from the spirit which guides both.

Anyway, that's a matter for the ordained to deal with. I've just stepped out of my comfort zone.

Talking of comfort zones, I should add that half of those polled said they 'wanted to find the *true* meaning of Christmas' in church. At which point, vicars everywhere nursed their beards and claimed to have *just the thing*. With 51% of those canvassed agreeing with the statement 'The birth of Jesus is irrelevant to my Christmas', the vicars have work to do. As the earlier Samuel Pepys extract testifies, it was ever thus.

Coca-Cola (Holidays Are Coming)

'Holidays are advent, holidays are advent,' as they used to sing in ancient Rome.[2]

Used as a measure for whether 'it's, like, properly Christmas now' by people on Facebook, the Coca-Cola Christmas ad's popularity shows no sign of abating, swallowed and burped back up each year with gusto. The familiar scenes of the articulated lorries rolling through a snowy Midwest conurbation deliver joy

---

[1] They may also argue that the stern, lofty Jehovah of the secular imagination - and, sadly, many sermons - wouldn't be worth spending the morning with anyway.

[2] There's that 'advent' joke I promised you back on page 3.

to millions[1] and will, I boldly predict, continue to do so, whether broadcast in 4D or as a mind projection, for the rest of our lives and beyond.

Watch out
Look around
Something's coming
Coming to your town

Only Coke aficionados and imbeciles who write books about Christmas know that there are, in fact, three different *Holidays Are Coming* ads. Rather horribly, the adverts are officially called *Christmas Caravans I* (1995), *II* ('96) and *III* ('98). The 1998 edit is the version we see each year, with its trucks magically lighting up the town as they pass through.[2]

So popular is the ad's jingle, a full 4-minute version called *Wonderful Dream (Holidays Are Coming)* was released in 2001 by the US singer Melanie Thornton.[3] For reasons that cannot be known, but which may be down to the Germans' need to sneak their way into nigh on every entry in this alphabet, Thornton's

---

[1] As well as a frightening supply of Coke to that Midwest conurbation's general store. I mean, do they really need that much?

[2] Hard to believe now, but when the ad first aired, the visuals were considered quite stunning. They were produced by Industrial Light & Magic (of *Star Wars*, and, to a lesser extent, *Flubber*, fame). One of the Coke trucks now tours our beloved country each December, stopping at towns and cities near you. 'I'm sure it's the most photographed truck in Britain,' said its driver. Well, I can think of no other contender for that hollow crown. (FYI, there were only three trucks used in the filming of the ads, but the wizardry of TV created the illusion of more. It's the *TOTP Christmas Special* all over again...)

[3] A jingle preceding a song is like a film preceding a book, which, as anyone who's read *Independence Day: Resurgence* will tell you, is seldom a good thing.

54

song is a constant presence in the Deutsch music charts each December. They consider it something of a classic over there, which would be a tempting reason to mock them were it not for our own annual dalliance with East 17's *Stay Another Day*.

On a darker note, young Melanie Thornton died in a plane crash in 2001, two days after her single was released. I expected this book to be Victorian-heavy and German-heavy, but I didn't foresee it being death-heavy. Believe me, as far as tragedy goes, we've only just got started. Altogether now:

Tragedies are comin'
Tragedies are comin'

And this isn't the end of the Coca-Cola Christmas story, either. Just you wait til you get to the F-section.

Crackers

Originally called 'Cosaques' because they sounded like the fire of a Cossack's rifle,[1] Christmas crackers were invented by a London confectioner called Tom Smith in the 19th century.[2]

Smith had visited France and, as confectioners are prone to do, admired the way the natives wrapped their bonbons (as it were). A sense of nationalism surged within Smith and he went home to set about devising an Anglo-Saxon response. His first move was to wrap *his* sweets in paper, too, à la France. But he wasn't content with merely mimicking the wrapping methods of la République. He wanted to go further, pushing the boundaries of confectionary design. To spice things up, he slipped love

---

[1] Not sure why they weren't called 'Cossacks', then, to be honest.

[2] When else?

notes between the sweet and the paper.[1] Alas, Smith had underestimated just how sexually repressed the English were, and the love note innovation failed; his sweets were no more popular than before. Then, one crisp winter's night, destitute, staring into his crackling fireplace, he had an idea:

'Wouldn't it be great,' he exclaimed, 'if my new invention involved an explosion of some sort!'

His wife pretended not to hear him and went up to bed, muttering something about an early start, but Smith stayed awake, envisaging a sweet which cracked like a firework when opened.[2]

Smith's new exploding wrappers were a sensation, ensuring parties went off with a bang, not just at Christmas, but all year round.[3] Bored of sweets, he replaced the wrappers' contents with toys and trinkets. So successful was his innovation, Smith was commissioned as master cracker-maker for a range of national events and exhibitions. When weaselly competitors entered the fray, offering their own range of crackers, Smith went even further with his designs, stunning all and sundry with his creativity. The cracker gene was clearly hereditary. It was

---

[1] Nothing sordid, of course. They were phrases, instead, in keeping with the standards of Empire at that time. Things like 'Come hither', 'Tell me, dear woman, are you betrothed as such?' and 'Get yer ankles out'.

[2] I should point out that this is Tom Smith's own version of events. Some people think he stole the idea and devised this little anecdote as a cover story.

[3] Some Australians still call Christmas crackers 'bonbons', which is decidedly highbrow by their standards. You'd think they'd call them Snazzy Whizz Bangers.

Smith's own son who, in the 1950s, produced the classic joke/ hat/toy cracker combo that we know and love today.[1]

The toys inside crackers have a charm and history all of their own and, for all the different brands of cracker now available, seem to be omnipresent. I was personally partial to the 'mystery calculator' and the plastic frog, but there was also room in my heart for the spinning top and ball-bearing maze. The only thing I didn't like - besides the plastic earrings - was the little goldfish who revealed your inner emotions. You could only watch as it curled and writhed on your open palm, revealing to onlookers that you were deeply in love with your gran.

Then there's the paper hats. One can chart one's life through one's response to paper hats, can't one? As a baby, one will wear the thing unconsciously, eventually pulling it from one's head to eat it. When a toddler, one will wear the thing happily, thinking its crown to be an apt reflection of one's standing in the world. When slightly older, one will feel like a dickwad and refuse to wear it for fear of appearing uncool. In late teens, one may condescend to wear the hat sarcastically. Then, later on, grudgingly. Later still, plump with middle-age and good health, one shall wear it with sincere content. Until, finally, once again, one shall don the thing unconsciously, pulling it from one's head to eat, causing the care-worker on minimum wage to wonder if one is choking.

For all their evolution, crackers still have an amazing capacity to underwhelm in their key duty: to make a cracking sound. How often are you left in a scenario where, having pulled a cracker, you have to then manually unwrap its contents and

---

[1] The Smith family company merged with Caley Crackers in 1953, setting up shop in my beloved Norwich. Also, there's a belter of a BFI documentary called *Making Christmas Crackers* available to watch for free online. It was made in 1910.

yank the snapping strip independently of its casing? I know I've done it plenty of times. Even when the bang has worked, I have *never* seen a cracker split neatly down the middle when pulled. It's always lopsided carnage, with shrapnel flying around and plastic frogs landing in the gravy jug.

As a nation, we buy around 154 million crackers each Christmas. Oh, and it's illegal to take them on planes.

OK. What else do you want to know?

D is for...

Dates

Not just the name of the very best episode of *Only Fools & Horses* (and it was a Christmas special to boot), dates were once a staple of the British Christmas. Or, should I say, a staple of the British *new year*. The truth is, although bought with Christmas in mind, dates would usually spend the season looking on helplessly as every other treat was devoured. Then, on the eleventh or twelfth day, with the Quality Street tins licked clean and with the television idents back to their non-festive normality, the dates would have their moment in the sun.

'Eat Me,' said their glasses-case-shaped box.

'If we must,' came the general reply.

Dates were memorable for their texture more than their taste: a cross between a sweet found under the sofa and a bollock. Chewy and leathery to start with, they'd slyly soften. Then, somehow, by the end, they'd be rock hard. Black magic. No wonder they were held into position in their box by a white, plastic version of the devil's pitchfork.

I always felt dates had a high opinion of themselves, as though they thought they were Christmas royalty. How wrong they were. Although still loved in other corners of the world - it's often a food that Muslims choose to break their Ramadan fast - modern Britons tend to feel the same way about dates as they do the Cold War: they're not sure why they put up with either for so long but are glad both have been left in the 1980s.

Deaths, Celebrity

Famous Christmas Day birthdays are legion and include Sir Isaac Newton, Jesus and Dido, to name but three (in no particular order), but it's the Christmas Day deaths that grab the glory. Among the many victims reaped by yuletide's tinsel-wrapped scythe are Dean Martin, James Brown, Eartha Kitt and George Michael. Perhaps most famous of all is Charlie Chaplin, who passed away in 1977.[1] Fittingly, even French film pioneer Charles Pathé, the man who first brought celebrity video news to the masses, kicked the festive bucket on December 25th, 1957.

And don't think celebrities are the only ones bereft of oxygen at this time of year. Statistically, and it is a genuine pleasure to bring you this news, we are *all* more likely to die around Christmas than at any other time; the cause of which being, most likely, heart disease. The other reasons for this annual festive bloodbath are cause for great debate. One theory is that people delay seeking medical advice 'until the new year'. Another is that unwell people subconsciously hang on to see

---

[1] I find it hard to comprehend Charlie Chaplin being alive in the 1970s; I associate him too much with the distant past. I can't imagine him being around at the same time as Hot Chocolate and *The Generation Game*.

one more Christmas Day, then get out of the game sharpish before the prospect of watching yet another *Jools Holland Hootenanny* presents itself.

On the plus side, suicide rates are usually at their lowest in December.

So, you know, every cloud.[1]

Decorations

Estimates of how much we proud Britons splash out on festive decorations per annum range from £30 to £300. Depending on which publication you read, the average Brit is either a refined spender with an eye for a bargain, or an electricity guzzling Christmas tycoon who drenches the house's exterior in fairy lights and fifty-foot inflatable snowmen. My hunch is that the real figure is closer to £30 than £300. Regardless, it doesn't matter how many new decorations *I* buy each year, nothing warms my heart more than my box of old ones.

I suspect most families have a box of Christmas decorations that means more than all their other boxes combined. Full of priceless school-made artefacts, they harbour gems such as angels depicted in dry spaghetti, poorly proportioned gingerbread men made out of clay, and weak-gripped drawings of Father Christmas (complete with a green beard, four sets of teeth and a handful of extra noses). And all, of course, with miniature calendars glued to the bottom at clumsy, vulnerable angles. Children's Christmas decorations are so joyous that

---

[1] Although it goes against everything we're told on TV and in Facebook memes, this is completely true. The stats prove it. Christmas Day is regularly the *day* with the fewest UK suicides, and December is regularly the *month* with the fewest.

Homebase should switch suppliers and hand the toddlers of Great Britain next year's production contract.

The only negative about cherished Christmas decorations is that hanging them requires an operation worthy of a trained conservationist. It's like handling the earliest surviving copy of Shakespeare's *First Folio*. The slightest fumble can break hearts.

Even the box that the old decorations live in is often adored. If I catch a glimpse of mine in the summer, whilst doing something mundane like looking for a sleeping bag, it transports me frantically back and forth to Christmases past and yet-to-come. The one at my mum's house is a Frazzles box from a time when Frazzles were new kids on the block, in crisp-eating circles.[1] I only need to see a flash of the box's logo and I'm lost to the past.

With good reason, gone are the dangerous tree decorations of yore, although they leave fond memories: the knife-sharp glass stars; the lights that hummed when you switched them on at the wall; the pink sugar mice that could give you Type 2 diabetes with one lick. The Christmases of my own childhood were made particularly thrilling by a set of glass baubles which had a deadly inverted concave designed to simply invite fleshy, investigative little fingers. Whenever my sisters and I went within five metres of them, any adults in the vicinity would drop everything and shout:

'DON'T TOUCH THEM! THEY'LL RIP YOUR HANDS OFF!'

Considering the risk my parents thought these baubles posed, it's surprising they were brought into the house in the first place. It was as though they'd invited an Iberian wolf to live with us for a couple of weeks.

---

[1] Some time around the sinking of the Belgrano.

Dickens, Charles

'I wear the chain I forged in life,' replied the Ghost. *'I made it link by link, and yard by yard.'*

Charles Dickens, *A Christmas Carol*, 1843

Upon release, *A Christmas Carol* was considered something of a return to form for Charles Dickens. Having gone from one roaring success to the next with his serialised tales - *Oliver Twist, Nicholas Nickleby, The Old Curiosity Shop* - the slow sales of *Martin Chuzzlewit* caught the superstar off-guard. His reckless spending and ever-expanding family had taken their toll on the coffers. Suddenly, despite having penned a string of hits already, he found himself needing to produce yet another.[1]

Inflamed by his meandering night walks, where he would pace hauntedly around London's backstreets for hours on end in search of peace and inspiration, Dickens dreamt up an idea for a Christmas story. Writing furiously by day, walking furiously by night, this new novel took him just six weeks to write. The story consumed him. As his friend and biographer, John Forster, reported, 'He wept over it, and laughed, and wept again, and excited himself to an extraordinary degree'.

Dickens, excited to an extraordinary degree, wanted his new Christmas book to be fully illustrated with colour pictures. His publishers, as publishers tend to do, refused the lavish request, wondering if good old black & white sketches wouldn't do the

---

[1] Technically, *Martin Chuzzlewit* still had time to become a hit. Like most Dickens books, the story was serialised in monthly episodes. The first instalment came in December, 1842, but there was still a third of the story left to write by the time the comparatively short *A Christmas Carol* came out in 1843. The last issue of *Chuzzlewit* was released in July, 1844. Sales did pick up but they were dwarfed by those of the Christmas book.

trick instead. Rather than backing their star man, they threatened to reduce his pay if his festive venture failed. To eliminate the risk of losing money on publishing costs, they wanted the story to be slipped into a magazine or an anthology. Dickens was adamant it be a standalone novel. Defeating the entire object of the book as an opportunity to get him in the black, he decided that *A Christmas Carol* should instead be beautifully bound and kaleidoscopic, a gift which people would buy for one another and take delight in. With Christmas fast approaching, he threw his own money into the project, paying the bulk of the vast production expenses out of his ever-decreasing private funds. He could have chosen to print the book cheaply, of course, but what good would an ugly book be at Christmas time? Where's the fun in that?

We accept coloured pictures as a given these days, but in 1843 they required busy production lines of artists neatly painting each image by hand.[1] *A Christmas Carol* was eventually released on the deliciously festive date of December 19th, mere weeks after its final word had been written. In today's money, these first editions were priced at around £20 - not costly enough to turn much profit. But Dickens couldn't price them any higher without financially alienating his audience. So, already against the ropes, he took yet another hit. The first run of books sold out in under a week. Dickens made just £230.[2]

---

[1] With their wages all paid by Mr Dickens.

[2] First edition sales were often the most crucial in terms of royalties. In the days before effective copyrighting (another cause Dickens successfully championed), once a book was released, it was pray to all sorts of unofficial rewrites and plagiarisms. Theatre companies, for example, would adapt popular novels, change huge parts of them, rake in a fortune, and owe nothing to the original authors. Worse still, wholly new bootleg versions of books, with edits and new characters and God knows what else, would be sold on street corners.

For a man who had already knocked out a handful of English literature's best-loved works, it is astonishing to think that in 1843 Dickens was still only thirty-two. Equally astonishing is that his finest material lay ahead of him (and that his publishers considered it to lay *behind* him[1]). At the time of writing *A Christmas Carol*, the wisened old bearded incarnation of Dickens - of ten pound note fame - was barely half-formed. The 1843 Dickens model was still an excitable, clean-shaven dandy: England's first literary titan, leading a course for other literary titans to follow.

Although often surrounded by crowds[2] or friends and family,[3] I can't help but think of Charles Dickens as a lonely soul. He was a man who liked to travel alone, walk to London alone, walk *around* London alone. At night. ('I would get up directly after lying down,' he wrote, 'go out, and come home tired at sunrise. My principal object: to get through the night.') He would sometimes walk as far as thirty miles, until he was deep into Kent, lit by the sunrise. Even some of his Christmas traditions were solitary. Despite spending much of the season playing the all-entertaining celebrity host, two of his routines involved walking the East End markets on Christmas Eve, then, on Christmas Day, wandering through the city's poor districts

---

[1] In retrospect, I guess he *was* kind of washed up by that point. He only had *Little Dorrit*, *David Copperfield*, *Great Expectations*, *Dombey & Son*, *Bleak House* and *Our Mutual Friend* ahead of him. And *Hard Times*. Oh, and *A Tale Of Two Cities*.

[2] In America, his arrival was greeted with Beatlemania-like euphoria, with women wildly snipping off pieces of his coat and begging for locks of his hair.

[3] He referred to his family - eventually comprising of ten children - as his 'menagerie'.

alone, unnoticed, to secretly watch families preparing their dinners through their windows.[1]

Many biographers suggest Dickens' love of Christmas was inspired by the happy Christmases of his early years of semi-wealth and semi-plenty, before his father was incarcerated in Marshalsea debtors' prison. That the bulk of Dickens' output, including *A Christmas Carol*, is rife with social commentary is likely a result of such an upheaval. By the age of twelve, Dickens' comfortable childhood had been aborted. He was removed from public school and sent to work in a factory near Charing Cross. The job required him to paste labels onto jars of boot polish. His wages - six shillings a week - went towards supporting his bankrupt parents.[2] He was so traumatised by the experience that he kept it secret for most of his adult life. Driven by private demons and a desire to exorcise them, he frequently visited poorhouses and penal institutions as an adult, and, whilst there, saw children - of an age who, today, would be

---

[1] His observations of which almost certainly make an appearance in *A Christmas Carol*, in the chapter where Scrooge watches the Cratchit family eat their dinner unawares. Dickens' excursions weren't just fanciful, they were immensely brave. He would knowingly walk through diarrhoea-scented slums - riddled with typhoid and numerous air-borne killers - seemingly oblivious to the accepted wisdom of the day that 'all smell is disease'. On occasions where he visited these downtrodden areas with friends, he would often have to watch on stoically as they were physically sick in the street. Biographer Peter Ackroyd perhaps most strikingly sums up life in the capital by saying 'most people felt sick virtually all the time they were in [Victorian] London'.

[2] While in the factory, Dickens worked with a raggedy boy by the name of Bob Fagin. 'I took the liberty of using his name, long afterwards, in *Oliver Twist*,' he revealed.

performing in school nativities and learning how to spell 'cat' - being forced into deadly manual labour.

For all our sleepy mythologising of the 19th century as Great Britain's heyday, the fact is that life in industrial cities was close to hellish for most.[1] In Manchester at the time of *A Christmas Carol*'s release, half of all working class children died before their fifth birthday; in Liverpool, the average age of death for factory workers was fifteen; in Dickens' own London, around half of all funerals were for children under ten.[2] It was the plight of these neglected inner-city children that inspired *A Christmas Carol*. Dickens knew their world because he had lived in it. His book was a call to action for those with the power to force positive change.[3] Today, the fashion of the intellectuals is to write off much of the author's work as sanctimonious. It is just about the cruellest thing we can have done to his legacy. And, I suppose, the most inevitable.

After the popular success of *A Christmas Carol*, the young Dickens produced a new Christmas tale or essay nigh-on every year. They always sold well but none have had the staying power of Ebenezer Scrooge and his late-night visitations. The story

---

[1] It was no picnic out in the country, either. The reason why populations of cities such as London swelled in the 1800s was that thousands were trying to escape the plight of rural famine.

[2] And those that survived were often subjected to a life of misery, incest and prostitution. One especially unpleasant passage (of many) in Peter Ackroyd's *Dickens' London* tells of a man who'd 'had sexual intercourse with the child he had begotten of his own daughter'.

[3] Scrooge's profession is never made clear (in the novel, at least). Dickens deliberately meant for him to represent all wealthy men from all trades.

Dickens wrote in those frenetic six weeks in autumn 1843 is now so well-known that its phrases and ideas remain part of our own festivities almost two centuries on. Where would our modern Christmas be without expressions such as 'Bah, humbug', 'God bless us, every one',[1] and even 'Merry Christmas' itself?[2] Not to mention the numerous parodies made by near enough every TV programme ever.[3]

We now know the story so well that it's easy to forget how outrageously gorgeous its premise: that acts of human cruelty lock their perpetrators in invisible chains and, when they die, the chains become visible to them. These shackled spirits, the book says, now wander among us, looking on, wishing they could help the needy, but are unable to act.

Scrooge watches them from his bedroom window:

'Every one of them wore chains like Marley's Ghost; some few (they might be guilty governments) were linked together; none were free. Many had been personally known to Scrooge in their lives. He had been quite familiar with one old ghost, in a white waistcoat, with a monstrous iron safe attached to its ankle, who cried piteously at being unable to assist a wretched woman with an infant, whom it saw below, upon a door-step. The misery with them all was, clearly, that they

---

[1] Not, let it be noted, 'God bless us, *everyone*'.

[2] The phrase 'Merry Christmas' went back centuries but was re-popularised by the book. Dickens also helped forge the connection of snow to Christmas. His famous *Pickwick Papers* instalment featuring Mr Pickwick on the ice was published just as England was gripped in its 1836 Christmas tundra (the very tundra which, as mentioned in a previous chapter, has been depicted on Christmas cards ever since).

[3] Including, in 2016, an *Eastenders* reimagining (performed by the 'Walford Players') which remains the single worst piece of television ever produced by fully grown adults with actual jobs.

sought to interfere, for good, in human matters, and had lost the power for ever.'

The time to act, *A Christmas Carol* tells us, is in fullness of life. The only way to break free from your past and improve your yet-to-come is to change in the present. 'It has,' wrote G.K. Chesterton of it, 'the same kind of artistic unity that belongs to a dream.'

Viewed by one critic on publication as 'a new gospel', the book was in tune with the growing public consciousness of the time. Even Dickens' lifelong literary foe, Thackeray, called *A Christmas Carol* a 'benefit to mankind'. Numerous anecdotes of the age tell of real-life Scrooge-like characters reading the story and changing their ways, throwing their money and weight around to make things better, lest they feel the tug of the ghostly chains.

What *A Christmas Carol* also served to do was stoke the fire of growing Victorian interest in archaic Christmas traditions (we already know how fixated they were with the medieval age). Although it was the title of an unwatchable turd of a 2017 movie, Charles Dickens was not *the man who invented Christmas*.[1] He certainly helped make it fashionable again, though. Seen beforehand, largely, as a rural holiday to be celebrated in lowly villages and backwaters, the novel brought yuletide traditions back to the swelling towns and cities of Britain.[2] Why Bob Cratchit so tentatively asks Scrooge if he can take Christmas Day off is because shops and businesses generally stayed open

---

[1] More eagle-eyed readers may have noted, for instance, that the year *A Christmas Carol* was released, 1843, was also the year Sir Henry Cole produced the first Christmas card. Proof enough that Christmas was already finding new favour.

[2] Towns and cities which were now swelling, interestingly, with people from lowly villages and backwaters.

on Christmas Day. That Scrooge gloomily consents is a sign that the book dwells in the realm of fantasy. In real life, at that time, it would've been a no-go; the modern equivalent would be asking your boss if you could have Valentine's Day off.[1]

Prior to *A Christmas Carol*, newspapers and advertisers seldom mentioned Christmas. After it, they sensed its commercial potential. I suppose the tempting thing to ask is, 'What would Dickens think about how Christmas has been monetised and over-hyped?' My suspicion is that he would raise a smile. To pinch a line from Claire Tomalin's excellent biography, Dickens saw 'good cheer, food and drink shared, gifts and even dancing, [as] not merely frivolous pleasures but basic expressions of love and mutual support among all human beings'. We have to think that he would not encourage getting into debt or the proliferation of Easter eggs in Sainsbury's on December 24th, but he would be happy that Christmas Day has become an event, the only event in the whole year when you can guarantee the 'dull principles as bargain and sale' get short shrift and the Cratchit families of the modern world can spend the day at home.

For now.

When *A Christmas Carol* was written, the bustling, snowy, goose-roasted idea of a Victorian Christmas that the story depicts was largely a feat of its author's imagination. It was what Charles Dickens *hoped* Christmas would become. A time of games, family, food and merriment. By and large, thanks in no small part to the great man's own endeavour, he got his wish.

---

[1] Things were even less festive north of the border, where Christmas Day was only made a public holiday in 1958. Boxing Day followed suit in 1974. (For a country in which Christ-mass was banned for the best part of four centuries, it should be of little surprise to learn that Scotland is comparatively barren on the 'festive tradition' front.)

At the end of the story, Ebenezer Scrooge throws open his bedroom window on Christmas morning in a fit of ecstasy. If you're on your own at this precise moment, I'd sincerely recommend reading this passage aloud:

'No fog, no mist; clear, bright, jovial, stirring, cold; cold, piping for the blood to dance to; Golden sunlight; Heavenly sky; sweet fresh air; merry bells. Oh, glorious! Glorious!'

It's difficult to say those words and not feel better afterwards.

In his preface to *A Christmas Carol's* first edition, Dickens hoped that the spirit of his 'Ghostly' book would find favour with his readers.

'May it haunt their houses pleasantly,' he said, 'and no one wish to lay it.'

Donkeys

Little donkey, little donkey, had a heavy day
Little donkey, carry Mary, safely on her way

Eric Boswell, *Little Donkey*, 1959

Finally, a Christmas tradition rooted firmly in biblical traditions.

Well, not quite.

The idea that Mary rode from Nazareth to Bethlehem - about eighty miles - on the back of a creature that tends to flag after twenty yards on a seaside beach, is possibly too hard for even the converted to believe. They'll accept a virgin birth, but, like a donkey, their beliefs will only go so far. Luckily for them, they don't have to believe it, as this particular little donkey isn't in the Bible. The Gospels make no mention of which creature

Mary rode into Bethlehem on.[1] It's most likely to have been a horse or camel. That being said, donkeys *were* cheaper and, in that respect, fit the narrative neatly. Then there's the pleasantly circular aspect of the Easter story, in which Jesus, now out of the crib and fully bearded, rode into Jerusalem triumphantly on a donkey...

Oh, who knows? Perhaps Joseph gave her a piggy back.

Beautifully odd, it is perhaps the sombre gait of a donkey that warms it to people's hearts. Donkeys have always been looked upon fondly by artists and writers, from A.A. Milne's Eeyore to G.K. Chesterton's 'tattered outlaw of the earth'. But perhaps the best-loved ass - oh, come on, grow up - is the beautiful ass that children everywhere sing about in *Little Donkey*.

It may sound as though it's of a finer vintage, but *Little Donkey* was actually written in the late 1950s by a physics lecturer from Sunderland.[2] Gracie Fields found the song too complex for her ageing vocal cords and the physics lecturer simplified it on her

---

[1] This is true of a lot of nativity traditions, as you doubtless already know (and, if you don't, will have hammered home to you later on in the book). The idea of Mary riding a donkey is likely to come from the Gospel of James, one of the many gnostic gospels (effectively, a series of 'unofficial' gospels with even zanier tales than the ones that made the New Testament's final cut. Gnostic gospels have served to fuel endless conspiracy theories about Jesus and the church. Without their wacky yarns, Dan Brown would still be doing bar-work to make ends meet). The gnostic gospels may be out of favour now, but they were widely recited and believed across Europe until the 16th century, at which point the emerging Protestant church disavowed them, causing the Catholic church to follow suit in an attempt to look cool/ hard.

[2] In all honesty, have I not done well to keep this book down to 400 pages? I mean, this fact alone feels like it deserves several passages of specialist attention.

behalf. His new arrangement not only made it effortless for Mrs Fields, but for music teachers up and down the land. They slotted the song into school carol services with ease. Although recorded by a host of stars, its popularity with teachers truly brought home the bacon. Sheet music sales to schools ensured a lucrative longevity for the little donkey.

To this day, the simple tune can cause a whole generation to float back in time to their school hall nativities, barefoot and giving it plenty:

Ring out those bells tonight
Bethlehem, Bethlehem
Follow that star tonight
Bethlehem, Bethlehem

It's hard to conceive how anybody could fail to covet their neighbour's ass after hearing so sweet a ditty.

Oh, now, look. Do grow up.

The 12 Songs Of Christmas

#3

Peace On Earth/Little Drummer Boy - David Bowie & Bing Crosby

No matter how many times you see the video, it never stops being strange. The sight of David Bowie, aged thirty but looking ten years older due to his former hankering for cocaine,[1] standing beside a cardigan-clad seventy-four-year-old Bing Crosby is difficult for our brains to categorise. It's like seeing a selection of continental cheeses laid out on the bonnet of a monster truck. We don't know what to do with the image.

The video is actually an excerpt from *Bing Crosby's Merrie Olde Christmas*, a 1977 US TV special[2] in which Mr Crosby spends a weekend at the manor of Sir Percival Crosby, a long-lost relative. Bing visits the house with the intention - and this is where the premise thins further still - of retracing his family history by perusing the deceased's belongings. Surprisingly, for all its soft-focus and Stateside aesthetics, the show was filmed

---

[1] Bowie is said to have existed for a while on crack, milk and red peppers (a diet idea taken from *Mary Berry's Kitchen Favourites*). A year previous to his duet with Bing, he'd released an album called *Station To Station*, the recording of which he famously remembers nothing.

[2] The 42nd consecutive Christmas special Bing Crosby had presented.

in merrie olde England. Perhaps because of this fact, Sir Percival's home is visited by a host of British celebs who just so happened to be near Elstree Studios that day (including half-forgotten film-star Norman Baxter and the model Twiggy.[1])

Bowie's unexpected appearance on the show was down to three factors. The first was that Bing's real family felt somebody hip and young was needed to give the programme vitality (some hip-replacement, if you will). The second was that the drug-free Bowie was still in no fit state, mentally or physically, to tour his new album, *Heroes*, and needed to promote his music on TV as much as possible to make amends. A third, and more polite, version of events claims that Bowie appeared on the show because his mum was a Bing Crosby fan.[2]

Typical of the man in his full 1970s swagger, Bowie arrived on the set of *Merrie Olde Christmas* with little awareness of what he was expected to do. When he heard the song the producers had lined up for him - *Little Drummer Boy* - he was less than impressed. ('I hate this song,' was his exact critique.) Panicked, the show's musical team spent an hour writing an entirely new song, *Peace On Earth*, which they hoped Mr Bowie might be willing to sing instead, over the top of Bing Crosby's *Little Drummer Boy*. Bowie consented, leaving he and Bing scant rehearsal time for the all-new arrangement. They sang at one another initially. Then, together. To the surprise of everyone

---

[1] Who'd appeared on the cover art of Bowie's *PinUps* in 1973, looking effete and slightly unwell.

[2] Closer to the truth is that Bowie himself had always been a lover of the crooners, particularly Frank Sinatra. The feeling wasn't mutual. When Bowie was touted to play Sinatra in a biopic, Sinatra barked that he wasn't going to be played by 'that faggot'. Bowie went to see him play in Vegas and requested to meet Ol' Blue Eyes backstage. Ol' Blue Eyes sent a note back denying Ol' Discoloured Left-Eye the privilege.

watching the unlikely duo practise on the studio floor, their voices blended with rare beauty:

Come, they told me, parump-pa-pum-pum

A new born king to see, parump-pa-pum-pum

Also a thing of rare, albeit bizarre, beauty, was the scripted dialogue between the two, as they made their way to the piano under the bold studio lights of Sir Percival Crosby's home:

'Now tell me,' says Bing, cameras rolling. 'D'ya ever listen to some of the older fellas?'

'Oh sure,' Bowie replies, 'I like, er, John Lennon.' He scratches his thin white chin. 'And the other one, Harry Nilsson.'

'Mmm,' Bing smiles, 'you go back that far, huh?'

'I'm not as young as I look,' says Bowie, looking ten years older than he actually is.

One noteworthy part of their exchange is Bing's pronunciation of 'Bowie'. As a boy from the American heartlands, he knew the word was pronounced 'boo-ie', not bow (as in 'bow tie') or bow (as in 'take a bow'). *Boo*. As in a *boo*-ie knife, which is exactly what the young David Jones had named himself after. The pronunciation of Bowie has long been a cause of debate. In an interview with *Newsnight* in 1999, Bowie claimed that even he didn't know how it was pronounced anymore. In his earlier years though, he said it was bow as in 'bow tie' (as that's how *he'd* thought 'bowie knife' was pronounced). It's intriguing to hear the All-American Bing Crosby tell it like it is (or like it should have been).

Throughout their duologue, Bing glances off camera, as though seeking assurance that all is going well and that this young crackpot isn't talking bollocks. Then the music starts up. Bowie pretends to play the piano. The camera closes in. All awkwardness fades. And out of the mess we're left with two icons from two different planets singing two different songs, all the while achieving a curiously moving unity:

I pray my wish will come true

For my child and your child, too

At this point, Bing looks at his production team again, and smiles to himself, singing up to the rafters.

He'll see the day of glory
See the day when men of goodwill
Live in peace, live in peace again

The song fades. Bowie attempts to make eye-contact. Bing holds focus on the middle-distance instead. They share the final line:

Can it be?...

Silence.

'It's a pretty thing, isn't it?' Bing concludes, in his Baloo-like voice.[1]

Whereas Bowie looked the closer to death at the time of filming, it was Bing Crosby who would pass away first, just five weeks after the shoot.[2] Their duet, however, wasn't released as a single for another five years, and was done so without Bowie's permission, denting his credibility months before his perfectly cultivated upcoming 1983 comeback *Let's Dance*. Regardless, their duet shifted close to half a million copies in the UK alone and has, to this day, outsold the majority of David Bowie's other

---

[1] Quite gloriously, this final snippet of dialogue remains on most edits of the single.

[2] A similar fate had befallen Marc Bolan of T-Rex. Just *two days* prior to *Merrie Olde Christmas*, after recording a 1977 TV special with David Bowie, he was killed in a car crash. (I'm not suggesting anything untoward here, although Bowie himself later admitted 'I was getting seriously worried about whether I should appear on TV again'.)

releases.[1] As he had no songwriting credit, it was far from the cash cow that other Christmas hits have proved to be elsewhere in the biz. Luckily, he had a few bob tucked away in his Current Account for rainy days.

Even if you hate *Peace On Earth/Little Drummer Boy*, which would be wholly understandable, I'd still encourage you to look up the full segment of *Bing Crosby's Merrie Olde Christmas* on YouTube. It's like watching a controlled explosion in reverse, creation forming out of rubble. Predictably, with David Bowie also now passed, lots of the viewer comments claim that the two of them are now duetting in heaven, singing for the angels and so on.

Music can make people very soppy sometimes.

Isn't a pretty thing, isn't it?

#4

A Winter's Tale - David Essex

Talking of soppy.

Initially somewhat forgotten, *A Winter's Tale* has now, almost forty years on from its original release, become a standard of the Christmas compilation album (usually appearing towards the end of disc two, between Steeleye Span and Kylie Minogue). The cream rises to the top, as they say. Even where Christmas songs are concerned. Although, in all honesty, I wouldn't necessarily class *A Winter's Tale* as cream. It's more like a little

---

[1] As the singer of *White Christmas*, Mr Crosby would've sniffed at a measly half million sales. He was used to his own Christmas songs selling closer to fifty million.

sprinkle of chocolate for on top of the cream, which you can't particularly taste but is inoffensive nonetheless. Either way, it's a nice enough song, that's what I'm trying to say. The reason I want to write about it, though, is that, like *2000 Miles*, it has a backstory of note. Except this time, nobody is found overdosed in a bathtub.

And that's a promise.

A *Winter's Tale* was written by Mike Batt after David Essex had called him in late October, 1982, requesting a Christmas single.[1] Batt himself had recently *become* a Christmas single after his girlfriend had swanned off to Australia to focus on her acting career. They'd still loved each other but, to quote Batt, their relationship was 'terminated' for 'geographical' reasons.[2]

'I wanted to send a message to the girl,' Batt said. *A Winter's Tale* would be that message. Well, international calls weren't cheap back then, and he wasn't made of money.

Mike Batt, for the benefit of those who have a social life or value utilising their memory for more important information, had made his fortune as chief songwriter for a criminally underrated early 70s glam rock outfit by the name of The Wombles. Cleverly, Batt had rejected a £200 fee from the BBC for creating *The Wombles'* theme tune[3] and, instead, retained copyright for all future wombling musical endeavours. He wrote

---

[1] *Oh, what a night - late October back in '82*
Essex called Batt for a Christmas tune
What a feeling, what a night...

[2] Ah, the sweet poetic language of love. I'm certain that Wordsworth mentions an affair 'terminated' for 'geographical' reasons somewhere in *The Lucy Poems*.

[3] Still an absolute banger.

78

numerous huge-selling hits for the band,[1] until their star finally faded and the boys succumbed to the usual rock-star addictions, making good use of the needles they found on London's commons. By 1975, The Wombles had, as Batt might put it, been terminated.[2]

Post-wombles, Batt branched out and worked with other underground-dwelling mammals, penning the song *Bright Eyes* for the bunny massacre that is *Watership Down*. He also wrote Katie Melua's two best-known songs: *The Closest Thing To Crazy* and *Nine Million Bicycles*. And *she* is the first ever singer to perform live under the sea at the base of an oil rig - and you don't get much more underground than that. But that's a different story.[3]

Back in '82, with little else to do with his free time but mope about of an October evening, Batt set to work on his song for David Essex.[4] Not that he had much choice. Christmas was just around the corner and the as-yet-unwritten song needed to be recorded *and* pressed in time for December's all-important vinyl

---

[1] Including the classic *Wombling Merry Christmas*, which was kept off number 1 by Mud's *Lonely This Christmas*. Festive tunes galore in '74. Salad days, fellow Christmas fan. Salad days.

[2] But none had been found dead in a bathtub, let me make that clear.

[3] The performance took place 994 feet under the seabed in 2006. According to one report, she 'performed two concerts at the bottom of a hollow concrete leg that helps support an offshore platform'. How's that for rock 'n roll? Melua called the gig 'surreal'. 'Terrifying' would have been my word of choice, with 'pointless' a close second.

[4] It must be weird to work in showbusiness and have to field calls from the likes of David Essex, in which you're asked to quickly write a Christmas song. What face does one pull when they put the receiver down after *that* conversation? I mean, honestly, think about the subject of *your* last phone call and compare it to that.

sale bonanza. Batt speedily composed a melody and just so happened to have Sir Tim Rice round for lunch the next day. Over a bowl of stew that tasted suspiciously like womble meat, Batt gave Sir Tim the gist of his relationship woes, using the words 'terminated' and 'geographical' at opportune moments. Being the old pro that he is, Timbo bashed out a verse in next to no time, before buggering off on a prior engagement, leaving the recently-heartbroken Mike Batt to pen the rest:

And anyway the snow has covered all your footsteps
And I can follow you no more

Meanwhile, over in Australia, his ex-girlfriend had started a new relationship with a fellow actor which she was in no mood to terminate, especially as geographical issues were no longer a factor. Mike Batt had written the song as a message and the message was doomed to fall on deaf ears.

I wonder if you hear
I wonder if you're listening

Mike Batt's loss was David Essex's gain, however. To the singer's delight, *A Winter's Tale* was recorded *and* pressed in time for Christmas. Not only that, his record label also managed to film a drop-everything-and-YouTube-it video of Essex dressed like Frodo Baggins, hamming his way around a manor house, looking wistfully out of lead-slatted windows and stroking a frankly enormous - and confused - doberman by a fireside.[1]

Sales were modest at first but the tune eventually peaked at number 2 in the UK singles chart, albeit in January, long after the last pine needles had been hoovered from the nation's carpets. This slow burn in sales would mirror the song's gradual

---

[1] Somewhat mysteriously, this video has recently been replaced with an alternative featuring David Essex stalking around moorlands in Heathcliff-mode, stroking an average size - and content - border collie by a fireside. The original can't be found for love nor money. It's been *terminated*. I reckon it's something to do with the illuminati.

emergence as a festive omnipresence. Although far from being a knockabout party favourite, its melancholy chorus is sung, either in jest or sincerity, in many a home at this time of year:

It was only a winter's tale
Just another winter's tale
And why should the world take notice
Of one more love that's failed?

And for all its saccharine silliness, a real break-up, real pain, lies at its heart.

But, my friends, I'm not here to bum you out. This is a cheerful book, I swear. As promised, the cream - or, indeed, the little sprinkle of chocolate - has floated to the top of this particular coffee in more ways than one. Many years later, geographical forces made good their earlier errors: Mike Batt and the Australian actress met again. The spark remained. They got back together and remain happily unterminated to this day. *One more love that's failed?* Not on my watch, folks.

And aside from the occasional bifta smoked purely for medicinal reasons, The Wombles have all been clean for the best part of forty years, too.

The Yule Log

SEPTEMBER

Sat 1st -

The 'X Factor' is back. Christmas really is on its way.

The programme once had no peer, ruling Saturday night television, swatting aside all challengers. Look at it now. A rigid corpse. Every year, viewers are promised a revamp. Yet, every year, Dermot O'Leary presents it (wearing his blue suit and trendy - for 2008 - thin black tie). Every year, the theme tune remains the same (sounding like it was composed on a Playstation2 music-maker). And the staging. And the lighting. And the judges' comments:

'You know what, I totally believed every word you sang'; 'You know what, you have got the likability factor'; 'You know what, we're going to remember you...'

I couldn't tell you precisely when 'X Factor' died, but it was probably when its audience swelled to such a size that it encompassed grandparents. Suddenly the live shows were awash with singing brickies (stubble, acoustic guitar, home county mockney) and pudding-faced karaoke-hoggers with hearts of gold. For every half-decent winner, there have been three rotters who usually go on to release just two albums. (The first, called 'Moments', features the winner's big number 1 single and assorted cover versions. The second album, called 'Second Chance', sells an amount comparable to the number of Old Testaments which could be knocked out by a Guggenheim printing press in an hour.) They're next seen in some doomed West End production - 'Jurassic Park: The Musical' - and presenting competition features on 'This Morning', before going into 'I'm A Celebrity', then out on tour to the market towns with a song called 'Crazy Hearts (Of Gold)', which they wrote whilst in the camp.

There's only so much the public will stand.

Tonight's episode was distinctly hard to watch. Robbie Williams is a judge this year. He sat there lording it up at ringside. His wife was there, too, for reasons I couldn't fathom. Also at the judges' desk was some soft-featured, clothes-horse from One Direction. I think he's called Liam or Troy. They were all unpalatable, the lot of them. Screaming at each other and showing off, then, out of nowhere, pretending to cry out of one eye. All too much, even for me.

Part of the show's former charm was that it was crap. Now it's gone beyond crap, even with the alleged revamp. In terms of comebacks, it's reminiscent of Muhammed Ali's 1980 return against Larry Holmes. Like Ali, the show is bloated, past its best, but won't quit, won't submit to the wincing of the crowd. Bruised, bloodied, and dead inside, surely somebody will chuck the towel in soon.

Thank God 'University Challenge' remains in rude health.

Mon 3rd -

I hope nobody ever talks about the summer of 1976 again. 2018 has been piping hot since May. Even the grass has got a tan.

Weds 5th -

Back to work after eight weeks off. My body didn't know what to do this morning. Waking up at 7am felt like being startled by a smoke detector in the dead of night. Shocking and quite scary.

 This is the autumn term. In other words, Christmas. Doesn't particularly feel like it with England being all lush and green/clammy.

Sun 9th -

Another Christmas advert spotted. This was for one of those 'clubs' where a gloomy single mum pays in a teeny 'bit' each month and, by December, is rolling in it, her visage a picture of good cheer.

 One development I've noticed in the last five years is how early into October the real Christmas ads start. Generally, the big players now hit their yuletide stride long before the clocks have gone back.

Tues 12th -

Woke up humming Elton John's 'Step Into Christmas'. I do like the track, but can never make the lyrics scan the way he does:

 'Eat, drink and be merry, come along with me...'

It took me about twenty years to realise what he was singing. Went online and couldn't resist checking to see if the song had a b-side. It did. It was called 'Ho! Ho! Ho! Who'd Be A Turkey At Christmas?' and sounds like a Herman's Hermits track. In other words, I liked it for reasons I can't fully explain.

Thurs 13th -

Christmas cards are in nearly every shop now. The sun shines warmly on them. They've been out for a while. Retailers need to be ahead of the game with all this stuff, obviously, but I do wonder who buys cards this early. Not only are they doubly expensive but who on earth is that prepared?

Sat 15th -

'X Factor' is still terrible. Saw a couple of minutes tonight. It's one Christmas tradition I'm happy to ditch. Simon Cowell looked like he'd had some serious plastic surgery done. By somebody he'd met at a bus stop. His bloated cheeks reminded me of JFK at the height of his drug dependency.

Friday 21st -

Don't get up to much, do I?

Mon 24th -

Still not a lot to report, Christmas-wise or otherwise. So, why am I writing? Don't know. One day in 1930, the BBC radio news began with the announcer saying, 'There is no news today'. This was followed by fifteen minutes of somebody playing the piano.

Weds 26th -

News! Serious movement in Tesco. The Quality Street tubs have been designated a small section of an aisle which, by this time next month, I expect to be a cornucopia of chocolate money, selection boxes and those tins of shortbread with a picture of a stag on the front.

Thurs 27th -

There was a bit on 'The One Show' tonight about how 'barmy' it is that Selfridges have got their Christmas stuff out. Presenter Matt Baker held the predictably mundane belief that Christmas stuff should only be out in December, which is one of the many reasons why he isn't Chancellor of the Exchequer.
 Christmas items do hit the shelves pretty early but we aren't forced to buy any of it. Being surprised or upset by it ranks alongside thinking 'them footballers get paid too much' in the pointless-things-to-say list. What are businesses to do, sweat it out and see what happens come December? Christmas is everything to retail. It's fair enough to question why Easter stuff is in the shops on Boxing Day, though, as I don't expect chocolate eggs prop up the economy in quite the same way.

Fri 28th -

Isn't it weird that I'm writing this right now on the 28th of September and haven't got a clue what's going to happen over the next few months? Whereas you can flick through these pages and become a time traveller, leaving me locked in the moment. You could hop back and forth through the unlived months of my life, if you wanted. You can find out if I get murdered or find a girlfriend or buy a yacht. Or all three. I can't guarantee anything quite so exciting will happen, though. My only prediction is that Christmas Day will be unseasonably mild. You don't need to be a time traveller to know that.

ne 12 Things To Watch Of Christmas

#3

A Christmas Story

It's one of the most bestest films ever *ever* made, what do you mean you've never heard of it?

If I'm honest, *I* only discovered it by accident. On BBC Two. No kid ever switched to BBC Two on purpose, especially in the run up to Christmas. BBC One and ITV were where the action was. BBC Two was where you went for Burt Lancaster films and claymation Shakespeare re-imaginings. I couldn't tell you the exact year of my *A Christmas Story* discovery, but it was during a shadowy period of the mid-90s where our telly had no remote control and we had to get down to ground-level to change the channels. Our TV, like most 90s models, had a black plastic flap at the front - broken off within a fortnight of use - which you could pull open to reveal manual buttons for volume control and channel hopping. In order to get from BBC One to ITV using this no-remote method, you *had* to flick past BBC Two, careful not to look directly at its output for fear of turning to stone.

Something must have been wrong with me that day. Perhaps I was tired. Whilst flicking past BBC Two, ignorant of the dangers, I accidentally looked up, catching a burst of the channel's deadly rays full in the face.

But there was no fallout. My face refused to melt. Pushing my luck, I looked at the screen once more. Instead of seeing Burt Lancaster leaning on a ranch fence, or a claymation Desdemona claiming that Othello's unkindness would ne'er taint her love, I saw a boy in thick milk-bottle-bottom glasses being chased down a snowy alleyway by a red-headed bully. Transfixed, I took my finger off the button. The chase continued. I willed the boy to escape but the bully caught him and had his way. Going against my BBC Two instincts, I watched on. I couldn't stop. The film wasn't just about the incident with the bully, it was about the boy's whole manic life in the run-up to Christmas (mainly, how his request for a toy rifle was constantly refused on the grounds that he'd 'shoot his eye out'). It was like watching my own biopic. I'd never seen a film about someone I identified with. After twenty minutes of fixation, I was dragged into some duty or other by a parent. I never saw the end. I didn't know whether the boy got his rifle or ever bested the bully. I made a point of checking Teletext to at least see what the film was called, but I forgot until it was too late.

Ah, well, maybe I'd see it next year.

Nope.

The year after?

No.

Each year, I'd desperately scour the Christmas TV guide. Initially, because I wanted to watch the ending. Eventually, because I needed evidence that the film wasn't entirely a work of my imagination. To compound the issue, nobody else knew of its existence.

The legend grew. In full adulthood, I attached titanic affection for that distant afternoon screening on BBC Two. I still needed to see it one more time, for sanity's sake as much as anything. But, God, after almost twenty years, I'd given up hope.

Then I went to Homebase.

To buy a paint roller with an extendable handle.

Minding my own business in the queue, wondering who actually signs up for Homebase loyalty cards, I turned around to find myself face-to-face with a blonde-haired boy in milk-bottle-bottom glasses.

It was him!

Of all the places to end my quest, Homebase would have been somewhere near the bottom of my list. I mean, they didn't even have any paint rollers with extendable handles (I'd had to settle for a dull old regular roller), what chance would they have of selling an obscure Christmas classic on DVD? What they lacked in the home decor front, however, they more than made up for on the dream fulfilment front. Not only were they selling this legendary movie, but they'd deliberately placed it on a shelf at eye-level so as *I* would definitely see it.

It's easy to look back on our childhoods and cringe at our mistakes, but there are also things for which we ought to pat ourselves on the back. Watching *A Christmas Story* again that afternoon, I couldn't help but be proud that, aside from my copy of *Compliments On Your Kiss* on cassette and my loyalty to *Encounters* magazine, the younger me had a semblance of taste.

A Christmas Story really is the most beautiful ninety minutes of film. It has a style reminiscent of *Malcolm In The Middle* and early *Simpsons*. The casting, always especially vital when children are taking the lead, is perfect.[1] Had the casting been dreadful, the film would still be worth watching and re-watching for the

---

[1] Ralphie, the boy with the milk-bottle glasses, played by Peter Billingsley, was one of 8,000 children auditioned for the role. (The day of audition must have been reminiscent of the crowds in an *X-Factor* series opener.)

location shots alone: snow-blanketed Midwest streets[1] and detached wooden townhouses, complete with foot-long icicles hanging from the porch and clanky Oldsmobiles in the yard. *A Christmas Story* offers a vision of late-1930s America that is as aspirational to non-Americans as it is to real ones: a casually wealthy and comfortable depiction of the past glories of industry, where every man had a job, every family had food and every home had a growing collection of exciting new electronic appliances. *A Christmas Story*'s splendour, however, lies not in its retrospective aesthetics, but its script, specifically the thoughts of young Ralphie, as narrated to us by the real life Ralphie, Jean Shepherd.

Indiana born and raised, Jean Shepherd worked his way through local broadcasting before settling on the East Coast with a plum spot on New York talk radio. His one-man shows filled the Manhattan airwaves with stories from his, and his country's, romanticised past. The tales were so well-loved that 'Shep' received requests to tell the same ones over and over. Whereas most radio DJs would get requests for Frank Sinatra and Tammy Wynette, Jean Shepherd's listeners phoned in to hear classic Ralphie anecdotes.[2] The most popular requests involved childhood Christmases back in Indiana. Each year, on his last show before the big day, sometimes as late as Christmas Eve

---

[1] In true Hollywood style, the snow wasn't real. It had been shipped in from a ski resort.

[2] Ralphie was Shepherd's pseudonym for all children - a 'universal I', as he called it - although he was happy to admit that the boy was largely based on himself.

night, Shepherd would re-tell his holiday stories to his captive audience.[1]

'For the last six or seven years we've read this story,' he told his audience in 1974, 'and it's kind of a thing we always do now.'

One of Shep's audience that night, a young film director by the name of Bob Clarke, was so entranced that he parked his car and listened for an hour. He vowed to turn Shepherd's tales into a film. Twelve years later, he did just that. Having recently made his first major movie - bizarrely, the steamy-locker-room ladfest, *Porkies* - Bob Clarke's next project of note would be a retelling of Jean Shepherd's radio musings.[2]

Although Shepherd's radio career had slowed by the time Clarke came to prominence in the early 1980s, he remained an active performer and speaker, drawing crowds wherever he appeared. He allowed the film to be made on the condition he co-write the script with Bob Clarke.[3] He was also given the job of narrator.

Sir Isaac Newton claimed that 'the thumb alone' was sufficient evidence to prove God's existence. Jean Shepherd's narration in *A Christmas Story* is so immaculately suited for purpose that I wonder if that, too, doesn't offer similar promise of a world

[1] Some broadcasts were recorded onto reels and subsequently uploaded to YouTube by some goodly soul or other. They are the most magnificent things, all wholesome and cockle warming. (Shepherd also put the tales into a great fictional autobiography with the deeply off-putting title, *In God We Trust - All Others Pay Cash*.)

[2] In a move of which Charles Dickens would've approved, Bob Clarke waived his director's fee and pumped in $150,000 of his own money to see *A Christmas Story* over the line.

[3] Predictably, Shepherd and Clarke had different ideas about the best way to make the film. The director won out, leaving Shepherd a vocal critic of the movie.

beyond. Just look at this dialogue, describing a group of children gazing into a toyshop window during a Christmas parade:

First-nighters, packed earmuff to earmuff, jostled in wonderment before a golden, tinkling, display of mechanised, electronic joy.

And these other gems:

Every family has a kid that won't eat. My kid brother hadn't eaten voluntarily in three years.

The light was getting purple and soft outside.

My father wove a tapestry of profanity... He worked in profanity the way other artists might work in oils or clay. It was his true medium.

The film shows the workings of a child's mind so accurately that it borders on the supernatural. The insane thought-processes. The confusion. The fears. The loves. Perhaps its most famous scene involves Ralphie's friend, Flick, licking a frozen telephone pole in the school playground. He gets stuck to it and starts crying, saliva cascading out of his un-closable mouth. The school bell rings. The children do the done-thing and run away, back to class, leaving Flick to wail alone in an enveloping snow storm.

'Where's Flick?' asks the teacher, in the warmth of the classroom. 'Has anyone seen Flick?'

'Flick?' asks Ralphie's inner monologue, innocently. 'Flick who?'

Unlike the UK, where you have to hang around in home improvement retailers to find a copy, *A Christmas Story* is an established classic in the USA, up there with *Miracle On 34th*

Street and *Holiday Inn*. One channel shows the film round the clock, from the 24th of December to the 26th.[1] The cause of its relative lack of success in Britain may be that the film is *too* American: the schools, the streets, the cars, the clothes, the shops, the decor – even the milk-bottles (and milk-bottle glasses). It doesn't help that its first fifteen minutes suffer from ghastly sound editing, meaning the accents get lost, and with them, the heavenly dialogue.

When the Cleveland house where *A Christmas Story* was filmed came up for sale, fans of the movie clubbed together and bought it, viewing the act as a duty of preservation. They now run a museum across the street, full of props from the movie. You can book a night in Ralphie's house (for around $500 in December). Their official online shop sells *A Christmas Story* merchandise of such touching detail that it could put fans of the film into a state of capitalistic arousal.[2]

The very next day after my Homebase discovery, somebody mentioned *A Christmas Story* at work. The odds of that happening must have been on a par with a Lusitania survivor having their suitcase safely returned. Then I saw it in HMV. Then it was on TV. Out of nowhere, *A Christmas Story* had come back into my life in style, running into my open arms. And now I watch it every December. Each viewing is as fresh as the Hollywood snow outside Ralphie's house. It brings my Christmas to life.

I simply must go to Homebase more often. And I guess BBC Two isn't all that bad, either.

---

[1] The channel is TNT, by the way, not some obscure regional station.

[2] They sell a model of Ralphie's house for $68. I've never wanted anything so frivolous so much. There's also a quite beautiful model of Flick licking the telephone pole.

#4

The Snowman

'I don't have happy endings. I create what seems natural and inevitable. The snowman melts, my parents died, animals die, flowers die. Everything does. There's nothing particularly gloomy about it. It's a fact of life.'

Raymond Briggs, 2012

A couple of years ago, I went to a special screening of *It's A Wonderful Life*. What made the screening 'special' was that a local DJ was to give a 'special' talk beforehand. What made the *talk* 'special' was that the DJ in question was going to dress up as James Stewart and do the entire skit in an American accent. I couldn't miss it. I bought seventeen tickets to make sure I didn't.

Until then, I'd never watched *It's A Wonderful Life* properly. By *properly*, I mean without losing consciousness halfway through. For a chap so fond of all things festive, having no appetite for what was considered one of the season's finest films left a sour taste. My hope was that *It's A Wonderful Life* would have a more appealing flavour on the big screen, preferably spiced up by a 'special' talk from a local DJ beforehand.

Our host for the evening, James Stewart, walked on stage in a winter coat, with a scarf wrapped around his neck. As the applause died down, he talked nervously about how much he loved Norfolk. In an Australian accent. After a few minutes, though, Mr Stewart calmly remembered his Pennsylvanian roots and his distinctive American accent returned. He told us about his time in the 'USch Air Forsch' which he 'schure did enjoy, deschpite the dangersch'. In 1943, he said, his squadron

95

was 'schent' to Tibenham in Norfolk and 'schpent' many happy days there.[1] Then he told us about *It's A Wonderful Life*. It was a 'schlow burner alright' and 'loscht almoscht half a million dollarsch at the boxsch offisch' when first released way back in 1945.

Schlow burner was an understatement.

Such was the disregard for the film on release, the copyright was removed almost instantly. Decades later, with the rise of cable television - and its many channels, all in need of cheap programming - *It's A Wonderful Life* was repeated ad infinitum. It went from barely anybody having seen it, to being repeated so often that even caged parrots could recite key scenes.[2] Year after year, the legend grew until *It's A Wonderful Life* became a holiday staple both sides of the Atlantic. To all except me.

After years of not paying it full attention, I was trapped in the 'special' screening. For all one-hundred-and-thirty minutes.[3] It's hard to pinpoint exactly what it is about *It's A Wonderful Life* that makes it so euphoric. It may be that its wholesome finale feels completely out of keeping with the rotten chain of events that befall James Stewart's character beforehand. Even though the title is in itself a spoiler, the ending still caught me out.

---

[1] In fairness to the *real* James Stewart, his record during the war was outstanding. He was the first major Hollywood star to offer his services and, on his many flights over Nazi Germany, took risks of which the scriptwriters back home would've been proud.

[2] The little girl who delivers the movie's now-famous, 'Every time a bell rings, an angel gets its wings' line, didn't see the movie herself until one of those copyright-free TV screenings in 1979, a full forty-four years after she'd filmed it.

[3] Which, added to Mr Stewart's autobiographical musings, meant I'd been in the cinema long enough to open a new door on my advent calendar by the time I got home.

Another factor in its success may be that much of its plot occurs at different points in the year. It builds *towards* Christmas, rather than using it as a starting point.

Walking home through town after the screening, lit by zig-zagging streams of electric Christmas lights swaying in the wind overhead, I felt wholly ready for the season. Regardless of the monochrome, *It's A Wonderful Life* had coloured my night. I went home, sent texts to people I hadn't spoken to for ages, drank a cup of hot chocolate and went to bed, floating off to sleep in a spirit of goodwill. Obviously I awoke the next day as grouchy as a bin man, but for one night, after years of trying, *It's A Wonderful Life* had worked its trick.

Fortunately, not all Christmas classics take quite so long to make an impact.

Is there a more beguiling sequence in the history of British film than the opening minute of *The Snowman*? The autumn woodlands fading to winter in front of our eyes; the thinning black snow-covered branches; the owl flying into view; the sombre piano notes, accompanied by the soft rolling timpani and the stirrings of the orchestra; the journey leading us past the woodland, over blanketed white English fields until we arrive at a cottage, then up, into the bedroom of a sleeping child.

The Snowman is exquisite from the off. Confusingly, though, there is more than one 'off'. A number of versions of the film exist. Some feature the author himself, Raymond Briggs, narrating the opening sequence:

'I remember that winter because it had brought the heaviest snow I had ever seen. Snow had fallen steadily all night long and in the morning I woke in a room filled with light and silence. The whole world seemed to be held in a dream-like stillness. It was a magical day. And it was on that day I made the snowman.'

97

When Channel 4 sold their film to the international markets, however, US broadcasters thought the intro a little shy on the glitz front. They wanted a superstar narrator to open the film, not some gloomy illustrator from Wimbledon. So, a new live-action scene was filmed, in which the boy in the story, now an adult, climbs up into the old cottage's loft. Whilst there, he finds the scarf given to him by Father Christmas on that fantastic evening of his childhood. David Bowie was chosen to play the part. Clean-cut and cocaine-free, fresh from his sell-out *Serious Moonlight* world tour, he was the perfect choice, lending the scene a suitable air of mystique.

Imagine if they'd picked Phil Collins.

This all-new American introduction provided a major addition to the plot. The existence of the scarf all but confirmed that the boy's snowman experience was real and not, as Raymond Briggs' tale might suggest - to its older readers, at least - a childish flight of fancy.

When it comes to the story, the British animators were just as loose with the source material. In Briggs' original picture book,[1] the Snowman and the boy do 'walk in the air' but their tropospheric hike only takes them as far as the south coast. They pay no visit to Father Christmas, as they do in the film. In fact, the book has no Christmas references at all. It's set in winter, but not Christmas. There's no tree in the boy's lounge,

---

[1] A book wholly without dialogue. Children's illustrator, Posy Simmonds, described it as 'as quiet as when it snows'. Because of the silence, it didn't sell well, at first. People would flick through it in the bookshop and think they'd already read it. It was the film which made a hit of the book.

no bunting hanging from the ceiling. The addition of Christmas was further artistic licensing on behalf of the production team.[1]

There are other amendments. In Briggs' book, the boy and the Snowman sit in a parked car and play with the headlights. In the film, however, they ride a motorbike. One of the artists had just bought a bike and wanted to animate it, so the motorcycling scene was shoehorned in[2] (in a similar vein, the false-teeth on the parents' bedside were modelled on those belonging to an animator's gran).

Perhaps the biggest change came in the naming of the book's previously unnamed boy. 'James' is written on the gift-tag of the present Father Christmas gives him (named after an animator's boyfriend). Such was the film's success, James is what the boy is now universally known as, even in reprints of the book. The film is infused with these personal touches,[3] which is perhaps why the people who worked on it have always talked so lovingly of the project:

'There was something intangibly pure in the end result,' said its executive producer, Iain Harvey.

Not all of the film-makers' new ideas came good. One plan was to have the Snowman and James fall down a hole and partake in a badgers' tea party. Luckily, when put under the heat of the spotlight, the idea met the same fate as the film's title character.

----

[1] Not a bad addition, to be fair. 'Perfectly good,' Raymond Briggs said of it (a man who has something of a reputation for seldom thinking things are perfectly good).

[2] She even went so far as to give the Snowman's bike her own registration number.

[3] The TV big-wigs got in on the act, too. They noticed that James' television set only had three buttons. As the film was funded and broadcast by a then-young Channel 4, they ensured the set was reanimated with that vital *fourth* button.

For all its tweaks and changes, as adaptations go, *The Snowman* is near-faultless. The decision to animate it using hand-drawn sketches, in pencil,[1] lends it a unique, crabbed beauty, making an impact on par with Walt Disney's *Pinocchio* and the first *Toy Story*. To quote one of its artists, 'The charm of *The Snowman* is that it is not perfect'.

Used commercially from toilet-seat covers to fried chicken containers,[2] *The Snowman*'s smiling face retains worldwide appeal almost forty years on.[3] Although requests for product placement are filtered, millions of new *Snowman* products and lines are produced each year.[4] Even the theme song, *Walking In The Air*, largely achieved popularity through a TV commercial. In 1985, a re-recording of choirboy Peter Auty's version (as heard in the film) by a young choirboy gunslinger called Aled Jones was featured in a Toys R Us advert, putting the song back into the mainstream on a nightly basis. It was Aled Jones, not Peter Auty, who was asked to go on *Top Of The Pops* (and told to steer well clear of the presenters backstage). His performance sent the song soaring/walking up the charts. Meanwhile, Peter Auty sat at home, plotting his revenge in a broken voice.

---

[1] Strictly speaking, they used wax. Coloured pencil wouldn't work on film cells. Wax was the next best thing.

[2] Japan had a KFC-style *Snowman*-adorned family bucket. The film was a sensation over there.

[3] Yep. Forty years. Depressing, eh? The book is already older than that, coming out in 1978.

[4] One of the few requests that *has* been turned down is for a *Snowman*-themed condom.

To this day, *The Snowman* is a vital fixture in Channel 4's festive schedule. Aired without fail on Christmas Eve (which is the single best time to watch it), it also tends to get an outing on Christmas morning and at several other points in December. The film has proved so profitable for Channel 4 that they've since created a *Snowman* spin off, a near like-for-like retelling of the story involving a snow*dog*.

'It is a tribute to the very strength of Raymond's creation,' said Iain Harvey, 'that none of this commercial spin-off has seemingly done any harm to the perception of *The Snowman* as an iconic element of the Christmas season.'

It's hard to believe *The Snowman* will age, that it will lose any of its charm with the passing decades. The opposite is more likely: that it will become more and more adored as more and more children fall under its spell. The story will go on. 'Like Beatrix Potter or something,' its grumpy author once mused, proudly.

A friend once told me that he'd bought his children a hamster 'to teach them about death'. After reassurances about how he intended to treat this new hamster (rest easy: his plan was to let it die of old age), I wondered why he didn't just show them *The Snowman*. What better example is there of letting children know that the party doesn't go on forever?

'*The Snowman's* success,' said Raymond Briggs in 2012, 'is about a simple thought. We all have favourite people we become fond of and then they pass away. It touches a chord of loss. Even for young people, someone dies.'

There are two things children love that so many adults think they hate: fear and an opportunity to emote. They're bigger hams than Brian Blessed. Other than Peter Auty's testicularly-challenged singing voice, *The Snowman* offers little in the way of fear, but few can resist its power to rattle the emotions. That final scene, as James awakes to see his new friend reduced to a watery memory, as he picks up the scarf and rubs it against his cheek, as the camera pans away, taking us with it...

Oh. Goodness.

Even now.

I guess there *is* a more beguiling sequence in the history of British film than the opening minute of *The Snowman*.

The Christmas Alphabet

E is for...

Easter Eggs

You know the drill. You pop out to Tesco Express late in the day on Christmas Eve (after realising that you've got plenty of stollen, but no Hovis; plenty of eggnog, but no semi-skimmed). Inside the store, you notice that the Christmas posters have been taken down. The selection of cheeses has thinned. Mince pies are thirty pence a box. Overhead, the sounds of Wham! and Wizzard have been replaced by Adele and Maroon 5. Then, on a shelf by the till, you spot an arrival from another planet: Cadbury's Mini Eggs in £1 bags.

One psychotherapist has claimed that the sight of Easter eggs is unpleasant because 'people need to compartmentalise Christmas'. I would argue that the sight of Easter eggs is unpleasant because we've just spent hundreds of pounds on enjoying Christmas and are already being reminded of upcoming costs to look forward to in the new year. Seeing Mini Eggs on Christmas Eve is like getting a gas bill and discovering that your supplier has also slipped in an estimated bill for the next quarterly:

'You Owe Us: £387.29. Oh, and you'll probably owe us about £400 in March as well, m8'.

Most supermarkets get their eggs out early because, they claim, they sell well. A more likely factor is that it's cheaper to store them in a shop than a warehouse. We oughtn't complain, I suppose. Christmas is capitalism's birthday, too. It's only right that the festival is hijacked by further spending demands before it's even started. Currently, it's only Lidl who hold off putting their chocolate eggs on the shelves until March, stating that they've 'always sold Easter eggs at this period as this is when we see demand from our customers'.

Good on them. It's true what they say: every Lidl helps.

Electronic Mail Christmas Cards

I'll treat this subject with the same time and effort that those who send them treat us.[1]

F is for...

Father Christmas

'And so I awaited Christmas Eve, and the always exciting advent of fat Santa.'

Truman Capote, *One Christmas*, 1983

As any regular quiz-goer will tell you - as you desperately reach for the exit - it's Coca-Cola who are responsible for popularising the image of the big, red Father Christmas.

---

[1] Carbon footprint, my eye. I notice these people are more than happy to go on long-distance flights to Indonesia when the chance presents itself, uploading photos of themselves dicking around on mopeds and annoying the locals. The one thing I can say in favour of the Christmas email is that it at least has the originality to not be German or from the 19th century. Although Charles Babbage *did* design the first computer in, ooh, when was it, 1833?...

As much as I'd love to tell you these regular quiz-goers are wrong, they're not. However, if you did wish to stick something in their pipe for them to smoke, you could tell them that a very similar red-clothed 'fat Santa' also appeared long before Coca-Cola's, in a 1923 advert for White Rock soda. He'd featured in numerous other publications, too - most notably *Harper's Weekly* in the 1870s - looking all red and white and rotund. Generally, however, until Coke got involved, there was no definitive Santa.

In 1931, in hope of creating a more consistent Father Christmas for their advertising campaigns, Coca Cola employed an artist by the name of Haddon Sundblom. Borrowing heavily from descriptions of St Nicholas in the poem, *'Twas The Night Before Christmas*, Sundblom designed a jolly, fat Santa with a big white beard and a red hat to match his jacket. Variations on the image have been used in Coke promotions ever since, helping to die the cast. Coca-Cola did for Santa what the King James Bible did for the English language. They standardised him.[1]

Therefore, instead of milk, I shall leave a glass of Coke out for Father Christmas this year. Perhaps we all should. It's only right. Mind you, imagine the effect on his innards. He'd be dead by the time he got to Rotherham. And who could blame him?

But what, I hear you cry, of all those *other* Santa-like figures whose existence pre-dates carbonated drinks?

Originally based on the Turkish St Nicholas of Myra - who, at some point in the 4th century, gave his neighbours some money

---

[1] Less successful, however, was Coke's short-lived experiment at creating an elven sidekick. Spriteboy was his name. I'm not kidding. It was only slightly less disastrous than their attempt to sell Dasani spring water in 2004, using the slogan 'Bottled spunk'. (The company have openly confessed that the drink in question is actually just purified tap-water with added table salt. It's still popular in the US.)

when they, like, proper needed it[1] - a whole host of variations on the character have since come into being. In England, the idea of a benevolent festive cad took off in the 16th century. Until the 20th century, he was oft depicted wearing a daringly revealing green cloak (it parts far too close to his 'jingle bells' for my liking) and sometimes went by the name Sir Christmas. Rather than being escorted by reindeer, he used to make his way on foot or, on some occasions, sitting on a goat, which couldn't have been comfortable for either party. Instead of giving gifts, the olde Englishe Father Christmas offered 'good tidings' and wishes of peace (which are obviously just as good).[2]

He wasn't all hearty belly laughs and good cheer, though. One 18th century folk song paints a frankly unsettling image of Father Christmas:

'hare comes i ould father Christmas welcom or welcom not...'[3]

Elsewhere, the Scots once had their own character called 'The Old Man of Christmas' (not to be confused with Rod Stewart). And the Welsh had 'Chimney John', who sounds less like a figure of yuletide joy and more like a nickname for one of those thin-haired shandy-sippers you see idling near social club fruit machines, rummaging through the sandwich-bag of phonecards and loose baccy that they keep in the pockets of their imitation-leather jacket.

---

[1] More of which later. Technically, St Nick was Lycian, not Turkish, as Turkey didn't exist in the 4th century (leaving the people of Europe to make-do with Lycian Delight and Lycia Twizzlers).

[2] It was Sir Christmas who was first festively associated with the phrase 'Eat, drink and be merry', taken, of course, from that all-time classic Christmas book, *The Bible* (which, as we know, did for the English language what Coca Cola did for...).

[3] It resembles something my nanny would type using predictive text.

The most eye-catching of the world's many manifestations of Father Christmas has to belong to the Netherlands. Their Sinterklaas[1] is dressed like a bishop and swanks around on a white horse. It is his sidekick who is most alarming, though. Zwarte Piet, or *Black* Pete, was created in the 19th century by a poet inspired by the jolly sight of a member of the Dutch royal family berating a slave. However, the idea of painting faces black and handing out presents goes back centuries more. Part of the myth is that Black Pete came to Holland from Spain to give Sinterklaas the lowdown on who had been naughty or nice. If children were nice, they were given sweets and presents. If they were naughty, Black Pete would tie them in his sack, give them a good hiding, and lug 'em back to Spain.

All good-natured fun.

Naturally, Black Pete causes controversy today. In 2017, a group of Dutch white supremacists - with the noble of desire of protecting cultural traditions, you understand - stormed a primary school while dressed as Black Pete and told its foreign teachers to 'go back to their own country'.[2] The character has been tweaked in recent years, with him sometimes being referred to with the less confrontational name 'Chimney Pete'. It is a matter of great national debate. The United Nations have even chipped in, suggesting that Black Pete is perhaps somewhat passé. Most importantly, though, and something that has largely been ignored, is that many Dutch children find the character frightening. But, you know, as I said, it's all good-natured fun. I'm sure there's no long-term harm in making white children think black people are dangerous.

---

[1] I'm sure you can translate that one for yourself.

[2] A phrase, one may hazard a guess, that the Dutch white supremacists in question may well yell at those of Black Pete's own skin colour during the other eleven months of the year.

Also following Sinterklaas' lead in preferring horses to reindeer is Russia's Grandfather Frost, who, after an early history of kidnapping children, now turns up on New Year's Day bearing presents. Russian children still have to remain on their best behaviour, though, because Baba Yaga - the Christmas witch - is always on hand to snatch the presents back should the little scamps get on her wick.

The differences around the world are so weird and wonderful that they could fill their own book: the Finnish Santa, for instance, politely knocks on doors to enquire about behaviour before delivering any presents (rather than tempting fate with an arse-scorching trip down the chimney); Hungarians are visited by Little Jesus himself on Christmas Eve; Père Noël galavants around France on a lively donkey;[1] Italian children are visited by a witch who, like Baba Yaga, beats them senseless with her broomstick if mood dictates; Japanese kids have three visitors, including a fat monk who only arrives if the house is tidy; in many Spanish speaking countries, the Three Wise Men are the ones who bring the goods; and the figure of Christkind - a blonde depiction of you-know-who - remains popular in Germany, Austria and Switzerland, arriving at the ringing of a Christmas bell.[2]

Don't let those quiz-goers have the last laugh. The old boy goes back further than Coca-Cola. And he's twice as bubbly. To get to every child on his list, our own modern Father Christmas must zip along at 650 miles per second and visit 49,320 houses every minute. Going from door to door at that rate, he puts Jehovah's Witnesses to shame. Frankly, where Christmas is concerned, it's a good job they don't get involved.

---

[1] Noël is a derivative of the French term for good news: 'les bonnes nouvelles'. (In case you were interested.)

[2] The name Kris Kringle is an Americanisation of 'Christkind'.

Finding Out

'How deceitful, how cruel, grown-ups were! They had exiled my dear old friend, Santa Claus, to eternal oblivion.'
George Mackay Brown, *The Lost Boy*, 1983

The game ends for all of us at some point. The question is, how did *you* find out?

I know of someone whose parents took them to one side and gave them the facts of the matter, aged eight, *on Christmas morning*. At least that person reached such a luxurious age. The flame on my own wonderful candle of make-believe was blown out long before. My sister told *me* after discovering a list of presents and how much they were going to cost, all in my mum's handwriting. I was five or six. I'm forever curious as to how long it would have taken to have worked it out for myself.

Like most kids, the revelation about Santa's existence knocked the Paxo out of me.[1] From then on, adults and magic were not to be trusted again. The revelation left me sad and angry. When Father Christmas falls, he drags the whole fantasy family down with him: the Easter Bunny, the Tooth Fairy, Jack Frost, the elves, Rudolph, everything. The gateway to enchantment is bolted shut. It takes a lot to jimmy your way back in and even then it's not quite the same: playing along is nowhere near as fun as genuinely believing.

Some parents never even create the magic to begin with, opting to tell their children from the off that the presents come from their own hard graft. And a number of children are born ready-terrified of visits from a large man in red, needing to be reassured about his non-existence else they spend Christmas

---

[1] Couldn't resist the Paxo/stuffing gag. Sorry.

Eve night shivering by their bedside door, holding a crowbar and muttering positive mantras.[1]

The official policy for parents, according to one child psychologist, is to break the news 'as soon as they ask'. It's a policy I'm not sure I agree with. Children pose Santa-questions from a *very* young age. It would be a cold-heart indeed who could respond to a four-year-old's enquiry so bluntly:

'Daddy, iss Farva Krismuss weal?'

'God. *Finally*! The penny's dropped has it, bird brain?'

I should add that the psychologist in question *was* being interviewed by the *Daily Mirror* and could easily have been a figment of a desperate copywriter's imagination. A more learned study from the University of Exeter claims that children generally, to quote Greg Lake's Christmas classic, '*see through him and through his disguise*' of their own accord at around the age of eight or nine. Of course, some little cherubs are grossly distorting this number with their, let's call it, *innocence*. I've seen hard evidence of this. In my previous life as a college tutor, I always made a point of enquiring. Some kids told me they got *well* into high school before they sussed it. Others needed to have it written at the bottom of their GCSE results slip:

'FYI - Santa isn't real. Think about it. Enjoy Sixth Form!'

The teens of today might know how to put a bunny-ear filter on their Snapchat selfies and how to embed GIFs into their WhatsApp comments, but more than a few remain - let's stick with it - *innocent* when it comes to the land of make-believe.

It's all solid ammunition, bear in mind, for when one of the little blighters cockily zips around the highstreet doing

---

[1] Top tip: if you want your own kids to develop a cost-effective fear of Father Christmas, show them the unintentionally terrifying 1898 short film (v. short indeed: 2 minutes), *Santa Claus* online. They'll never write to him again.

wheelies on a mountain bike between slow-moving traffic, swearing out loud and being purposefully hideous.

'Oi, mate,' you can shout. 'Father Christmas isn't real. Yeah, you heard me.'

G is for...

Games

'Peace and good will and plenty and Christmas games and mirth.'
John Masefield, *Christmas*, 1903

The world may be spinning at an ever quicker pace, but when it comes to games, nothing beats the classics. From charades[1] to Trivial Pursuit, we Brits love an opportunity to create tension where previously none existed.

Around 84% of Britons claim to play a game after their Christmas meal each year. What begin as fun, friendly endeavours more often than not turn into grouchy, passive aggressive bouts of mumblings about 'getting all the easy questions', all leading, inevitably, to a mass un-biting of lips in which your mother admits she's never known true love, your brother reveals he left the Royal Navy in April for a career in 'modern dance', and your sister-in-law tells your step-uncle what she *really* thinks about his decision to remortgage the house in order to install a cricket net with undersoil heating.

---

[1] French in origin, as you'd expect. Became popular in the you-know-what century. It gets a mention in *Vanity Fair* (the novel, not the mag) and *Jane Eyre*, but its status was assured with ITV's 80s quizshow, *Give Us A Clue* (a series that, oddly, for the first few years, shared a famous theme tune with *Grange Hill*.)

With the exception of Cards Against Humanity and Articulate, few modern games manage to push their way into the nation's festive selection. A 2018 survey of the top ten family games was so full of established classics - Monopoly, Cluedo, Scrabble, Chess - that it could easily have been conducted in 1953. The refusal to embrace change on the festive board game front is likely down to people's unwillingness to have to tax themselves with the rigmarole of learning something new on Christmas afternoon. There's little joy to be had in spending fifty minutes faffing around with the packaging of a new game and decoding its double-sided sheet of jumbled rules in red print (font size five). Nobody wants to spend their afternoon having to drunkenly decode this sort of thing:

'For each player who lands on an Optimum Choice card, the player to have scored the second highest total on the earlier Stamina Wheel challenge must deduct four Axe Credits (or two, should the player in question have fewer than four Axe Credits remaining). This penalty can, however, be avoided if the tallest member of Team C can throw an eight using any possible combination of numbers from the available green and/or purple dice. If not, the aforementioned penalty is applied.'

Often, all these new games serve to create is confusion and arguments (and, as the afternoon turns to night, the opportunity for someone to proudly declare, 'Oh, *now* I get it!').
It's much easier just to play Monopoly. And argue about that instead.

❋❋❋

Ghost Stories

'Certain London spiritualists for some years past have decked out a Christmas tree with presents that have each the names of some dead children upon it, and sitting in the dark on Christmas night they hear the voice of some grown-up person, who seems to take the presents from the tree, and the clamorous voices of the children as they are disturbed. Yet the presents still hang there and are given next day to an hospital.'

W.B. Yeats, *A Vision*, 1925

Perhaps the most unlikely of Christmas traditions, the festive ghost story goes as far back as the days *before* the little lord Jesus lay down his sweet head.

It was believed, millennia ago, that bringing evergreen sprigs into the home/hole-in-the-ground during the lean winter months would ward off evil spirits and remind people of the eternal cycle of life.[1] As the evenings drew in, families and communities considered themselves more susceptible to attacks from those things that go bump in the night. Sitting around their fires, they would ease their worries by sharing tales of myths, legends and all things untoward. After all, what better way to calm the nerves than to scare the faeces out of one another? Still, at least they had the sprigs to protect them.

Dickens, as we know, re-popularised the ghost story form with *A Christmas Carol* in later centuries, but many other writers have ghoulish links to the season, perhaps none more so than M.R. James, whose stories were brought to haunted life in the 1960s and 70s by the BBC. Inspired by the critical success in adapting the sleep-wrecking James story, *Oh, Whistle & I'll Come*

---

[1] Possibly a pre-cursor to Christmas trees, one might wonder, if one was particularly short on things to wonder about. (On that note, there's plenty more sprig news to come!)

To You, My Lad, the BBC annually produced festive adaptations of his work for the best part of a decade.[1]

The Victorians had yet further part to play in the proliferation of the ghost story. When Catholicism was banned during Elizabethan times, it had made a crime of rosary beads and crucifixes. Also a victim of this new anti-Catholic vogue were ghosts. With belief in purgatory and its wandering souls firmly disregarded as Catholic nonsense, the number of reported hauntings fell close to zero. For centuries in England, very little was written or spoken about ghosts and, as a result, very few sightings were reported. However, with three hundred years' breathing space, tensions eased between the C of E and Rome. Relaxed restrictions on Roman Catholicism in the 1800s meant that the idea of meandering spirits slipped back into the public consciousness. With style. Soon there were spiritualists and mediums everywhere, channeling last-minute will amendments of deceased aunts, whilst foaming at the mouth and discreetly making the table move with their feet.

We often associate Victorians with the occult. Such is our cerebral blending of the two, one of the most commonly seen ghosts *is* a Victorian male, complete with black top hat and perturbed grin. Three out of five people in Britain today claim to have seen a ghost of some sort (often of family members or pets). According to one report, men are twice as likely as women to 'run away and scream' when confronted with one. So, if you do ever see the top-hatted Victorian fella loitering at the foot of your bed one night, show him a mirror. He'll cack his breeches.

❄❄❄❄

---

[1] *Lost Hearts* is my particular favourite, with its faces at windows and figures gliding silently up moonlit staircases. Like all horror, it is best watched alone. At night. But perhaps not Christmas night...

Grinches

'Do not select the merriest of the three hundred and sixty-five [days] *for your doleful recollections.'*

Charles Dickens, *Christmas Festivities*, 1835

We all know the sort of rotter we're talking about here. The kind of person who takes the tree down on Boxing Day or gets so sozzled on Christmas Eve that they don't emerge from their crypt until gone midday, smiling wanly and complaining of a sore head. The sort of stinker who tuts during school plays, doesn't lick the envelope of a card, and wraps presents in a carrier bag.

For some people, being a grinch is an understandable reaction to a December-time trauma from an earlier chapter of their lives, or an innate Charlie Brown-style pessimism.[1] What alternative reasons one may concoct to be a miser each year are beyond me. The beautiful thing is, I can slag these non-entities off as much as I like because, unlike you, dear Christmas lover, they'll never read this book. The sour-faced, soulless, witless, feckless, pointless dregs.

In one of Josef Goebbels' December diary entries in 1940, he reported how his line manager, Mr A. Hitler, had, during a working lunch, talked passionately about a number of upcoming business initiatives, namely the Jews being 'hurled out of Europe' and Winston Churchill 'ending up on the scaffold'.

'The Fürher,' Goebbels added, 'does not intend to mount any air raids at Christmas.'

---

[1] 'I know nobody likes me,' he says in the sumptuous *A Charlie Brown Christmas*. 'Why do we have to have a holiday season to explain it?'

Even Adolf Hitler, king of the rats, could find it in his black heart to rein it in a bit on December 25th. If that doesn't offer a grinch pause for thought, what will?

H is for...

Holly

Holly's religious significance pre-dates Christianity.[1] Previously associated with the Sun God, displaying holly was once a key Pagan custom at this time of year. As well we now know, other ancient religions - whose very names are too boring for me to expect you to read - used holly for protection, decorating doors and windows with it in the belief that doing so would ward off evil spirits.[2] The Christian church knew a good thing when it saw it and adapted this tradition for itself in medieval times, using holly to symbolise the crown of thorns laid 'pon our saviour's brow. The church's story goes that holly berries used to be white, but Christ's blood stained them forever red.[3] As the words to *The Holly & The Ivy* tell us:
The holly bears a berry as red as any blood
The holly bears a prickle as sharp as any thorn
Then Noddy Holder shouts, 'It's Chriiiistmaaaas'.
Henry VIII was so enraptured with the sprig in question that he composed his own song, *Green Grow'th The Holly*, which proved him to be, in the words of one contemporary critic

---

[1] Here's that sprig news I promised on page 113!

[2] A belief yet to be given the green light by scientists.

[3] A belief yet to be given the green light by scientists.

116

eager to please (and keep his head atop his neck), 'the finest lyricist of his age'. Admittedly, it *is* a jolly nice song:

As the holly groweth green
With ivy all alone
When flowers cannot be seen
And greenwood leaves be gone

Then Noddy Holder shouts, 'It's Chriiiistmaaaas'.

Do give *Green Grow'th The Holly* a listen on Spotify if you get a chance. One can do such quietly miraculous things nowadays, with songs written by Henry VIII.

The 12 Songs Of Christmas

#5

Sleigh Ride - The Ronettes

'I have devils inside that fight me.'

Phil Spector, 2003

What are we to do with these people who produce moments of artistic beauty yet are otherwise unpalatable? History is loaded with the blighters. We've got the fascist Wagner and his masterful concertos, the racist poet Ezra Pound, and the wife-beating John Lennon. Almost every creative of note has a hideous blot on their copybook: Caravaggio (murder); Virginia Woolf (elitism); Roald Dahl (anti-semitism[1]); Pablo Picasso (misogyny); Michael Jackson (everything). Even the recently sanctified David Bowie made some pretty raw remarks, albeit

---

[1] 'There is a trait,' Dahl said, 'in the Jewish character that does provoke animosity... even a stinker like Hitler didn't just pick on them for no reason. I mean, if you and I were in a line moving towards what we knew were gas chambers, I'd rather have a go at taking one of the guards with me; but they [the Jews] were always submissive.' (This quote was taken from *The News Statesman* in 1983, by the way, not *Matilda*.)

in the crack-addled guise of his 'Thin White Duke' persona.[1]
And the less said about Morrissey, the better.

What's the plan, though? Do we disregard these people and
their works because of their views, and, by doing so, become all
the poorer for it? Or do we ignore the negatives and enjoy their
art? I tend towards the latter. There are swines aplenty anyway -
at least these ones give us something positive. Most other
fascists, for instance, just clog up market towns of a Saturday
afternoon, their gnarled faces wrapped in JD Sports scarves,
waving England flags bought from Poundland.[2] They haven't
dished out a neoclassical masterpiece or swaggering inter-war
novella between them.

To the sorry list of tainted geniuses we must now add Phil
Spector (slotting him in somewhere towards the top of the
chart). Famed for his distinctive 'Wall of Sound' production -
string arrangements, harmonies, orchestral percussion[3] -
Spector reached a creative zenith in the 1960s and early 70s,
masterminding such classics as *Be My Baby*, *Da Doo Ron Ron*,
Then He Kissed Me, *You've Lost That Loving Feeling* and *River Deep-
Mountain High*.[4] They are among the most beautiful melodies

---

[1] 'I believe Britain could benefit from a Fascist leader. After all,
Fascism is really nationalism,' Bowie said in 1976. Throughout his life,
Bowie otherwise appears supremely liberal, so these comments are
that bit easier to sweep to one side.

[2] Poundland being one of the few foreign 'lands' these people are
willing to embrace.

[3] Ironically, the Jewish Phil Spector referred to his 'Wall of Sound' as a
'Wagnerian approach to rock 'n roll'.

[4] A song whose chart failure - it reached number 88 in the US - caused
Spector to retreat to his mansion, watching *Citizen Kane* on repeat for
the best part of two years. We've all done that before, though. Right?

ever composed. For most musicians, these songs would represent their finest work. But Spector saved his very best for a Christmas album.

It's sometimes hard to believe, all things considered.

Born[1] and raised in the Bronx to parents of Ukrainian descent, Phil Spector's early childhood was somewhat typical of the era. The relationship between his parents was less so. To this day, rumours persist that they were cousins. His father's suicide, seemingly out of the blue, in 1949, caused his mother to move her family to the other side of the country when Spector was in his early teens. Life started again on the West Coast. The gangly, asthma-sufferer taught himself guitar and the laws of music composition, while his doting, over-zealous mother taught him French and how to be weird. After high school, his linguistic skills were such that he moved back to New York to work, improbably, with the United Nations. The job didn't last. Music was too much of an obsession. Instead of checking into the UN, he formed a band and wrote songs, several of which became radio hits.[2]

'Success,' to quote Spector's biographer, 'went to his head like helium.'

The party was off and running. By twenty-one, Spector owned a record label, becoming the youngest person ever to do so (and, at five foot tall, possibly the shortest). Searching New York for acts who could do his compositions justice, he quickly built a roster of artists. Writing and arranging tracks of fierce beauty, his work spoke to the youth of his generation. He called

---

[1] On December 26th, no less.

[2] One of them, the divine *To Know Him Is To Love Him*, got its title from the epitaph on his father's gravestone.

the songs his 'little symphonies for the kids'. Elvis had gone to the army and come back a movie star. The rock 'n roll fire had gone out. Spector sensed that America needed something fresh.

'Every baroque period,' wrote Tom Wolfe in 1965, 'has a flowering genius who rises up as the most glorious expression of its style of life: in latter day Rome, the Emperor Commodus; in Renaissance Italy, Cellini; in late Augustan England,[1] the Earl of Chesterfield[2] - and, in Teen America, Phil Spector is the bonafide Genius of Teen.'

Spector knew why his output proved popular:

'It's very American. It's very today,' he said of it. 'It's not what it means, it's what it makes you feel!'

A master of the pop single, Spector's first full-length album would be so off-piste that even the Earl of Chesterfield might have raised an eyebrow. Instead of an ultra-hip collection of new material, it would be a selection of 'holiday' songs performed by acts on his label. It would have the ghastly title *A Christmas Gift For You*[3] and consist of eleven festive standards and one original,[4] all given the lavish Spector treatment.

Recording the album consumed his life:

'Christmas meant a lot to Phil,' said Darlene Love in 2013. 'It was one of the biggest projects he ever took on because it was something that had never been done before.'

The recording process lasted over three months with Spector devoting his all to the project. One colleague noted that Spector arranged his musicians 'like he was going to invade

---

[1] Excuse me? When?

[2] Excuse me? Who?

[3] It sounds like a tacky website: xmasgifts4u.com

[4] Darlene Love's epic, *Christmas (Baby, Please Come Home)*.

Moscow'. He lambasted performers and engineers[1] until every detail was perfect. The singers weren't excused from his ire, either:

'I would be there from 1pm to 1am as a teenager,' said Crystals' singer, La La Brooks. 'It was like child abuse.'

'It was August when we were recording,' recalled Darlene Love in 1999. 'We never knew what time of day it was because we were working with Phil Spector, who worked us until our tongues were hanging out of our heads.'

Fittingly, considering its heated creation, the album was released on one of the most turbulent days in world history. As music stores stocked their shelves with the mad, young New Yorker's latest masterpiece, another young madman was awaiting his moment in the sun.

The day JFK was shot was just about the worst day possible for releasing a sugary, festive hoopla of a Christmas record.[2] *A Christmas Gift For You*'s chart failure was all but guaranteed when the panicking US government swiftly imposed an indefinite ban on the sale of popular music. The kids were no longer allowed their subversive little symphonies. Spector's masterpiece stalled

---

[1] Among them, a then-unknown Sono Bono and a young Brian Wilson, whose piano playing was cut from certain tracks for not being up to scratch. (Despite this slight, Wilson would call *A Christmas Gift For You* his favourite album of all time).

[2] Nov 22nd, 1963, was a big news day all around. Elsewhere, Aldous Huxley and our Narnia friend, C.S. Lewis, had also died, crossing off two possible suspects from the FBI's shortlist in the process. For all the events of that day, you'll be pleased to know that the BBC evening news still found time to interview Nigel Farage.

outside the top ten and wouldn't go any higher until The Beatles' re-released it on their Apple label in the early 1970s.[1]

A Christmas Gift For You's standout moment is *Sleigh Ride* by The Ronettes.[2] Beginning with the sound of a reindeer clopping and neighing through the snow, the song then bursts into life, rattling along without pausing for breath.

Our cheeks are nice and rosy, and comfy and cosy are we

The voice of all voices. Ronnie Spector.[3] Straight from the Spanish Harlem:

We're schnuggled up togever, like two boyds of a fevver would be

Completely charming. An instant tonic. Wholly alive with good cheer. Provided you can ignore that it was composed by a maniac.

Just hear those sleigh bells jingling, ring-tingle-tingling too

Ronnie Spector revealed the extent of her husband's frenzied nature in a 1990 autobiography.[4] In an effort to keep his wife in check, she wrote, Phil Spector had surrounded their infamous Spector mansion with barbed wire and guard dogs. He regularly

---

[1] The band's own breakthrough US album, *With The Beatles*, was released that fateful 1963 day, too. Spector would go on to produce their final album, *Let It Be*, and do such an unseemly job that Paul McCartney remains uncharacteristically grumpy about it to this day.

[2] Prior to *A Christmas Gift For You*, The Ronettes had also recorded perhaps Spector's finest song, *Be My Baby*, which, musically, has more than a little in common with *Sleigh Ride*.

[3] Veronica Bennett. Until she married the madman.

[4] He once bought her a pair of twins for Christmas. They were five-years-old. She'd originally asked for gift vouchers. That way, she could buy whatever she wanted i.e. *not* twins.

123

pulled a gun on her and once bought a glass coffin as a gift, telling his wife it was so he could 'keep an eye on her' after he'd killed her. Whenever Ronnie *was* allowed to leave the mansion, she had to drive with a life-sized dummy of her husband in the passenger seat. She escaped, barefoot, in 1972, after an intense three-day scope-out of the mansion's security system.

'I knew that if I didn't leave,' she said, 'I was going to die there.'

In 2003, someone did die there. The body of a young actress was found in that very same mansion. She had been shot in the head. Chips of her teeth were scattered on the carpet. She'd only known Phil Spector a matter of hours.

After years of trying - and failing - to forge a career in movies, Lana Clarkson resorted to making ends meet with a security job in an LA nightclub. One evening, a frail old woman had entered. A special guest. She sported an eye-catching coiffure that was part-Hollywood siren, part-Huddersfield dinnerlady. Clarkson spoke to the frail old woman and eventually deduced two surprising facts. First, that her name was Phil. Second, that she was a bloke, thank-you-very-much. Initial confusion put aside, the couple fell into deep conversation (about what, exactly, I can't begin to imagine). The young bouncer was smitten with the megastar hitmaker. She agreed to go back to the mansion. Possibly for a nightcap. Possibly to run her eye over his top-end security system.

What precisely happened that night remains a mystery. Spector called it an accidental suicide and suggested Clarkson had tried to kiss one of his pistols.[1] This story was somewhat undermined by his chauffeur, who claims Spector ran out of the house soon

---

[1] Unsurprisingly, he collected guns. Well, they're more exciting than stamps.

after the shooting, carrying a gun and saying, 'I think I killed someone'.

Phil Spector, composer of some of the most life-affirming music ever made, was convicted of Lana Clarkson's murder in 2007. The case went to retrial and the pint-sized genius from the Bronx was found guilty for a second time. Some corners of the media suggested that he revelled in the attention the case brought him. After thirty years of relative quiet (with a brief re-emergence in 2003 to produce, of all things, a Starsailor album), Phil Spector was box office again. He now has nineteen years to look back over the newspaper clippings.

Thank God he never stayed on at the UN.

With his health deteriorating to the point where he can now no longer talk, it's expected that the man whose musical flair gave a heavenly touch to songs such as *Imagine* and *My Sweet Lord* will soon meet his maker. And have a lot of explaining to do.

'Insane is a hard word,' he confessed in an interview weeks before Lana Clarkson's murder, 'but it's manic-depressive, bipolar. I take medication for schizophrenia, but I wouldn't say I'm schizophrenic. But I have a bipolar personality, which is strange. I have devils inside that fight me. And I'm my own worst enemy.'

Deeply respected and deeply hated by nigh-on every person who ever met him, Phil Spector remains one of pop music's true oddities. A monster, yes. Yet, somehow, also, the creator of *Sleigh Ride*. And of an entirely perfect Christmas album of such cheery soul that just one listen can make you feel everything is worthwhile.

Let's take the road before us and sing a chorus or two
(Ring a ling a ling a ding dong ding)
Come on, it's lovely weather for a sleigh ride together with you

I mean, what can you say about it all? My goodness. What curious treasure for the devils to leave behind.

#6

In Dulci Jubilo - Mike Oldfield

For all its wackiness, *In Dulci Jubilo* hides behind the most serious of facades: a folky, progressive rock interpretation of a German hymn.[1] The title roughly translates to *Good Christian Men Rejoice*[2] and dates back to the early 1300s. It has had several rewrites over the centuries, the most familiar being John Mason Neale's 1853 reworking.[3] But it was Mike Oldfield, fresh from his multi-million seller, *Tubular Bells* - written and recorded when he was only nineteen - who brought the Deutsch ditty kicking and screaming into the 1970s with his wildly silly musical interpretation.

'Act as if what you do makes a difference,' said the philosopher, William James. 'It does.'
It's a theory popular amongst modern psychologists. In short, if you smile, you'll instantly feel a little happier.[4] If you sit upright, you'll feel more motivated. And if you don't watch *Match Of The Day*, you can't get annoyed by Alan Shearer's

---

[1] Come on. It's been at least ten minutes since we mentioned Germany.

[2] Or else.

[3] Come on. It's been at least ten minutes since we mentioned the 19th century.

[4] Try it - it works.

platitudes.[1] And so on. With this philosophy in mind, listening to *In Dulci Jubilo* whilst prancing about can *only* make you feel better. They should play it in Boots as you queue to collect your repeat prescription. Bank managers should listen to it before deciding on offering mortgages. I don't want to sound glib here, but do you honestly think the disastrous shooting in the Spector mansion would have happened if Mike Oldfield's *In Dulci Jubilo* had been whistling out of the sound system? Whole chapters of world history would be different if only this song had piped up at key moments. There'd have been no Carthaginian solution, no Stalingrad, no massacre at Peterloo. People would've been too busy grinning and asking their adversaries, 'I say, by what name is this delectable ditty known?'

It must be queer for Mike Oldfield to reflect that not only did he create one of the most famous horror compositions (*The Exorcist* theme) but he also chimed in with this merry jig. I can think of no other artist whose two most famous songs conjure such wildly differing images. One brings to mind medieval circular dancing around frosty mulberry bushes, the other makes you think of a fully-rotational head. Throw in the fact that Oldfield also revamped the *Blue Peter* theme tune and you've got a curious career all round.[2]

Mike Oldfield now lives out in the Bahamas: a move partly fuelled by the classic English middle-aged sensitivity to *political*

---

[1] Such as: 'If anything, he's hit it *too* well'; 'Hey, but what a nice headache to have, though, eh?'; 'And who should arrive at the back post but Yours Truly?' (For thoughts of this calibre, Mr Shearer receives £420,000 of licence fee money per annum.)

[2] 'I've still got my [*Blue Peter*] badge proudly in a box somewhere,' he said in 2014. 'Forget *The Exorcist*, winning a Grammy or having a number 1 – *Blue Peter* came to see me!'

correctness gone mad[1] and partly fuelled by the idea of being isolated:

'I've got more lawyers than friends,' he once quipped, whilst possibly not quipping.

Something of a reluctant pop star, Oldfield always disliked touring and performing. He was happiest when making music in a studio. By his own accounts, he had a difficult upbringing:

'[It was] a very disturbing childhood, with my mother being mentally disturbed. And my father as well, being a doctor, trying to cure her. But you're not allowed to treat your own family. So there were doctors and hospitals and ambulances. There was fighting, there was violence.'

By the time *In Dulci Jubilo* was released, Oldfield, was still only twenty-two. Most twenty-two-year-olds spend their days wondering what use their degree has actually been, whereas Oldfield was writing and performing enormous hit albums, playing every instrument himself. Although ostensibly a Christmas song, *In Dulci Jubilo* only entered the charts *after* Christmas, 1975, making a lowly appearance at number 22 on the 27th December. As with David Essex's *A Winter's Tale*, it performed better in the new year, where it reached number 4. It was still in the top 40 on Valentine's Day.[2]

❄

---

[1] 'I read about a chap getting a ticket for eating a KitKat while driving! It's like being at prep school!' he fumed in 2012.

[2] He followed this success with the equally silly *Portsmouth* in Christmas '76. Despite faring better in the charts than *In Dulci Jubilo*, *Portsmouth* has never stood up as a Christmas single, possibly due to the title. Portsmouth is the last place people want to be thinking about in the season of goodwill. If the song had been called something like *Dance Ye A Christmas Capriole*, I suspect we'd still be hearing it in shopping centres nationwide.

When compiling this list of twelve songs, I was torn between including *In Dulci Jubilo* or its homely b-side, *On Horseback*. A recent discovery for me, *On Horseback* is a great *post*-Christmas song. It has spoken word vocals above an early electric synth, with folky strings, making it sound somewhat like a cross between Brian Eno and the theme to *The Riddlers*. Oldfield's label, Virgin, were so enamoured with *On Horseback*'s Christmas market potential that they put both songs out as a double a-side. The radio stations thought the track a bit odd and opted to play the still odd, but admittedly slightly less odd, *In Dulci Jubilo* instead, thus lessening public exposure to one of the true British Christmas classics.

To this day, *On Horseback* is a git to find. Oldfield's tight copyright control[1] means that it's quickly removed when uploaded to YouTube. It can only reliably be heard by tracking down his *Ommadawn* album and skipping to minute thirteen (and forty-six seconds) of the title track, then waiting for the silence to be replaced by the song's improbable opening line:

I like beer and I like cheese

What follows is a twinkling ode to the Hertfordshire countryside and the joys of traversing it by steed. Yes, it has a touch of Father Ted's *My Lovely Horse*, but that's not necessarily a bad thing:

Hey and away we go
Through the grass
Cross the snow
Big brown beasty
Big brown face
I'd rather be with you than flying through space

Why is *On Horseback* a Christmas song? A mention of snow, perhaps. Also, the mention of pastoral English countryside and inclement weather. It's one of the few seasonal songs to laud

---

[1] Who needs friends when you've got lawyers?

grass and mild westerly breezes (a rare admission of realistic British weather in December). On later choruses, Oldfield's nasal spoken word is joined by a children's choir. Ah, it's a soppy affair but, well, you're a harder soul than me if you aren't warmed by it:

Some find it strange to be here
On this small planet, and who knows where
But when it's strange and full of fear
It's nice to be on horseback

It's also nice to hear someone say it's 'nice' to be on horseback. That it's nice to go outside and smell the wintry air. Nice to go out in it alone. Nice to be in England at this time of year, with its log fires and green hills, its real-ale and stilton. All so very nice. Even if the person lauding these very nice things has slunk off to the Bahamas.

The Yule Log

OCTOBER

Mon 1st -

It's the 1st of October. With regards to Christmas, anything goes!

Tues 2nd -

Nothing went.

Weds 3rd -

Saw my first advent calendar of the year. In the toy shop. (The shop doubles up as a post office, which is why I went in, rather than to look at toys.) No chocolate ones yet, only Playmobil and Lego. £25 each. A lot of money for an advent calendar. If my maths is correct, you could get twenty-five Peppa Pigs advent calendars for that at Poundland.

It was nice to see that as well as the top-end calendars, the shop also sold those traditional, flat cardboard efforts. The artwork was reminiscent of something you'd see on a Christmas card from your gran: vaguely Catholic images of Jesus in the manger, the three wise men on a starlit sand dune, or a pack of bemused shepherds pointing leeward.

Thurs 4th -

The mornings aren't fully dark yet but today was the first time I've felt reluctant to get out of bed and attack the day on account of the air in my bedroom having a distinct mountainside-tent chill. It's so much easier to get up on warm summer mornings, when the room is so bright it's hard to find a shadow.

Sat 6th -

Talk of an Indian summer this week. That should slow the sales of Quality Street. Not that the tubs are flying off the shelves anyway, especially after the Gambian summer we've already had.

I wonder if supermarkets put their mini autumnal Christmas selection out as a psychological ploy. Perhaps it's all about jamming their foot in the doors of our minds, alerting us to the importance of Christmas shopping. It sounds ever so slightly like a conspiracy theory, but supermarkets do stuff like that all the time, don't they? Filtering the fake scent of freshly-baked bread in through the air ducts to whet our appetites, and placing milk at the back of the shop so we have to walk down the aisles, impulsively loading our baskets with Hobnobs and Pringles en route. There'll be think-tanks out there who study all this consumer manipulation stuff. Imagine being that intelligent then dedicating your career to supermarket layouts.

Sun 7th -

Absolute classic run of the mill weather forecast on 'Countryfile'. The presenter said how this isn't an Indian summer because an Indian summer has to meet requirements x, y and z. Nothing is ever as it seems with weather presenters. They never let us call anything <u>anything</u>:

Indian summer?

'Well, actually...' they say.

Red sky at night?

'Well, actually...'

First day of winter?

'Well, actually....'

They're like that bloke in the pub who undermines everything you say with a contradictory fact they misheard on 'QI'. In an age where the media are lambasted for over-egging every pudding they can get their oven gloves near, TV weather presenters love to strip away the hyperbole and let us know that our modern meteorological experiences will always dawdle in the shadow of yesteryear:

'If you think today is cold,' they say, 'try going back to 21st January, 1973, when...'

Everything is <u>almost</u> the hottest/coldest/wettest it's been since records began.

That said, I do like it when they present the weather for the week ahead on 'Countryfile' and, instead of wearing their usual designer suits or flowing gowns, they dress like teachers on a school trip: blue jeans, chunky jumpers and - best of all - brushed cotton shirts with the top buttons undone to show that, hey, woah, they're not squares.

Mon 8th -

Signed two copies of my book, 'Kismet Quick'. Both bought as Christmas presents. Wrote 'Merry Christmas' in each. I wanted to add something along the lines of, 'I'm writing this in October!' but when the reader unwraps the present - with a facial expression that could be best described as bemused - on Christmas morn, they won't give a fig that it was signed in October. They'll be well into the festive swing by then. Like those Christmas specials of 'The Chase', the fact they were filmed on a sultry June afternoon won't register to those watching it on a dark December one; they'll see holly and mistletoe and Bradley Walsh wearing a Santa hat, and the illusion will be bought into.

Tues 9th -

A white van in town tonight. Parked up. Its back door was open. Resting on the pavement beside it was a star-shaped, decorative Christmas light to line the streets.

Being a seaside resort, there are novelty lights up in my town all year round - and they never look too dissimilar to the Christmas ones. Yet, every year at around this time, white vans arrive at the day's close, and volunteers in orange jackets climb ladders and shout 'hoy' at one another.

I won't lie, I was excited to see the van. The season is drawing close. Or is it? I just looked at the 'Experience Sheringham' website (yes, that's really what it's called) and it says the light switch-on is November 16th, more than six weeks away. The length of a school summer holiday. And that's just until the lights go on, which itself is almost a further six weeks from the big day.

Weds 10th -

The Indian summer (which isn't an Indian summer, remember) supposedly reached its peak today. It hasn't been too warm at all, just pleasantly sunny. Although it was mild, the wind shook the leaves off the trees like rain this afternoon. I've noticed that, in some rooms, the low sun now shoots in from new angles as our planet performs its annual twizzle. It's supposed to be warm tomorrow, too. Someone told me that it was misty inland. The coast was blue and sparkly, though.
 I'm ready for autumn.

Sat 13th -

So much for Wednesday being the peak. So much for being ready for autumn. Today has been like a particularly hot summer's day. Record temperatures were officially recorded up the coast in Lincolnshire (take that, weather presenters!). We couldn't have been far off in north Norfolk. Went to the beach with Sarah (who does my cover art) and her husband, Dan. They were both dressed for the occasion: short sleeved and sock-free. I refused to buckle in the heat and clung to October by wearing trousers and a shirt. We had tea at a café, outside. Wasps and flies landed on everything. It does make you wonder what the future holds for the planet as we all, and I include myself in this, greedily leave our mark. In honour of those thoughts, I spent the afternoon whistling 'Saltwater' by Julian Lennon:
 'We are a rock revolving/ Around a golden sun/ We are a billion children rolled into one/ So when I hear about the hole in the sky/ Saltwater wells in my eyes...'

I loved that song when it came out. 1991. I was eight. I thought it was the most profound - although it would be at least another five years until I knew what that word meant - song ever written. When you're very young you have an inchoate sensitivity to mawkishness. The most uninspiring thing can move you to tears. In today's out-of-season heat, the clunky lyrics rumbled around my brain once again:

'We climb the highest mountain/ We'll make the desert bloom/ We're so ingenious we can walk on the moon/ But when I hear of how the forests have died/ Saltwater wells in my eyes...'

Then, in the cool of this evening, I heard my first Christmas classic of the year.

Guess which one:

'A very merry Christmas/ And a happy new year/ Let's hope it's a good one/ Without any fear...'

From son to father. Julian to John. It featured in a rudderless documentary called 'The US vs John Lennon'. I'd seen the film before but only realised this, worryingly, about seventy minutes in.

Although it gets played to exhaustion, I still completely love 'Happy Xmas (War Is Over)'. It reminds me of the Christmas tape we used to have in the car. I didn't know back then that the man singing was the father of the man who had sung the terribly profound 'Saltwater'; instead, I was swept up by the ringing of the guitar strings, the distant Japanese voice creeping over the top of everything, and the choir of children who sang like the children in our school assemblies. It sounded like nothing else on the cassette. And those lyrics. Harrowing to a child - especially when hidden within a Christmas song:

'War is over, if you want it/ War is over now...'

Christmas songs are much more powerful out of season. In the height of summer, their sound can induce nausea, but slightly later in the year, as the evenings draw in, a snippet of a particularly fond one can elicit warmth and melancholy in equal measure. Hearing Lennon's song tonight, in isolation, will likely put all December airings of it in the shade.

Sun 14th -

Rain. All day. Fourteen degrees and blustery. The living room was so dark at lunchtime that I had to turn the lamps on.
 That's more like it.
 Take your Ambre Solaire and liberally apply it where the sun don't shine.

Tues 16th -

Lots of gnats about. My walk home from work was effectively an exercise in seeing how few of them I could eat. I kept my total down to about 257. The last time I saw the air so pregnant with bugs, we had a ladybird invasion. There's talk of one happening this autumn. This could be the week.
 Invasion is such a dramatic word. Especially when preceded by the word 'ladybird'. Ladybirds are too delightful to invade. They should call it a 'ladybird garden party' or something along those lines. That said, the last invasion was hellish. The sort of thing that needed to be seen to be believed. When described, it sounds an implausible exaggeration. Along our stretch of coast, Cromer was worst hit. A rolling, ankle-deep, black carpet of ladybirds clogged the pavements along

the seafront. In certain corners and crevices, the writhing mess went a foot deep. This was in midsummer, bear in mind. The holidaymakers weren't to know what awaited them. They arrived en masse, as always, strolling their crunchy way through the orgiastic bug detritus in sandals, as though it wasn't there. They let the little things fly into their faces, onto their ice creams, into their candy floss, between their arm hairs, as though it were all part of the charm of a trip to the English seaside.

Even in the height of that invasion, I still didn't think less of ladybirds. There's something terribly cute about them, from their little multicoloured jackets to their very name. If any other insect had chosen to invade, it might have been a different story. Imagine a fly invasion or worse, a wasp invasion. England would be in free-fall. The Daily Express would be well on the case, warning us of the 'Killer Death Plague To Kill Thousands'.

God, I can feel my face tickling as I write this. Invisible bugs creeping across my skin. Possibly real ones. They certainly feel real. I shall soon find out. Must admit, I didn't expect to write about a ladybird invasion in the run-up to Christmas.

Thurs 18th -

No ladybird invasion. Britons never never never shall be slaves etc. Apparently, the ladybirds are now going to invade Russia instead, which they claim to have been their plan all along. A likely story... I hope for their sake they've packed their winter coats.

Fri 19th -

Tonight is officially chilly. Outside, the air is fresh and cold around the ears. Just went to the shop to get dinner and thought I saw my breath.

Sat 20th -

In town, the shops are readying for the big push. Chocolate advent calendars, wrapping paper, spray snow in the windows, Christmas magazines, cards, festively-themed carrier bags.

Talk of a cold snap next weekend ('Well, actually...'), a driving northerly forcing an icy front into a blocked pattern for a good few days. That would be lovely. I haven't worn a scarf this autumn. Plus it would really give those remaining summer bugs something to think/die about.

Saw 'Kismet Quick' in a charity shop. It's the first time I've seen one of my books in a state of rejection. I knew it had to happen eventually. It was an odd feeling. The first thing I did was check if it was a copy I'd signed and personalised, so I could collar the bastard who donated it. It was unsigned. There are so many reasons why it could end up in a charity shop but, naturally, my assumption was that somebody hated it and gave it away, stopping for a moment to think about re-selling it online before deducing that it was unfair to demand cash for such an item.

The shop wanted a fiver for it. An outrageous amount. I almost offered to sign it but wondered whether I'd look particularly pathetic.

To console myself, I imagined the previous owner had died and that the book had, in a moment of madness, been prised from their cold, leaden hands and lumped into a box of other books and mistakenly taken to the charity shop by a loved one.

I am a terrible person.

Mon 22nd -

Half term. I've always loved this half term, but my current job has <u>two</u> weeks off, doubling the joy.

Went to Great Yarmouth with my mate. What a place. It's like a live action Lowry painting - if Lowry ever took LSD. Even on a windy October afternoon there were revellers on show, wearing shorts and eating ice cream. But it was nowhere near as busy as the summer season. The fruit machines sang to no one. The rollercoasters and miniature trains rattled along, almost empty. The donkeys, with nobody to ride them, brayed under the pier, chattering amongst themselves about their plans for the festive season (one was doing some work at a carol service; another had a few gigs at market town Christmas light switch-ons).

Sellotaped to the windows of the arcades and bingo halls were notices about opening hours for the winter season. Most were closing at the end of this week. A strange life these proprietors must lead. From May to September, they're raking it in, working, sweating, from sunrise to sunset and beyond. Then everything slows down until they stop altogether. They lock the doors, switch off the machines and go home to hibernate, trying to make sure their stockpile of nuts lasts til the clocks spring forward again. Such a mysterious existence. They should do a feature on their habits on 'Autumnwatch'.

We played bingo. I was lured into the hall by an unfounded belief that, as I'd walked past, the girl calling out the numbers had looked longingly at me and smiled for reasons other than attracting my custom. Sensing the most unlikely of romances, I took a seat. The minute we crossed the threshold, her flirtatious advances ceased. The oldest trick in the bingo callers' book. Ah, well. It was only 10p a go. Bargain. After a few attempts, I was hooked. I got annoyed when other people kept winning. I wanted to stand up and break the studious silence by announcing that it was all a game of chance and that any smugness should be restrained. Then my numbers came up, one by one, in a diagonal line. I panicked, then slammed my hand on the button. House! Bingo! Me!

'Winner on card twelve,' sighed the girl. 'That's a winner on card twelve. Eyes down and we go again. Any line, four corners or diagonals...'

Not so much as a flicker from her to acknowledge my greatness. Regardless, I glanced across at the room to let my rivals know that, even though this was a game of chance, I had won it. Then a lady handed me a winner's voucher and said, 'No one don't leave Great Yarmouth empty handed'. The voucher entitled me to any one of the number of prizes behind a protective glass casing. I went for a miniature rip-off version of Connect 4, called something like Connect One More Than Three.

On the way home, we passed through the beautiful dune-swept villages of Winterton, Waxham, Happisburgh. At Horsey, we drove alongside a thin stream of still, Broadland water; I looked across and saw a one-man sailing boat, complete with white triangular sails, sweeping along at its own steady pace. We were the only car on the narrow road. She was the only boat on the narrow water. Around us, green flatlands and autumn trees. The sky above was vast and clear as water.

No one don't leave Great Yarmouth empty handed.

Tues 23rd -

Spent the day indoors waiting for deliveries. One was a new mobile phone. My old mobile died over the weekend so I had to bite the bullet and buy myself out of my Vodafone contract early. £75 was my punishment. To make matters sillier, the best new tariff available also happened to be with Vodafone. So I'm paying £75 to effectively re-join the same company. I bickered on the phone with them all morning. At one point, out of nowhere, they claimed I had to pay an additional £20 cancellation fee to add to the £75. I asked to cancel my contract. They said they understood my concerns and would call back with a new offer to tempt me to stay.

'OK,' I replied. 'But it has to be less than what I'm currently paying. It categorically have to be less than £23 a month and with the same handset. Otherwise, it's pointless.'

'I think you will be most pleasantly surprised, Sir,' the operative chirped. 'I will call you back in half an hour.'

More time lost. The afternoon vanished. A delivery of books arrived in the interval. I'd already wasted the morning chasing that up after they'd been delivered to the wrong house. When they finally arrived, the delivery lady went to my back door. This happens a disconcerting amount. If you ever saw my property, I find it hard to imagine you'd be confused as to which was the front door. The path leads directly to it, the number is on the door, and it's under a porch. I opened

142

the door and barked, 'This is the back door!'. The lady gently replied that she'd know better next time and I was sad that I'd taken my ire out on her.

An hour later, the Vodafone operative called back regarding that offer of categorically <u>less</u> than £23 a month.

'Here is our fresh offer, Sir,' he continued. 'As a loyal customer, we can offer you the same minutes and data, Sir, with the same handset for a mere £37 a month.'

I waited for him to add something else, like a free car or timeshare villa. But nothing came. That <u>was</u> the deal.

'Now what do you think to that, Sir?'

'I think it's higher than £23,' I replied.

I was so angry I wanted the head of Vodafone on the phone - or preferably a plate. The operative said all his supervisors were busy but that one could call me back in 24-48 hours.

'Do you promise?'

'Yes, Sir.'

Weds 24th -

No call from a Vodafone supervisor.

Thurs 25th -

No call from a Vodafone supervisor.

Fri 26th -

Set my alarm for half-six for a deeply embarrassing reason. To buy a computer game: 'Red Dead Redemption 2'. It's a cowboy/Western thingy from the makers of 'Grand Theft Auto'. Yesterday, I asked somebody in the supermarket whether she knew if they would be selling the game (therefore saving me a trip to Norwich). She said she 'dint' know. I asked if she could find out. She said she'd 'troy'. Having disappeared into one of the backrooms on my behalf, she returned several hours later saying she still 'dint' know 'fer shur'. I walked home and rang the store instead. An automated voice said that if I was calling to enquire about 'Red Dead Redemption 2', then worry ye not, the store <u>would</u> have copies in the morning.

My alarm jolted me out of a vivid dream. Groggily, I put my loungewear on - including a bobble hat on account of the icy wind - and somnambulised my way in the dark to Tesco on the stroke of 7am. I'd been expecting a queue outside. This is the most anticipated game release in years. But I was alone. It did nothing for morale that I was clearly more excited about the game than its target audience of fourteen-year-olds. The staff looked at me incredulously, moodily, as though I were an unwelcome guest in their house. The newspapers hadn't even been laid out yet. There was no pop music, no electronic beeps, no screeching of trolley wheels. Just squeaky footsteps and yawns.

I made a beeline for the computer game shelf. No 'Red Dead Redemption 2'. I asked another lady whether they had the game. She, too, said she 'dint' know but would 'troy' to find out. She wrote the name of the game on a clipboard. 'What did you say it was called, moy darlin'? "Red Automatic Gun"?'

'"Red Dead Redemption",' I said. '"Two".'

She vanished into the store's ever-mysterious backrooms and came back excitedly waving a copy of the game in each hand.

'Here we go,' she said, proudly. '<u>Two</u> Red Dead Redemptions!'

❄

From a surreal beginning to a surreal conclusion. I ended the day watching a George Michael tribute act on Cromer pier. The wind had strengthened. The waves were cutting in on the old gaff at a cruel angle, smashing into the structure and splashing high over the promenade. In short, it was the sort of weather you might look at and say to yourself, 'Corr, I wouldn't like to be on the pier tonight.'

I'd booked months in advance, when the idea of a dark, tempestuous autumn evening seemed the stuff of fantasy. Now it was here. Tonight. October the twenty-sixth. The poor fella had originally been scheduled to play in March but the show had been cancelled due to the snowy Beast From The East. Now he was expected to play over the sound of waves crashing into the antiquated scaffolding beneath. The tickets had been a birthday present to my sister. A woman sitting next to us said that she worked on the pier and there was 'only one layer of floorboards between us and the sea'. This is the equivalent of a pilot walking down the aisle before lift-off and whispering into your ear, 'We've probably got enough fuel to get us there but I wouldn't bank on it'.

George was good. The voice was excellent though not exactly like George's, but the mannerisms were spot on. Middle-aged women walked to the front, stretching their hands out for George to touch, momentarily forgetting that this wasn't the man himself, but some bloke from the Midlands. About ten people stayed dancing for the whole two hours, congregating in a dark corner of the

145

auditorium and clapping along on the offbeat. After a few songs, they fell into an unspoken straight line. All the while the sea roared beneath us, shaking the floor.

The highlight was when George dashed offstage and came back, to the disco beats of 'Outside', dressed as an LAPD cop, baton and all.

'And now...' he said, 'we're going to get <u>naughty</u>.'

Sat 27th -

Bought my first decoration of the year. I'm trying to cut down on buying new Christmas things but this couldn't be avoided. It was a miniature leg lamp from the film, 'A Christmas Story'. I swooned over it.

Sun 28th -

After almost a week of waiting to hear from a supervisor, I called Vodafone, going straight to their complaints department to see if that made any difference. It did. They waved every cancellation fee (£95 in total) and reduced my monthly contract by £8 a month for its 24-month duration. Crazy. And annoying. Especially as that dippy bloke quoted me £37 a month as a 'loyalty deal'. I'm now paying £16 for exactly the same thing.

Clocks went back last night, so I've now also had a little horological compensation to add to my financial.

Mon 29th -

Closed my curtains at four this afternoon. One thing even the harshest critic can say in defence of winter is that it's ideal weather for hiding. Light summer nights make the early closing of the curtains feel as though you've failed at life. Shutting the world off at tea time, though, immersing yourself in lamplight and a book, makes you feel like you've got it sussed. Talking of books, I just started 'The Forsyte Saga'. I seldom read novels anymore. This is making me realise what I've been missing.

Tues 30th -

One of the highlights of this half term is my annual October pilgrimage to a Christmas shop. It's not really a Christmas shop, as such, but a dedicated festive section of a garden centre. It's a cutesy wooden barn bursting with decorations, one of those places where you daren't turn around too quickly for fear of your coat brushing £70 worth of baubles off a display table. Placed next to a tea room, it inevitably smells of tinsel, coffee, and cheese toasties.

 The garden centre is in the middle of a wood. The gravel car park was busier than normal. The place had changed its name, too. I didn't like the look of this. New owners tend to have radical ideas. And those radical ideas oft involve getting rid of things that, after a close study of the accounts, bring in little money i.e. Christmas sections that smell like tinsel, coffee, and cheese toasties.

 Luckily, the Christmas section had survived. Only it wasn't like before. The displays were more rigid. Gone were the round tables stocked high with trinkets. In their place were faux-rustic wooden shelves with everything neatly aligned. There was less stock but it was more orderly and colour coordinated. The smell of tinsel was still there, but only just. There was no music playing, just the clinking of the diners next door and the creaking of the roof in the high wind.

Weds 31st -

All Hallow's Eve. My, how Halloween has mutated in the last fifteen years. When I was a kid it barely got a mention. Now it's a full-on event with social media photos of zombified kids, mummified mummies and blood-lipped, rat-arsed, vampire students. Halloween even has its own aisle in the shops. An unimaginable thought pre-2000. Back then, if by chance you were invited to a Halloween event (I think, up to 1999, the combined total of Halloween events ever held across the UK stood at forty-three), you had to go to fancy dress shops to get your fake blood and witch hats. Today you can buy them with your groceries. I'm not against it. The more celebrations, the merrier. If I were king, and if kings had any sort of power, my first move would be to slap six or seven additional bank holidays into the calendar. Halloween: off. Remembrance Day: off. VE Day: off. Valentine's Day: off. I'd scour the calendar, day and night, to find quasi-significant events which would warrant a day off. The anniversary of the first broadcast of 'Blue Peter'? Off.

 When I moved into this flat, a huddle of miniature trick or treaters turned up on my doorstep. I had nothing to give the little mites. I opened a packet of chocolate digestives for them. The following year, and each subsequent year, I've made sure I'm well-stocked with sweets, jam-packing my kitchen with Swizzlesticks and Haribo.

 I've had zero visits since.

＊

Realised today how nobody talks about Brexit in real life. It exists only on the internet and in newspapers. I only mention it <u>now</u> to point out that nobody does mention it. The subject almost never crosses my mind. Like everyone else, I've got more important things to think about: is it worth paying that bit extra for slightly nicer tasting toothpaste?; are my trousers suitable for the day ahead?; how is my phone already down to 63% battery? Yet, in the history books and documentaries of the future, there will be a consensus that the nation shook at the prospect of exiting Europe, when, in reality, as far as I can see, we didn't shake at all. There was deep despair and elation in the days directly after the referendum (the result of which, for the record, I thought was a permanent mark on the reputation of the British character) but, two years on, most people just want the show-offs in charge to earn their keep and sort it all out.

There's a great bit in Dominic Sandbrook's book about the 1960s, 'Never Had It So Good', where he talks about the notorious 'Lady Chatterly's Lover' trial and how little interest the masses paid to it at the time. What transpired, however, according to Sandbrook, is that those who <u>did</u> have an interest in the case - writers, publishers, artists, politicians et al - were the ones who went on to write the history books and, obviously, inflated the trial's importance. I expect the same thing will happen with Brexit. Just imagine Owen Jones' take on the matter in his inevitable 2060 release, 'Message To My (Adopted) Grandchildren'. He'll be telling the world how, in his younger days, we <u>all</u> marched for freedom (when we didn't).

In Christmas news, which, if memory serves me correctly, is what this diary's supposed to be about, I went to a hardware store to see if they sold artificial Christmas trees (mine has broken). No luck. It wasn't a total waste of time, though. Whilst there, I may have stumbled upon my favourite ever human observation: that, when in hardware stores, men upgrade their nervous whistling to a more relaxed 'pom pom pom, de da de'. It's like they're still uncomfortable but more comfortable than in other shops, where they feel only bold enough to whistle. If I were Michael McIntyre, I could raise the domed roof of the O2 with an observation of that quality:

'Have you ever noticed, right, right, you're in the hardware store, aren't you, right, buying things for the Man Cave, when all of a sudden you hear...'

The 12 Things To Watch Of Christmas

#5

Chas & Dave's Christmas Knees Up

Recorded for television in 1982, this show features the self-proclaimed 'rockney' duo in a mock-up of a London boozer, belting their way through their greatest hits, accompanied, in its weaker moments, by old school (racist) musicians and old school (racist) comedians.

How and why *Chas & Dave's Christmas Knees Up* was commissioned is anyone's guess, but thank God it was, and thank God the production team took the project so seriously. Or, quite possibly, not at all seriously. Whatever their approach, they nailed it.

Despite being filmed in a TV studio, the setting and lighting is so richly reminiscent of the sort of drinking establishment that died before the millennium that you can almost smell the fag smoke and Brut. It captures the bygone age of pub perfectly. The brown suits. The flat caps. The drunken old dears sat around small, circular tables with handbags on their laps. The mixture of generations, from underweight teens to underweight octogenarians (all stick-thin on account of the lack of plenty). The steamed-up stained-glass windows. The bawdy conversations, shouted from one side of the room to the other, above the shouts of other shouted conversations. The old man wandering around on his lonesome, never settling. The single girl inch-deep in pink blusher. The young mum in her ruffled mock-Edwardian frock. Cravats. Rugby shirts. Cigarette machines. Sing-alongs. Clap-alongs. Mountainous ashtrays on mysteriously abandoned tables, surrounded by white, frothy empties. The noise. Lord, the noise. A carnival. At one point in the show, a wobbly lady in the crowd goes arse over tit with such clout that you wonder whether she saw another Christmas. Her slip is ignored in the beery chaos.

Screened almost every year by Channel 5, *Chas & Dave's Christmas Knees Up* was originally broadcast on London Weekend Television. The picture quality is mercifully terrible.[1] It doesn't strike me as a programme that will ever be upscaled to HD. It belongs in its original 1982 wrapper, where the streams of silver and gold tinsel hanging from the studio rafters glare with blinding majesty. Whereas modern music programmes like to treat us to close-ups of the most attractive people in the audience (to lend a bit of aspirational glam), the *Christmas Knees Up* makes a point of drunkenly focusing on the *least* desirable. The smokers by the fruity. The out-of-time clappers. The angry barmaid, momentarily pretending to smile.

Atop Chas' piano is a glass of thick red port. It might be tobacco spit. Dave stands throughout, plucking his bass, working off his last ounce of fat. The duo smash their way through the tunes - *The Sideboard Song*; *London Girls*; *Ain't No Pleasing You* - with mastery of their craft. Occasionally they shout things out to one another mid-song - 'Come on, Charley boy' - or tell the audience before each chorus, ''Ere we go'.

For all its beauty in encapsulating a lost era, the *Knees Up* does also offer a festive reminder of the benefits of cultural

---

[1] You wouldn't want to see some of its characters with too much clarity.

evolution. Between the songs, there are a number of comedy spots that are so bad they almost pose a risk to the viewers' mental wellbeing. One of the 'spots' is from a duo called Cosmotheka, who perform a Jake Thackray-esque attempt at a bawdy music hall number, with jokes about things being 'stiff' and needing 'tucking in'. Then there's a stand-up set from Cookstown's own Jimmy Cricket: humankind's worst attempt at a comedian. Almost every joke feels stolen. He arrives on stage with an umbrella and stands on a mini pedestal, firing off dead punchlines to howls of canned laughter:

'I love Christmas,' he says. 'In fact, I think we should have it every year... Me boss asked me to sing *The 12 Days Of Christmas* - I said I'm only off for a week!... I went to get a job as a Father Christmas. I needed four ho-ho-ho levels!...'

Sometimes, before a joke, he'll say, 'Come here' and motion the punters towards him.

It's shite.

Alas, the world's worst comedian doesn't give the show's worst performance. That honour goes to an up-and-coming young comic by the name of Jim Davidson, who sings a reggae version of *White Christmas* in a Jamaican accent. The Jamaican accent was a big part of Davidson's act in the early stages of his career. He even gave the character a name: Chalky White. Naturally, Channel 5 edit Mr White's appearance out of their annual repeats. It isn't even on YouTube (although an audio version of *White Christmas*, put out by Davidson as a Christmas single in 1980, is). We can only try and imagine it; which is actually fairly easy.[1]

---

[1] In 2014, Davidson told *The Telegraph* that he'd stopped doing the Chalky White skit because 'you rarely hear West Indian accents now', as though the character was an entirely affectionate reflection of the joys of a multicultural society.

Another star guest who may also have found funny the fact that Homo sapiens who descend from warmer countries have more melanin in their skin than those who don't, is guitarist Eric Clapton. After an eight-year absence from TV, he agreed to appear on the *Knees Up*. And there are plenty of racial skeletons in his closet:

'I think Enoch [Powell]'s right,' Clapton told a Birmingham audience in 1976. 'I think we should send them all back. Stop Britain from becoming a black colony. Get the foreigners out. England is for white people, man. We are a white country. This is Great Britain - a white country.'

Throughout the 1976 gig, he's said to have repeated the National Front's 'Keep Britain White' slogan, whilst, bear in mind, playing blues guitar and singing his most recent hit: a cover of Bob Marley's *I Shot The Sheriff*.

Clapton has since admitted he feels 'shame' about the comments, attributing them to drugs. Although, on the night in question, he reportedly yelled:

'I used to be into dope. Now I'm into racism. It's much heavier, man.'

His comments that night were the ultimate driving force behind the Rock Against Racism campaign. So, weirdly, some good came of his backwards rhetoric.[1]

Clapton aside, the *Knees Up*'s other musical guest, Lenny Peters, is a treat to behold. A cross between Dave Angel and, well, another Dave Angel, Peters sports a tight perm, eye-bag covering shades, a chunky sovereign ring, a gold medallion (hanging over his pale jumper) and grey trousers. He manages to sing without ever opening his mouth wider than a centimetre. Sitting on a stool, he croons a twelve-minute ballad about how

---

[1] 'I was so ashamed of who I was,' Clapton said in 2018, 'a kind of semi-racist, which didn't make sense.' Slight misuse of the word 'semi' there.

much he fancies Jesus - something along those lines - before standing to join Chas & Dave for a more up-tempo number (during which he increases his body-movements-per-minute ratio to about four).

You just have to watch this programme.

It wouldn't be right if I got to the end of a chapter without somebody dying, so now's the time to remind you that Chas (Charles Hodges) passed away from pneumonia in 2017, bringing the partnership to an abrupt end.[1] Theirs was a music career unlike any other. As well as a string of hits, they wrote the theme tune for *In Sickness & Health* and the kids' TV shows *Crackerjack* and *Bangers & Mash*. They were signed up to sing the *Only Fools & Horses* theme but were too busy touring after the unexpected success of their song, *Ain't No Pleasing You*.

'If I could describe what I was aiming for,' said Chas in 2009, 'I achieved it on *Ain't No Pleasing You*. A serious song, sung in me own accent. A cockney song being taken seriously.'

Both partners had impressive musical backgrounds before finding fame as a duo (a fame which arrived largely as a result of their song *Gertcha* being used in a Courage Bitter TV ad). Chas had worked with Gerry Lee Lewis and Gene Vincent in the early 60s and Dave (Dave Peacock) was in a number of bands who nearly made it. The latter's most famous piece of musicianship comes from his sessioning days: a bass-line on a 1975 Labi Siffre single. Dave's performance is perhaps better known for being sampled heavily on a 1999 track by a then-

---

[1] They'd originally retired in 2005 after Dave's wife had died. Dave reflected that his career had enabled him to take his 'wife around the world; luckily she saw some great places.' Rather than living the spotlit high life, Dave now spends his time carefully carving wood into old-fashioned wagon-wheels.

unknown rapper called Marshall Mathers. The song was called *My Name Is*.

Such was Chas & Dave's ability to craft infectious tunes, the duo scored a chart hit in 1986 with a song expressly about how much they enjoy snooker. They even had success with four separate songs about their beloved Tottenham Hotspur. It's hard to imagine we'll ever see their like again: serial novelty-songwriters with a sincere, brilliant back catalogue.

What is so endearing about the *Christmas Knees Up* is that it barely mentions Christmas, yet the spirit of the season, like the spirit of the age, runs throughout. Near the end of the show, a conga snakes its way around the studio pub set. When was the last time you saw adults in a conga? When was the last time you heard the word 'conga'? You should see them there, the people all lined up, kicking their legs, grabbing each other drunkenly by their tiny waists. *Chas & Dave's Christmas Knees Up* will be thirty-seven years old by the time you read this. What those years have done to its revellers, from the yuppies to the old Blitz-boys who worked on the river, who can say? But there they are, partying every year, after so many other parties have faded.

#6

Postman Pat Goes Sledging

Warning: contains spoilers

Although it's not a Christmas episode, and although I'm not sure if I ever watched it at Christmas, *Postman Pat Goes Sledging* is indelibly linked to December in my mind. When I was knocking up this list of films and TV shows, it felt wrong to leave it out. In order to write about it, I had to watch it again, for the first time in around thirty years.[1] It was precisely how I'd remembered it; my mind had treated the episode with great care.

For many years, *Postman Pat* was the *Fawlty Towers* of children's telly. There were only thirteen episodes in existence – as opposed to *Fawlty*'s twelve – but they were repeated and repeated without anybody really noticing. First broadcast in September 1981, *Postman Pat* became a staple of daytime pre-school programming, slotting into neat gaps in the BBC schedule on rotation. Seemingly eternally. It wasn't until 1997 that a second batch of episodes was commissioned, and *Postman Pat* stopped being the *Fawlty Towers* of children's telly and became more the *Twin Peaks*.

Those original thirteen *Pat* episodes represent the glory days, though. They really are the most magnificent things. Sensitively devoid of drama, their storylines involve Pat stopping to have a picnic, Pat stopping to have a cup of tea, and Pat's letters getting wet. In *Pat Goes Sledging*, he sledges his way along his snowy postal route after his van gets caught in a drift.[2] Everything is gentle and everything is soft in the land of *Postman Pat*. Yet children loved it. *I* loved it. *Love*. I'm not using

---

[1] Thank goodness for YouTube. Back in the day, as they say, I'd have had to buy one of those videos with a name like *CBBC Kids Classics* (also on the tape would be episodes of *Paddington*, *Superted*, *Charlie Chalk* and something left-field like *The Tooth Fairies*. It would have cost me a pretty penny, too).

[2] The village reverend, who has 'slipped on the ice' and broken his leg, avoids the ignominy of A&E and opts instead to bandage his leg and sit by the fire, hoping its warmth will weld things back into place. He is concerned that, what with his broken leg and the ten foot drifts, he won't be able to send out the parish newsletter. Pat agrees to deliver it, leaving the residents of Greendale to breathe a sigh of relief.

that word loosely. Shy of slick editing, pulsating lights, chorus-lines and explosions, so much of *Pat Goes Sledging* merely consists of his van driving carefully around the village. It is all so quiet, too. Very little but the squawk of birds, the van's hum and the occasional footstep crunching through the snow. I suspect if you switched on CBeebies or Nickelodeon right now, your television would flash and scream at you.

The creator of *Postman Pat*, and writer of the first series, John Cunliffe, knew he wanted to set a children's programme in the Lake District. It was a place he loved. It was where he lived and taught, writing children's books on the side, typing them up on a cranky old typewriter in his back bedroom. When the BBC asked him to produce some original scripts, his first thought was that he wanted the children to see as much scenery as possible,[1] and to show them a community where everybody was friendly. Cunliffe had been a victim of bullying growing up and, with his fictional village of Greendale, had purposefully created an Eden for children in a similar position. He wanted them to know that, wherever they were, when they were watching *Postman Pat*, they were safe.

The BBC suggested that the now-legendary animator, Ivor Wood, produce Cunliffe's scripts. Wood passionately researched the Lake District and designed a miniature landscape perfectly in tune with the writer's ethos. Having invested heavily to make the programme, Ivor Wood asked to buy the rights from Cunliffe, who agreed, on the proviso that he, Cunliffe, be the sole author of any new *Pat* books. That way, Cunliffe thought, he would retain creative control.

---

[1] The job of postman was deliberately given to Pat to enable his stories to travel the countryside. He could easily have been a milkman, or a presenter of property programmes: *Property Programme Presenter Pat.*

The marriage between Ivor Wood's vision and Cunliffe's spirit ensured *Postman Pat* was an instant success. Within years, it had become an industry. Cunliffe saw enough of the profits to live well, but his earnings were paltry by comparison to the fortune his character created. Repeat screenings on the BBC gave him no money. Nor did just about anything else, bar 10% of the royalties from annuals and TV tie-in magazines. Soulless new books involving Pat were published without Cunliffe's influence or permission. Things changed. Pat got stupider, wackier. Cunliffe had had his beloved character stolen from under his nose. Yes, he'd agreed a deal to write all official Pat books, but, as these non-Cunliffe books weren't technically *books* - i.e they were printed in magazines or on *card* instead of paper - the new writers could do whatever they liked. Elsewhere, Ivor Wood received much of the credit for creating Pat and the world of Greendale characters. Cunliffe quietly took his royalty cheques and watched on, helpless, as his hero mutated. Later in his career, he created other characters - notably the rag-dolls *Rosie & Jim* - but none met with anything quite like the success of his friendly village postman.[1]

On rewatching *Pat Goes Sledging* all these years later, I was surprised at just how delicate its sets were (and, for all the controversy, how excellent a job Ivor Wood had done). The opening sequence perfectly sets us up, with the green, bumpy hills and distinctive Cumbrian stone walls lining the narrow lanes. The model cottages and buildings capture the essence of that area's slate grey cosiness. The detail is exquisite. The houses have gutters and square windows, all with curtains. Mrs

---

[1] Those old enough to remember *Rosie & Jim*'s earlier series may remember that their canal boat was manned by an elderly gent called John. It was John Cunliffe himself.

Goggins' post office has handwritten notes pinned to the wall, little sweet tubs and boxes of detergent on wooden shelves, and milk bottles - with foil lids - on the counter. A broom leans against the wall. The old hussy herself is dressed in a finely woven shawl. All the characters are dressed with such care: shirt collars protruding over jumper collars (worn beneath wintry coats); tissues sticking out of pockets; buttons and zips; shoelaces; knitted scarves and winter hats. The houses Pat visits all have wallpaper (frayed at the edges!), bookshelves, grandfather clocks, skirting boards, biscuits on plates, lamps, plug sockets, flickering log fires.

 The only thing that lacked realism was that everyone had four fingers.[1] Oh, and that Pat took his cat, Jess, along on his daily route. In reality, this just wouldn't work. In the entire history of cats, I'd say only about eight of them have obeyed an order to sit, and that was probably because they intended to sit anyway. The idea that you could drive one around in a van is ludicrous. It would have to go in a crate, for a start. Anyone who's ever sat in an automobile with a crated cat will know that they seldom take warmly to the experience. Robbed of their free-roaming life of leisure, they squawk and wheeze as though intercepting messages from the spirit realm. Jess must have been on sedatives to sit there so placidly. In real life, the moment Pat

---

[1] According to a 2001 article by the BBC, Pat was given an extra finger in Japan so as not to create the impression that he was part the Yakuza mafia group, whose signature initiation move is to cut off a finger (apparently this is done to show you mean business; although I suspect *more* business could be done if you had five fingers. You could certainly make phone calls more quickly). How anyone could jump to the conclusion that Pat had joined the mafia, I don't know. Just imagine that episode: *Postman Pat Slits The Jugular Of A Grass.*

opened his van door, Jess would dash out, never to be seen again.[1]

There were a couple of other details I'd never picked up on. Firstly, that Pat's mouth is drawn onto his face and doesn't move when he speaks. Secondly, that Jess the cat is a *he*. I was convinced it was a girl. I even named my own female cat after her/him when I was six. Nobody pointed out my error.

The BBC went back for a third series in 2004 and ran the postman ragged, churning out a further 152 episodes since (now making it the *Midsomer Murders* of children's telly). Gone are the cups of tea and kites trapped in trees. Pat has moved with the times. He's been seen to drive speedboats, helicopters and snowmobiles. He delivers robots and jet boots. Yet not one of these episodes, I suspect, belongs in the nation's collective heart in the same way as *Pat Goes Sledging*, *Pat & The Windy Day* or *Pat In The Fog*, or any of those other quaint originals.

Pat even had to ditch the Royal Mail logo in 2000 after it was decided the character didn't fit with the brand's 'corporate image' (their corporate image being, presumably, rather hellish). Pat has had the last laugh there, though; I expect Postman Pat Ltd will have a fiscally stronger 2019 than the Royal Mail Group Ltd.

Postman Pat Goes Sledging ends with Pat and a moustachioed local farmer taking a sledge to finish the day's deliveries. I'd love to see that happen in real life: my postman and some farmer shuffling along in a silent snowy field. It would have a touch of *Brokeback Mountain* about it. But, done in that inimitable, gentle way of those first thirteen episodes, it does nothing but stir the soul.

---

[1] Like most cats when the going gets tough, Jess sits this frozen episode out, lazing it up in front of the fire.

In his last few years, John Cunliffe became disillusioned by children's television. You can understand why, but I hope he at least appreciated what a gift he'd given the children of Britain. Imagine being responsible for having created so much joy.

Anyway, back to my own attempt at leaving behind a gift of pure joy. The next entry in the Christmas Alphabet just about sums things up.

The Christmas Alphabet

I is for...

Irrigation, Colonic

One of the lesser-noted spikes in popularity, come Christmas time, is for advanced January bookings of colonic irrigation. Although as yet not scientifically proven to be of any health benefit whatsoever, the operation appeals to its patients as, primarily, an easy way to lose weight.

The NHS have steered clear. They've got enough mess to deal with. Colonic irrigation is only available privately, usually costing the drainee between £50 and £100.[1] We shouldn't laugh, really, but even the NHS' official description of the procedure sounds vaguely like they're mocking it:

'You lie on your side while warm water is passed into your bowel through a tube inserted into your bottom.'

And then the poo-poo goes out of your bot-bot and into a bucket.[2]

The joke soon ends when the NHS remind us of the common side-effects: rectal bleeding, anal fissures, punctured bowels.

And a partridge in a pear tree.

---

[1] Why these differences in price exist is a mystery; I shouldn't think the quality of service differs dramatically - a tube is a tube, is it not?

[2] I bet the bins round the back of colonic irrigation centres contain things that could make a mortician gag.

J is for...

January Sales

The world of retail has wreaked more havoc with the British calendar than the switch from Julian to Gregorian.[1] Thanks to the demands of capitalism, we're in a right old mess: Christmas starts in August; Easter starts on Christmas Eve; Father's Day drops the day after Mother's Day; and Black Friday kicks off on the previous Monday. Where that leaves Pancake Day is anybody's guess.

As further illustration of retail's calendar-meddling, the 'Sales' used to be widely called the '*January* Sales'. This was until, like most other annual occurrences, they were brought further and further forward to the point where they collided messily into the Christmas shopping period. The result of this is that the word 'January' has been eased out of action as seamlessly as the 1 from ITV1. The term 'January Sales' is now only used by people who still say things like 'the wireless', 'hand us an Opal Fruit' and 'on the never-never'.

Not on my watch. They'll always be January Sales to me. In fairness, this is largely because I couldn't think of anything else to put in the J section.[2]

Watch the evening news on Christmas Day and you can be sure that – other than a clip of the Queen waddling up the path of St Mary Magdalen church, Sandringham, accompanied by a ripple

---

[1] A switch which, incidentally, meant that people went to bed on Wednesday 2nd September 1752 and woke the following morning on Thursday the 14th, having lost the best part of a fortnight. Worse still, nobody had the foggiest as to when to put their green bins out.

[2] I eventually thought of *two* things to put in, as you'll see. If I had any sense, I could've put 'Jumpers, Bad' in here, too.

of warm applause – you'll see a report about 'expectant shoppers' camped outside Selfridges in the hope of saving 38p on a Boxing Day tea towel. My general reaction to these shots of queuing hordes is to tut, sneer and wonder, often aloud, whether these soggy parasites couldn't wait at least a week before getting back into spend-mode. But, come the 27th or 28th, my fingers get itchy and I, myself, begin to slather at the prospect of Marks & Spencer corduroys priced at £9.50, down from £38.

John Lewis Adverts

A 21st century rival to Coca-Cola's dominance in the Christmas advertising game, John Lewis Ltd like to pretend the tradition started in 2007 with the their shadow puppet Christmas advert However, the very fact that you haven't got a clue which 'shadow puppet' advert I'm talking about tells you that the tradition didn't truly start until 2011.[1]

Their 2011 TV advert featured a little boy counting down the weeks until Christmas morning. The reason for his eagerness, we discover, was that rather than receiving gifts, he wanted to *give* his parents a present. With its subtle blend of nostalgia and modern sentiment, the advert jerked tears up and down the land and is, I suspect, more likely imprinted in your memory than 2007's shadow puppets.

Another factor in the 2011's advert's popularity was that it featured a cover of The Smiths' *Please Please Please Let Me Get What I Want*, an altogether less saccharine tune than we're used

---

[1] 2009's ad was the *true* John Lewis prototype, featuring a dog receiving a stocking out in his snowy kennel, accompanied by Ellie Goulding's dippy cover of *Your Song*. The advert didn't capture the public imagination like 2011's effort, however.

to hearing on ads. The song was in keeping with the fashion of the time - still ongoing, in truth - of twee, plinky cover versions by boys called Tom or by girls who are so damn ethereal that they never wear shoes. Since 2009, nearly all John Lewis ads have featured dainty covers with similarly stripped-back arrangements:[1] the *Power Of Love* snowman; the *Somewhere Only We Know* animated bear; *Real Love* with the stuffed penguin; *Golden Slumbers* with the monster under the bed; and some dirge or other in that weird one with the old git crying on the moon.

The adverts are all the work of the Adam & Eve agency. Their services don't come cheap. Plumped up by a costly obsession with cover versions of songs you used to like, the fees John Lewis haemorrhage for the ads regularly run into the millions. Whether the final product reaps dividends for the retailer is a moot point. The company just shut its first store in thirteen years and is toying with suspending bonuses for the first time since 1953.[2] On the plus side, bosses crying into their Christmas pay-packets might be a good idea for next year's ad. I'd recommend a twee, plinky cover of *Money's Too Tight To Mention* to accompany it.

---

[1] Of songs that were, in most instances, reasonably stripped-back to start with.

[2] Their slogan, 'Never knowingly undersold', is partly to blame. After years of confusion as to what the devil the phrase meant, it has since been explained in the following terms: 'If you can buy more cheaply elsewhere anything you have just bought from us, we will refund the difference.' Which isn't as catchy, as slogans go. This promise to match competitors' prices is thought to be a substantial reason as to why the company has seen profits drop.

K is for...

Knees-Up, Staff

Eighty-six percent of all workplaces have some form of annual staff party and 54% of those invited dread going to it. This means, if I get my calculator out, that 46% *don't* dread going to it.

Small margins. Which side are you on?

Depending on the calibre of your colleagues, staff parties can either be annual highlights or excursions to hell. Many are the Christmas party pitfalls. The key to a good one is to pick your seat well. One false move and you're stuck next to somebody who never shuts up about their campervan trips to the Peak District. The worst thing is to be sat beside someone with whom you have nothing in common bar the name of your employer. It tends to lead to conversations like this:

'The meat was nice.'

'It was,' you reply.

'Really nice.'

'Yes.'

'Did you have the ham hock?'

'No, it's just the way my trousers hang.'

'Pardon?'

'Nothing. A joke.'

'Oh. Yes. Ha. That reminds me, did I ever tell you about the time my campervan got a flat tyre on the outskirts of Glossop?'

The staff party cliché is of a drunken orgy in which people photocopy their rump, snog each other in the stock cupboard, then find so-and-so from Accounts sobbing in the bogs. The reality is usually more sedate, however, generally consisting of a merry slosh-up between colleagues. The danger is if you miss the party for some reason (or purposefully avoid it) and have to spend the next three months being subjected to in-jokes:

'Whatever you do, don't end up like Gary with those teaspoons!'

Worse yet, is if the party was the stage for some scandal or other - an affray or eruption of volcanic discontent - which you then have to piece together in episodic instalments, like the lead in an ITV detective series:

'So, what did Jenny *actually* say?' you enquire, deftly.

'Well, I was at the bar at the time, but I heard her call Brian a bully.'

'And I,' a second witness chips in, 'saw her crying.'

'God. Really? Where?'

'The bogs.'

In the main, though, staff parties are a wholesome racket. Even more so when the company weighs in with the promise of free drinks all round. I've always pitied companies who have their Christmas party in November or January. They can't be much fun. Part of the joy of the annual party is that it takes place in the swell of December giddiness, when the night streets are filled with similar revellers, drunk on ale and wine and the promise of an upcoming holiday.

Having claimed that staff knees-ups are less wild than the clichés suggest, I may be completely wrong. In 2015, an *Independent* article claimed that 39% of people have had sex at Christmas parties. I should, I feel, point out that the statistics were compiled by Ann Summers Ltd. and are, like some of their returned goods, decidedly fishy. But even so. Thirty-nine percent! Maybe work-related parties *are* a world of fumbled carnal opportunism. Being the sort of person who goes home thinking he's pulled on the strength of a furtive glance, I'm perhaps not the best judge of such things.

❄❄❄

L is for...

Letters To Santa

'Did you post my letter to Father Christmas? Only I can't seem to find the Star Bird I asked for. Or me Batman cape. Or the ticket to the Bahamas.'

Bottom, 'Holy', 1991

In this white-hot age of technological marvels, the tradition of handwritten letters to Father Christmas has miraculously held firm. Santa tracker apps and Santa email initiatives may flood the market, but when it comes to contacting the North Pole, the children of today still lean towards the archaic pencil and paper.

One of the only real tweaks in the tradition is that, once upon a time, the letters used to come *from* Santa rather than being sent *to* him. Parents would get into character and write letters from the North Pole, giving their kids a kind of annual appraisal and letting them know whether they were in for any treats this year.[1] Eventually the power shifted from adult to child, and the appraisals morphed into requests. However, the

---

[1] J.R.R. Tolkien took the tradition to extremes, penning long, spectacularly illustrated letters from Father Christmas (and his sidekick, Polar Bear) to his family for twenty-five years. The collected book of these correspondences is an absolute treat. (The letters were also an ingenious way of letting his children know, straight from Father Nicholas Christmas, as Tolkien called him, why they hadn't received certain presents. Not a bad idea to pinch, if you've got the time to craft such elaborate musings.)

letters are still handwritten, before being burned on the fire and magically transported to the North Pole.[1]

If ever you were in doubt about the existence of good in the world, remind yourself that the Royal Mail have a policy of sending children free letters *from* Father Christmas (or, if needed, audio messages or braille). In the official FAQ section on the company website, the answer to the question 'Where do letters to Santa go?', the reply is:

'They go to the big man himself in the North Pole, of course.'

A touch of loveliness worth bearing in mind, I suppose, the next time one of their whistling employees hurriedly jams a council tax statement through your letterbox at twenty-to-three in the afternoon. Or, indeed, when the company declare that Postman Pat no longer matches their corporate image.[2]

Lord Protector, Oliver Cromwell

Poor King Charles laid his head on the block
January 1649, down came the axe and in the silence that followed
The only sound that could be heard was a solitary giggle from
Oliver Cromwell, Lord Protector of England

Monty Python, *Oliver Cromwell*, 1969

The original Christmas grinch. The grinch to whom all other grinches aspire.

Oliver Cromwell took a predictably dim view of how the religious festival of Christmas had lost its true meaning. What

---

[1] In Scotland, where the bairns are of hardier stock, they cut out the literary aspect and poke their heads up the chimney instead, shouting their wishes skywards.

[2] I'm still annoyed about that.

ought to have been a time of careful scriptural study - thought he and his Puritan posse - had, instead, become a twelve-day piss-up, laced with games, sports, singalongs and hearty feasts. To show what wits they were, the Puritans devised some alternative comedic names for Christmas in an attempt to shame those who celebrated it: 'Profane Man's Ranting Day', 'Superstitious Man's Idol Day', and the not at all tenuous 'Satan (That Adversary's) Working Day'.[1] Mirroring the (casual) puritans of today, the (official) Puritans of yesteryear lamented how Christmas had lost sight of its meaning.

Here's one old duffer's views on the subject, from the 1640s:

'The sins of our forefathers have turned this feast, pretending the memory of Christ, into an extreme forgetfulness of him, by giving liberty to carnal and sensual delights.'[2]

Yet even *before* Cromwell's rule, the Puritan-heavy Parliament was wary of how commoners had distorted the celebration of the babe's hallowed birth. To protect it from being tainted further, they enforced bans on parties or any such merriment occurring on December 25th and advised, with precious little uptake, that commoners spend the day, instead, in sombre reflection of the Christ child's message.

The 1653 crowning of Oliver Cromwell as King - although he strongly preferred the title 'Lord Protector' - stepped the pre-existing Christmas ban up a notch,[3] going so far as to officially

---

[1] Imagine if that last name had stuck. The effects on Christmas pop music would be tremendous:
*'And the boys of the NYPD choir were singing Galway Bay
And the bells were ringing out for Satan (That Adversary's) Day.'*

[2] And this was without him having seen the results of that 2015 Ann Summers staff-party sex survey.

[3] Just to be clear, Cromwell didn't ban Christmas. A ban already existed. Instead, he imposed a more organised lockdown.

forbid church services on the day itself.[1] Cromwell viewed *Christ-mass* as an ungodly overspill of Catholicism and yet another public exhibition of excess.[2] During his rule, hymns such as *The Holly & The Ivy* were considered as dangerous and controversial as *Anarchy In The UK* would be centuries later. Any festive gatherings, any public excitement, and Cromwell's elves - although he strongly preferred the title 'New Model Army' - would swoop in and make lists of who'd been naughty and nice.

Here's a ditty that secretly did the rounds at the time:

To conclude, I'll tell you news that's right
Christmas was killed at Naseby fight

Just as with any King - sorry, I mean *Lord Protector* - when Oliver Cromwell died, his son and heir, Richard, ascended the (non)throne. By this time, the Cromwell family name was synonymous with dreary, grey oppression.[3] The public had had enough. Sensing a groundswell of encouragement, Charles II returned to London from exile in Europe to a rapturous welcome in the capital. One of the first actions of the 'Merry Monarch' was to restore Christmas celebrations.[4] England was coloured with euphoria and song. Hooray for the Merry Monarch, Good King Charles, Man of the People etc.

---

[1] Easter and Whitsun were also given the same treatment, sending sales of Malteser Bunnies plummeting.

[2] A bit rich coming from someone who wanted his warts added to his portrait. I mean, how excessive is that? What a waste of oils.

[3] Privately, Oliver Cromwell was said to have an almost uncontrollable riotous side, leading historians to wonder if he was a manic depressive. Monty Python's '*solitary giggle*' isn't entirely implausible.

[4] He toyed with renaming it Satan (That Absolute Legend's) Day. (Not really.)

As always, the glee was short-lived. Within a matter of years, as the streamers and bunting were swept from city gullies, the English reached for their prescription-strength rose-tinted spectacles and saw, in their retrospective hue, how life wasn't really all *that* bad under Cromwell. If anything, they thought, things were quite pinkish and pleasant.

'Everybody do nowadays,' wrote Samuel Pepys during Charles II's rule, 'reflect upon Oliver and commend him, what brave things he did and made all the neighbour princes fear him.'

He sounds like a talking head from an episode of *I Love 1667*.[1]

He's an odd one, Oliver Cromwell. In terms of leadership, he is a paradox of light and shade. His treatment of his enemies – particularly the Irish Catholics – is justly infamous. As is his treatment of the necks of kings, specifically those belonging to Charles I.[2] And yet he built the navy into a global juggernaut, accelerated the expanse of the British empire (taking Jamaica

---

[1] Pepys had been aboard the boat on which Charles II had sailed back to England. In his diary, he mentions the king's dog, who 'did shit the boat, which made us laugh'. Me too.

[2] To be fair, Charles only had *one* neck, but Cromwell hated it anyway. He called Charles' execution a 'cruel necessity'. He famously flicked ink boyishly at confused onlookers as he signed the king's death warrant. King Charles' son, when reinstated on the throne, oversaw the digging up of Cromwell's buried corpse from Westminster Abbey on the anniversary of his own father's beheading. Cromwell's body – warts 'n all – was then hanged for a day and beheaded. Charles, too, may have though this a 'cruel necessity'. Personally, I'd call both acts 'megalomaniacal barbarity'. But whatever. Cromwell's head was stolen by an onlooker and is now said to rest in a vault in a Cambridge chapel. (Why it's only *said* to rest in the vault, I can't confirm. Can't someone can pop down there and check?)

from the Spanish) and greatly subdued the power of all future monarchs to the extent that, by the 21st century, they became little more than celebrity guests on DIY programmes presented by Nick Knowles.

Whether Cromwell's achievements were all morally sound is a discussion for more learned people than I to debate. However, in terms of how countries formerly measured their success, until the breaking up of the Old World in 1918, he more than made an impact. What *is* easier to agree upon is that he grossly misjudged the importance of eating, drinking and being merry, whether under the umbrella of Christmas or anything else.

The next time some bore cackles on about how Christmas has lost its meaning and isn't what it was *blah blah blah*, remind them that the 'true meaning of Christmas' has been enforced once before. At the expense of street parties and hooplas. And things, like Cromwell's warty nose, went pear-shaped.

Lynx Gift Sets

Many's the number who, having grown up in millennial Britain, have exited a passenger jet in Jomo Kenyatta International Airport in later years and remarked, on first sniffing the air, that the smell of Africa wasn't quite what they'd been led to believe.

Sales of Lynx's fruity intoxicants are mind-boggling. At the last count, they sold around ten million gift sets in one year. That's enough to supply around a third of all males in the UK.[1] The Lynx Gift Set (two items: shower gel and a can of deodorant) has replaced socks as the go-to present from somebody who places you in their £4-or-less present-buying category.

---

[1] And it's more than likely that the over-forties are left out of the Lynx demographic and that the true proportion of sales is around one gift set for every man under forty.

In the past, offering someone a can of deodorant for Christmas was tantamount to letting them know you thought they smelt like a kebab that had left on a charity shop windowsill. However, such has been Lynx's promotional drive in the last twenty years - with adverts that near-enough promise you'll be surrounded by an array of babes in knickers within seconds of application - receiving one of their gift sets could now be viewed as a comment on how urgently you need help with attracting the attentions of the fairer sex.

Ten million sets a year, though. Crikey. The waste doesn't bear thinking about: the cardboard box; the can of deodorant; the bottle of shower gel. Worst of all is their jet-black inner plastic casings, which won't biodegrade until a distant age when the sun is so big that everywhere will be as hot as Jomo Kenyatta International Airport - and, at which point, no amount of Lynx Africa will cease the sweating.

In truth, it might all be somewhat ironic.

The 12 Songs Of Christmas

#7

I Wish It Could Be Christmas Everyday - Wizzard

Considering how prevalent it is, it surprises me how few people class this as their favourite Christmas track. Anecdotally, it's the song most likely to get everyone singing at parties. Culturally, however, it lingers in the shadow of 1973's other huge selling yuletide standard, Slade's *Merry Christmas Everybody*.[1] But for those who like their Christmas smash hits to have a bit of jingly innocence (and to *not* have Noddy Holder screaming over the top of them), then Wizzard's Spector-esque masterpiece is the one.

Oh, well I wish it could be Christmas every day
When the kids start singing and the band begins to play

The story of the 1973 battle between these two staples of the Christmas mixtape is as over-told as the songs themselves are over-played. What *I* never knew, though, was that despite Slade's victory in the race to number 1, Wizzard's effort never

---

[1] If you want to pick up an extra point in a Christmas pub quiz, memorising the title of this Slade song would be a good place to start. Nearly everybody thinks it's called *So Here It Is Merry Christmas*. Losers.

reached any higher than number 4.[1] For all the legend of the two horse race - or two reindeer race, as we're being seasonal - Wizzard were outsold that week by two further acts: The New Seekers and innocent family favourite, Gary Glitter.[2] That's history for you. It does funny things to the memory. Even Wizzard's keyboardist thinks the song performed better than it did, telling the *Guardian* in 2011, 'Of course, Slade got the Christmas number 1 and we were number 2.'

I Wish It Could Be Christmas Everyday was recorded in August 1973. The children's choir - pinched from a nearby Birmingham classroom and beautifully referred to as 'Miss Snob & Class 3C' on the sleeve notes - were made to feel festive by singing in a studio decorated with Christmas lights and cooled to a wintry temperature with fans. Singer Roy Wood even found a woolly hat to wear. It was wild. This was an age, bear in mind, when kids were more easily pleased, happy just to spend the day away from crushing gypsum in the workhouse.

Unfortunately for Miss Snob & Class 3C, their moment of glory on *Top Of The Pops* was snatched from their grasp. The BBC insisted on hiring children from a London stage school to accompany the band instead. Roy Wood pleaded their case, but

---

[1] Wizzard did have two number one singles: one was the dubiously-titled *Angel Fingers*; the other was *See My Baby Jive*, which sounds so similar to *I Wish It Could Be Christmas Everyday* that the writer and producer of both songs, Roy Wood, would have a good argument for suing himself for copyright infringement. (Roy Wood also had a solo song in the top twenty at the time of *I Wish It Could Be Christmas*, a piece of doo-wop nonsense called *Forever*.)

[2] Glitter's own Christmas effort, 1984's barnstorming *Another Rock 'n Roll Christmas*, would have been a definite entrant in this list were it not for its performer's grim offences. Once ever-present on radio playlists and compilation albums, the song was rightly buried without a headstone after Glitter's conviction in 1999.

ultimately failed to bend the BBC's considerably inconsistent rules regarding what children were and were not permitted to do whilst in and around the *Top Of The Pops* studio. In hindsight, the children were probably safer at home. Although they weren't to know it at the time.

'It was devastating. I was so upset,' said Miss Doyle (AKA Miss Snob). 'We'd achieved this great thing. We were in the music charts and no-one knew it was us. I tell my children, "Listen, that's mummy on the radio", and they don't believe me.'

The children were right not to believe their mother's filthy lies, because Miss Snob & Class 3C's *Top Of The Pops* omission was just the beginning of their ordeal. Further pain awaited. When the song was slated for re-release in 1981, the record label realised they'd lost the 1973 master tapes. The entire track was hurriedly re-recorded, sans Miss Snob & Class 3C.

'It took a good few bottles of brandy before we even thought about how we would manage [re-recording] it,' said studio owner, Muff Murfin.[1]

With Class 3C well and truly past their best by 1981, a new choir was needed. Luckily, like last time, there was a school near the studio.

'Roy [Wood] just popped over and negotiated a deal with the music teacher,' said Murfin. 'A one-off payment was made to the school. So the kids came over and we taught them the song.'

And it is this version, the 1981 re-release, faultlessly recreated in next to no time, which we all know and love today. It's the version that plays on adverts, in the shops and on every Christmas compilation produced since 1981. The only way to hear the original choir of Class 3C is to look long and hard online. The 1973 master tapes are yet to be found.

---

[1] That really is his name, folks. He sounds like something from *The Moomins.*

✳

There are so many iconic moments in *I Wish It Could Be Christmas Everyday* that it almost feels like a medley: the cash register (real, bought especially); the relentless brass; the school choir(s); the big raspberry at the start; the legendary line, '*OK, you lot - take it!*'

The title alone is a thing of beauty. It came after Wizzard's saxophonist told Roy Wood, 'Being in this band, it's like Christmas every day'.

The song's buoyant spirit matched the band's own.

'We didn't go in for drugs,' Wood said, 'but mostly we were drunk. I can still smell every breath of vodka in that record.'

You can hear it, too, cutting across his delivery of those sumptuously silly lyrics:

When we're skating in the park
If the snow cloud makes it dark
Then your rosy cheeks are gonna light my merry way

The vocals are delivered with such gusto that the words get lost in the melody. How many people, for instance, are aware that these are the lyrics for the third verse?:

So if Santa brings that sleigh
All along the milky way
I'll sign my name on the rooftop in the snow
Then he may decide to stay

The physical sales of the record are frightening by current standards, sailing past the million mark (for a song which, as we know, only got to number 4). Streaming services ensure that it still ticks along today, making regular December chart appearances. It's thought the tune brings Roy Wood a Christmas present somewhere in the region of £150,000 each year. Were it not for what he classes 'a bad publishing deal', he would rake in much more. At his gigs, he plays it all year round. Even in the summer.

'I wanted to sum up the whole excitement of Christmas,' Wood said back in 2004, 'and have something that would stand the test of time, but I never thought it would still be going strong thirty years later.'

Fifteen years further on still, nothing has changed. *I Wish It Could Be Christmas* has lost none of its innocence, none of its power to charm. Long may it dwell safely in the shadow of lesser songs.

Now, come along, everybody. Altogether now:
When the snowman brings the snow
When the snowman brings the snow
When the snowman brings the snow...

#8 & #9

Wonderful Christmastime - Paul McCartney

&

Happy Xmas (War Is Over) - John & Yoko & The Plastic Ono Band

The Beatles, eh?

The greatest band there ever was. The Fab Four. Universally adored. Yet, their split in 1970 gave the world four solo careers that have left nothing like the same fab mark, despite them often hitting similarly fab heights.[1] The reasons behind this are not for someone of my calibre to tackle, particularly not in a jaunty stocking-filler such as this. So revered and cherished are Lennon and McCartney[2] that adding to the discourse is largely the duty of social commentators. The Beatles are historic. Their solo work, not so much, but it must still be approached with caution by amateurs like me.

Journalists and fans debate long and hard over who was the real genius of The Beatles. This is probably because it seems too coincidental that there might have been *two* of them in there. Genius shouldn't come in pairs. We're told that genius is individual, unique, all that. But here we are. We have to somehow pick the story to pieces and work out how The Beatles happened, how two of the finest songwriters who ever lived grew up in the same city and met by fate (at a fête, of all places). It feels intrinsically wrong. Human nature compels us to pick a winner. It would all be so much easier if one of the duo's solo work trumped the other.

The entire solo careers of Lennon and McCartney can be whittled down to their Christmas songs. Both sum their respective artists up: McCartney's *Wonderful Christmastime* is a plonky, synthetic singalong full of dad jokes; Lennon's *Happy Xmas (War Is Over)* is a wistful call to action against the Vietnam War. Both tracks are omnipresent come December. And both

---

[1] Less so, in Ringo's case, but his '73 single, *Photograph*, (written with George Harrison) is a treat.

[2] Not forgetting George Harrison, of course. But, for festive reasons, it's the other two I want to focus on here. Although, Harrison *did* have a seasonal single: 1974's *Ding Dong, Ding Dong*. The song is largely unspectacular but notable for its music video (a rare thing in 1974) in which Harrison dresses up in old Beatles outfits and, at one point, plays the guitar nude (very nearly exposing his *ding dong*).

were placed lower than Johnny Mathis' *When A Child Is Born* in a 2017 *Sun* poll.

The casual view is that McCartney was The Beatles' tunesmith and Lennon was The Beatles' artist. This isn't strictly true. It was McCartney, for instance, who suggested the revolutionary looping on *Tomorrow Never Knows*; it was McCartney who chopped up and edited *Abbey Road*'s spectacular second side; and it was McCartney who lived in the heart of 60s London, cavorting with the underground creatives. For whatever reason - and I suspect it was because he just liked writing hit singles - McCartney's solo years feature some wildly un-hip releases.[1] Yet, a core of exceptional music remains (with work such as *Junk*, *Ram On*, *Single Pigeon* and *Calico Skies* worthy of inclusion on any Beatles record). He refuses to slow down. Suitably, he has recently announced that he's working on his first ever musical: *It's A Wonderful Life*. He's already written most of the songs for it (and they have, according to the show's producer, 'exceeded expectations'). He will soon be eighty.

As middle-of-the-road as *Wonderful Christmastime* sounds to those who have had to hear it fifty times per annum since its release in 1979, there is more than enough of the surreal about it. It is the most unusual of songs. Think of the intro. Imagine it in your head now. That stab, stab of synths. Now think of those percussive sleigh bells. Think of how empty the song is, yet how full, how the breaks come at unexpected moments.

---

[1] Although I do wonder how Lennon's revered hits *Beautiful Boy* and *Woman* (from his 1980 comeback LP, *Double Fantasy*) would be perceived had McCartney written them. A number of scathing magazine reviews were held back from publication as the release of *Double Fantasy* overlapped with Lennon's murder. In the ensuing weeks, months, years, the reviews were generally much kinder.

Think of the sparse, but distinct, guitar lines. Then, the sound of McCartney himself imitating a choir of children singing *'their song'*:

Do-doo, dur-doooh

Then, his impression of a bell:

Ding-dong-ding-dong[1]

It's the definition of avant-garde. The title alone is kooky: *Wonderful Christmastime* rather than *Wonderful Christmas-Time*. I am now so familiar with it I almost forget how alarming the track was when I first heard it. Rightly or wrongly, it has probably become its author's most hated composition.[2]

Wonderful Christmastime was recorded during McCartney's short-lived, and mostly excellent, flirtation with synth pop, which culminated with the 1980 album *McCartney II*.[3] Written in around ten minutes, the production and structuring took decidedly longer. As with all songs recorded around the time of *McCartney II*, its author plays every instrument on *Wonderful Christmastime* and produced the track, alone, on his Sussex farm on a 'boiling hot' July afternoon. The track had a degree of

---

[1] Harrison should have taken him to court for ding-dong-related plagiarism.

[2] McCartney must like it, though. Despite only hitting number 6 in the UK on release, and *never* being a hit in the States, the song brings in around £250,000 a year in royalties. Money the poor chap sorely needs – and almost double what Roy Wood makes for Wizzard's yuletide classic. Perhaps poor old Roy really did get a bum publishing deal after all. Karma (of the non-instant variety) for Miss Snob & Class 3C, though.

[3] For a blinding exhibition of his creative powers at this time, listen to the other songs that, like *Wonderful Christmastime*, didn't make *McCartney II*'s final cut: *Check My Machine* and *All You Horse Riders* being the standouts.

significance in that it was one of the first McCartney released without Mrs McCartney and was a sign that he would be soon be flying the Wings nest, spelling a definite end for the band. (Maybe I'm being pessimistic, there, but I suspect they might have struggled without Paul.)

True to McCartney's homebody late-1970s lifestyle, *Wonderful Christmastime*'s promotional video was filmed in a nearby pub. In the age before MTV, the aim of the video was simply to spare him a public performance on *Top Of The Pops.*[1]

What, then, of John Lennon's Christmas hit?[2] Well, like much of *his* solo work, it is a straight down the middle shot at social commentary. Whereas McCartney's worst solo work makes him sound like he suffered a cranial injury in childhood, Lennon's low points are nearly always overtly political or overtly 'experimental', tinged with an undergraduate arrogance (for instance, his expectation that people would want to hear 25-minute recordings of him and Yoko doing cat impressions and pretending to have orgasms, as can be heard throughout their

---

[1] For all his modern day showboating across the stadia of the world, McCartney was something of an enigma in the late 70s. Although his output remained prolific, his public appearances were few and far between. It wasn't until Bob Geldof coaxed him out of semi-retirement for Live Aid in '85 that McCartney got the bug again. It was his first concert in six years.

[2] McCartney actually had a number of Christmas hits, including *Pipes Of Peace* and *We All Stand Together*. Neither were strictly Christmas-themed, though. The Beatles themselves had four non-yuletidey yuletide number 1s, as well as recording numerous festive ditties for their fanclub LPs.

best-forgotten late-60s LPs). At his best, he has a way of making your arm hairs prickle.[1]

Unlike *Wonderful Christmastime*, Lennon's song is altogether more chic. Recorded in New York City and produced by renowned sophisticate Phil Spector, *Happy Xmas (War Is Over)* has an opulent arrangement,[2] brought to life by the children of the Harlem Community Choir. The melody is beautiful[3] and, for all its overplaying, the song still manages to hit the spot, so long as it's heard in isolation and not preceded by Shakin' Stevens on a Christmas playlist.

Despite being called *Happy Xmas*, the chorus repeatedly sings of a 'very *merry* Christmas'. The only time 'happy' is used is in the intro when Yoko Ono whispers, 'Happy Christmas, Kyoko' (her son from a previous marriage) and when John whispers, 'Happy Christmas, Julian' (his son from a previous marriage). I don't know about you, but I'd always thought they were wishing one another a happy Christmas:

Happy Christmas, Yoko
Happy Christmas, John

---

[1] Some solo Lennon arm-hair pricklers of choice: *Mind Games*, *Mother*, *#9 Dream*, *Watching The Wheels*, *You Are Here*.

[2] 'I want five rhythm guitarists!' Spector ordered during the recording session. 'Get me some percussion! Bells! Celeste! Chimes!'

[3] Phil Spector claims it might have been pinched from one of his own songs: *I Love How You Love Me*. He'd have a point were it not the case that *that* melody was itself based on the traditional folk song, *Skewball*. So, in actual fact, it was Phil Spector doing the copying. (That aside, The Paris Sisters' *I Love How You Love Me* is one of the most divine pieces of popular music ever recorded. Bloody Phil Spector.)

The things you learn.[1]

Whether it's the production or the lyrical content, listening to *Happy Xmas (War Is Over)* sounds like we've tuned into a dispatch from our collective past. Lennon's voice may also be a contributing factor to this, having acquired an almost mythical poignancy since his murder. His vocal on *Happy Xmas*, especially, is sprinkled with indefinable spirit:

So, this is Christmas and what have you done?

Another year over, a new one just begun

'You've got the power,' Lennon once told a US TV audience, as Yoko sat beside him, channeling vibes with that ever-present expression as if she were trying to remember if she'd left the gas on. 'All we have to do is remember that: we've all got the power. That's why we said "*war is over if you want it*". Don't believe that jazz that there's nothing you can do, "*just turn on and drop out, man*". You've got to turn on and drop *in*. Or they're going to drop all over you.'

Their message was heavily advertised with now-iconic white posters - 'We're selling it like soap', Lennon said - slapped up around the major capital cities of the world, featuring the words in jet black:

'War Is Over - If You Want It'.

(Pedants everywhere must have itched to climb a ladder and add the words '*to be*' at the end.)

Lennon called it 'the advertising method', the difference being 'that our product was peace'. The posters went up in 1969. *Happy Xmas* itself wasn't recorded for a further two years. It

---

[1] Julian Lennon - who would go on to record *Saltwater*, mentioned earlier - was also the star of another world famous song, *Hey Jude* (originally called *Hey Jules*). It was written by Paul McCartney on his way to visit John's ex-wife, Cynthia, and baby Julian, who, Paul felt, had both been left out in the cold since Yoko Ono ghosted onto the scene.

performed poorly in the States due to clumsy promotion but did better the following year, reaching number 4 in the UK. The sincerity behind its platitudes has ensured that it arrives each December sounding like a very old melody with a brand new message.

'When we say *"war is over if you want it"*,' said Lennon, 'we mean that if everyone demanded peace instead of another TV set, we'd have peace.'

The song has since been covered by everyone from Miley Cyrus to REO Speedwagon to a gang of German Gregorian chanters. Only John Lennon has ever sold its message effectively. Like soap.

Who was the star, then? Who was The Beatles' driving talent? The one who was a bit silly? Or the one who took himself very seriously?[1] For my money, the plinky-plonky, balls-to-cool, self-produced madness of *Wonderful Christmastime* is in every way a match for the gorgeous, choir-led *Happy Xmas (War Is Over)*.[2] The debate will go on. Not for me, though. As unlikely as it is,

---

[1] For all his peace signs and free love, Lennon did have a habit, particularly in The Beatles' early days, of doing gruesome impressions of disabled people. He was also something of a brute around the house with his first wife, Cynthia: 'I used to be cruel to my woman,' he told *Playboy* in 1980. 'I was a hitter. I couldn't express myself and I hit. I fought men and I hit women.'

[2] Although I've suggested that both Christmas singles sum up their solo careers, so too do their b-sides. McCartney's was a reggae version of *Rudolph The Red-Nosed Reindeer*. Lennon's was written with, and performed by, Yoko Ono, and sounds like something you'd improvise whilst drunkenly singing to a newborn. I recommend steering clear of both.

I'm happy, and confused, to believe that there were two musical freaks of nature in The Beatles.

 That said, I know which one I'd rather sit next to at a Christmas party.

 Or do I?

The Yule Log

NOVEMBER - Part One

Thurs 1st -

Another Halloween passes without trick or treaters. Starting to think my gaff has a reputation as 'The House Where You Only Get Digestives'.

The first of November, eh? Weirdly, early November always feels further from Christmas than early October.

The leaves are still on the trees, despite a few days of cinematic wind and rain. The summer heat must have welded them into place. Maybe they won't come off at all. Yikes, what would happen then? There'd a be a leafy civil war come spring.

I need to get out more.

Fri 2nd -

Bought some Christmas-themed Walker's crisps: Pigs In Blankets, Turkey & Stuffing and Brussels Sprout. To quote Walkers, there are five 'exciting' new festive flavours in all, including Cheese & Cranberry and Glazed Ham. That's enough to concoct an entire crisp-themed roast dinner.

If you could transport somebody from the 17th century to the modern day, which of our marvels would impress them most? Television? iPhones? Cars? Planes?

Cookers? The height of everyone? Hot water? White teeth? The abundance of food? I wonder how many wonders of our technological age we'd show them before we finally got round to saying this:

'Oh, and if you think all of that's impressive, just try this potato chip. University-educated food scientists have designed it to taste like a sprout!'

I tried the sprout flavour first. There was a wonderful disclaimer on the packet, in capitals:

'IMAGE OF SPROUTS FOR ILLUSTRATIVE PURPOSES ONLY. PRODUCT CONTAINS NO BRUSSELS SPROUT.'

Talk about covering your back. Who would really ever need that information spelt out for them?

The crisps smelt of non-specific boiled veg but tasted vaguely like the uncooked leaf of a sprout. It's the first time in my life that I've left a bag of crisps unfinished.

I assume Walkers know their Christmas crisps are horrible. The aim is to draw attention to their brand. It's like when Kleenex recently renamed their 'mansize' tissues, knowing only too well that the thickos among us would scream at how mad political correctness had gone, whilst conveniently reminding everyone that Kleenex tissues are big and fluffy and that it's been a while since we all bought a box.

Sat 3rd -

I knew this book would be hard. It's going to be even harder in January, February, May, July... It's painful having to watch/listen to Christmas things when it isn't December. Have been watching some documentaries about 'The Snowman' and just hearing a snippet of its score is enough to melt my heart (I turned it down quickly, but not quickly enough). This is my life for the coming months. I hope people realise the sacrifice I've made. Not to be too melodramatic, but I'd put this act of selflessness on par with anything Florence Nightingale did.

Sun 4th -

Last night's telly was rammed with Christmas ads. The big guns getting their big guns out. Haven't seen the Coke one yet, though...

It's one hundred years to the day since Wilfred Owen was shot, one week shy of the armistice. I wonder if the man who shot him knew what he'd done, whether he pieced it together in later life. He's like the sniper who shot Nelson or the valet who poured petrol over Hitler and Eva Braun (on their honeymoon, the git). Silent legends of world history. Wilfred Owen's mother received the telegram about her son's death on the 11th day of the 11th month, just as the village bells rang out in celebration. And there's me complaining about the hardship of hearing 'The Snowman' soundtrack when it isn't strictly Christmas.

Love that bit in 'Blackadder' where Capt. Darling talks about the drudgery of war:

'The blood, the noise, the endless poetry.'

The poetry of WWI is what separates the conflict from all others. A collective anthem of doomed youths' disapproval at the old way of doing things. And here we are, years later, taking the piss out of it in sitcoms. Good. That's the way it ought to be. Collective anthem indeed. I wonder if, all things considered, Darling's line might be the most British joke ever written.

Mon 5th -

In love with Tolkien's 'Letters From Father Christmas' at the moment. Such effort. I hope his children appreciated them. He even wrote them in shaky handwriting, to make Santa look old. Occasionally, Father Christmas' assistant, the North Polar Bear, writes the letters instead, complete with spelling mistakes. In the letter I read tonight, the Polar Bear wrote, 'The Man in the Moon paid me a visit the other day... he often does about this time as he gets lonely in the moon.' I like that the letters were written mostly before Tolkien's 'Lord Of the Rings' success. Somehow, writing them as a relatively unknown academic makes them that bit sweeter.

Tues 6th -

Already looking at long-range weather forecasts from the meteorological part-timers on Twitter. Doesn't bode well. As per the last thirty-five years, it's looking like a mild Dec 25th. Some giddy optimists - people with account names like UKWeatherXtreme and BritWeatherCheq - are kind enough to inflate hopes with suggestions that, if the polar vortex does something or other, then this could be the snowiest December since records began.
 I oughtn't fall for it. But...

Weds 7th -

It's been heavenly walking home from work recently, just as the sun dips. An orange afternoon sky in autumn is nature's unrivalled beauty. I've been listening to my pre-Christmas playlists (songs that <u>aren't</u> Christmas-related but have a wintry feel). Bowie's 'Low' and Mercury Rev's 'Deserter's Songs' accompanied my walk this evening. Come December, the album chart in Tesco will be flooded with seasonal compilations with all the same songs in a marginally different order - 'Now That's What I Call Xmas III', 'The Best Xmas Hits In The World...Ever!', 'A Very Ratpack Yuletide' - but nobody has catered for the November, pre-Christmas music market: 'Now That's What I Call Autumn'.

Right. Enough's enough. I'm going on 'Dragon's Den'.

Thurs 8th -

Haven't had my heating on at all yet. Temperature is a fickle affair. It's funny how people in the same room, dressed similarly, will claim to be 'freezing' while others are 'f-ing sweltering'. You'd think such a blunt, scientific feature as room temperature wouldn't be so open to interpretation. It's usually the case that how cold you feel is influenced heavily by who is footing the gas bill. If you're in a church hall or cinema, you're likely to voice disproval at the chill; if <u>you're</u> the one coughing up for the next energy quarterly, however, chances are you're likely to adopt a more stoical approach and suggest that maybe people should wear extra layers if they wish to warm up.

Fri 9th -

Iceland have had their Christmas ad banned for being overtly political. It's a cartoon about an orang-utan trying to escape the (unspecified) jungle whilst man sets about destroying it to obtain palm oil. I don't understand quite why the advert was banned as it offers a message we've all heard a million times. It's a worthy sentiment, but deforestation won't come as news to anyone.

There is something suspect about all this. The ad doesn't make mention of Christmas and I can't help but feel the supermarket has got a spare Christmas ad up its sleeve, most likely involving a 'Loose Women' presenter and a trestle table overflowing with oven-baked party food. Obviously, Facebook and Twitter have gone mad at the ban. People are sharing the video and saying deeply profound things (whilst probably on the precipice of using some palm oil). Nothing raises my hackles like faux activism.

I expect Iceland are rubbing their hands with all the publicity, although I wonder how many people who have shared the advert on social media - and are so ardently behind the cause - will actually deign to do their Christmas shopping in Iceland. One tweet said something along the lines of, 'This is probably because big business have got involved and made the government ban it'; what they neglected to mention was that Iceland is a big business and, up til now, had never mentioned anything about palm oil or deforestation. Quite brazenly, the company have even admitted to only refusing to use palm oil in their own-brand products, meaning that their thousands of stores are all still loaded with the orang-utan-killing stuff.

Fair play to Iceland if they follow this up and do ban all use of palm oil in their stores, and if they make a point of returning to these themes in future adverts. My suspicion is that they won't. In 2012, Waitrose had an advert featuring Delia Smith and Heston Blumenthal in a half-empty warehouse talking about how, unlike some other supermarkets, Waitrose weren't going to do a crass, lavish Christmas ad and were, instead, going to spend the budget on 'local good causes'. Online, everyone applauded, wondering why other supermarkets couldn't do something similar.

Waitrose have done crass and lavish Christmas ads every year since. Meanwhile, 'Loose Women' presenters check their phones for missed calls.

Sat 10th -

Woke to find my bedroom window looking like I'd spent the night squirting it with a water pistol. I had a vent fitted in the summer. All it's served to do is make my bedroom that bit colder. Condensation is still king. I had a new central heating system put in a couple of years back and all the old vents were bricked off. Now every window in my flat is prey to night moisture. I can't keep on top of it. It has completely ruined my swanky curtains. The lining has strips of black mould in the crevices. I enquired about getting them dry cleaned but was quoted somewhere in the region of £4million for the honour.

Maybe it was because I was attuned to it, but amongst all the festive advertising hullabaloo I saw more adverts for anti-condensation gadgets today than I'd ever seen in my life. How's that for targeted advertising? Early November must be the condensation game's business-end.

One of the ads was for a sort of special moisture suction hoover for windows called the Glass Glugger 5000 or something like that. It didn't appeal. If ever an appliance was doomed to live its life in a box in a shed after being used twice, it's the Glass Glugger 5000. On the ad, it glided up the window pane, effortlessly drinking the previous night's exhalations. In real life, I bet it's heavy and weak and, rather than sucking up the water, sends it icily cascading down your sleeve, as well as up the curtains. Another ad was for a portable humidifier: the Air Clearer 4000. It looked a little like Mr Frosty. It sits on your windowsill, watching the moon creep along the sky, and, by breakfast time, has a fresh pint of night water in its belly. A far lazier option. I might get one. Hell, I might even buy a Mr Frosty.

Went to a Remembrance function at the local Victorian steam railway. We were given the impression that men - dressed as soldiers - were going to board the old carriages and that we, the masses, would wave them off, weeping into our white hankies etc. The station looked Christmassy as the afternoon darkened around it and archaic electric lights lit the crowd on the platform. We waited an hour or so for the send-off. And what a send-off it wasn't. Instead of men in uniform, we watched as railway staff lifted ten wooden cut-outs of soldiers onto the train. We would wave them off, yes, but they wouldn't be returning the favour. Several of the wooden soldiers' limbs fell off during the lifting process, serving as a poignant reminder as to the fate that befell the poor sods in real life.

Whilst waiting in the cold, I bumped into an old school friend who I'd always had a soft spot for. She asked what I'd been up to today. I watched her eyes betray a curious shock when I told her I'd been writing about 'Postman Pat', before passionately reeling off facts about him.

'It's for a book about Christmas,' I said, too late to undo the damage.

Sun 11th -

Remembrance Sunday. The centenary of the end of World War One.

'For our tomorrow they gave our today...'

Some did, anyway. Loads of them went to fight out of purposefully-misguided information about how easy victory would be. Loads of them went because society pressured them into believing it was the 'done thing'. Loads of them went because life at home was so abysmal that it was preferable to stand in a damp trench getting shot at. And even more of them went, and this should never be forgotten, because their beloved country forced them to go by law. Worst of all, our 'tomorrows' were largely unaffected by their sacrifices. I read and read and read about World War One but it never makes sense and I always forget why it started. Something to do with Belgium and trains.

War memorials get sadder with each passing year. The older you get, the more tragic those weather-beaten names appear. I imagine the ghosts of the soldiers all standing there, in their kit, reading their own names, as cars and busses zoom past.

I don't know where I stand when it comes to romanticising the wars. So much myth has seeped into history. A stat on the BBC website the other day said that 'actually' only one in ten trench soldiers were killed. And you think to yourself, 'Oh'. But then, actually, one in ten is an astronomical number. Now, when one solider dies, it makes the national news. Imagine one in the ten of the boys you went to school with dying young. We lost almost 20,000 in one morning on the Somme. What can our minds do with numbers like that? Nothing much. That's how romanticism slips in.

Mon 12th -

Put a status on Facebook tonight reminding people that my books exist. Had a pleasant burst of messages from people I'd never met. Social media is marvellous for things like that. I couldn't have created a similar spike in sales in years gone by without resorting to a paid newspaper ad or shuffling around the country wearing a sandwich board and clanging a bell.

Tues 13th -

Finished watching 'They Shall Not Grow Old'. Astonishing. I genuinely said 'Oh, my God!' aloud to myself when the chalky black & white images transformed to colour. It is as close as a modern audience can get to experiencing what 'Wizard Of Oz' viewers must've felt when Dorothy entered the colourful kingdom in 1939.
 Found out today that someone I work with rang the bell on the original 'Postman Pat' theme tune. She'd won a colouring competition, aged seven (blew all her competitors away etc.), and was sent to a recording studio in my home village of West Runton to ring the now world famous bell:
'There'll be knocks - knock knock
 Rings - ring ring
Letters through your door...'
  She brought it into conversation in such a blasé manner. If I had been the one ringing that bell, the whole world would know about it. I'd walk around with

it written on my t-shirt. I'd have published a memoir called 'Postman Prat: The Boy Who Rang The Bell'.

Weds 14th -

As I write this now, the sky outside is frozen pink and orange. My lamps are all lit. It is 16:22.

Had to meet one of the unknown people who messaged me on Facebook. She bought all three of my books. I suggested meeting outside the library as that was the ideal place to conduct a shady literature street deal. She said she'd pick her daughter up from school first. As I waited outside the library, I watched a top-end people carrier pull up on the pavement. The driver looked at me, as did her school-uniform-wearing daughter. For a good few seconds. Maybe they were having second thoughts about the purchase based on my appearance. I waved and smiled, regardless. Then another car arrived, with a school-uniform-wearing daughter in tow, and I knew I'd contributed a fresh entry into my long list of accidental waves.

After that I walked to the post office, through town, to send a batch of books across the land. The post office no longer has that little shelf with a pen chained to it. You have to go in fully prepared to send your parcel. There's no standing there and addressing envelopes on the premises anymore. I hadn't pre-addressed my envelopes, though, and was damned if I was going to walk home only to come back again. So, in an act of rebelliousness which would make the female of the species perspire and yearn for some alone time, I stole one of the pens in their stationery department so I could write on my envelopes. Then, like Brando flicking a cigarette stub, I tossed the pen back into the pot, to be bought by some square or other at a later date.

- To Be Continued -

The 12 Things To Watch Of Christmas

#7

Disney's Robin Hood

Walt Disney was a peculiar cove. A hater of communism and an alleged supporter of US Nazi organisations,[1] his ideologies appear at odds with your common or garden visionary genius. He was slow to allow female animators in his factories, claiming 'women do not do creative work' and was so conservative that, despite sporting a dodgy pencil moustache himself, he enforced a strict 'no facial hair' stance at his company theme parks.[2] Perhaps most bizarrely of all, his last words were, reportedly,

---

[1] An accusation that has never been satisfactorily settled, either way. He did hob-nob with Nazi film-maker Leni Riefenstahl in 1938, however, and perpetuate a number of anti-semitic stereotypes in his movies. He also made a film so morally suspect, from a racial standpoint, that the Disney company to this day generally refuse to acknowledge its existence (*Song Of The South*). Disney made a number of anti-Nazi propaganda cartoons during WW2, but it's thought these were largely created as a way to make money for the studio. For what it's worth (a cheap laugh), *Snow White* was one of Hitler's favourite films.

[2] A rule that they only lifted in 2012.

'Kurt Russell', which he scrawled onto a scrap of paper from his death-bed.[1]

Owner of the world's most famous signature, Disney was otherwise useless with a pen and had to be taught how to draw Mickey Mouse by his artists.[2] Not that he let it hold him back. His greatest triumph was in defying his critics by producing full-length animation features which attracted adult audiences. His studio's first few releases are indisputable classics of cinema: *Snow White*, *Pinocchio*, *Fantasia*, *Bambi*. By the 1950s, however, Walt Disney had lost the fire he once had for animation. He wanted to expand his output. He wanted to make live-action movies. He wanted to build a theme park. Most importantly, he wanted to play with his elaborate train sets.

'In one way or another, I have always loved trains,' he once said, whilst putting on a conductor's hat and making a chugging noise.

Part of Walt Disney's disillusionment with animation came from the outlay involved in that particular medium. Done properly, his cartoons cost so much that even when they were a runaway success at the box office, profits were comparatively slight (and left little leeway for flops). Hence, rather than a progressive quality to his company's animated films, Disney cartoons became more and more ragged.[3] Budget cuts led to

---

[1] The story about Mr Disney's head being cryogenically frozen is, however, a fairy tale. But not the sort of fairy tale you'd want to make into an animated film.

[2] Even that world famous signature isn't technically his, but instead, a stylised version written by an artist.

[3] Compare, for example, the crabby, hurried look of 1961's *101 Dalmations* to the picture-book visuals of 1940's *Pinocchio*.

many of the company's post-war cartoons using recycled snippets of animation.[1]

'We're through with caviar,' Disney famously mused at the time. 'From now on it's mashed potatoes and gravy.'

It's easy to forget now, but until the company's 1989 comeback hit, *The Little Mermaid*, Disney Pictures were in a creative slump that - with few exceptions - had lasted the best part of forty years, having fired out costly duds such as *The Black Cauldron*, *The Rescuers*, *Basil The Great Mouse Detective* and *Oliver & Company*. One exception was the universally adored *Jungle Book*. The other forms the subject of this piece.

Although released in 1973, seven years after his death, Walt Disney had laid the foundations for *Robin Hood* way back in his 1930s pomp. He'd wanted to make a film about the medieval rogue, Reynard The Fox, but was advised against it due to Reynard's anti-establishment ethos. The idea was kept on the back-burner and when the story of Robin Hood - with his overtones of Reynard - was mooted as a potential feature film, it didn't take long to decide what animal the title character should be. Deciding how best to anthropomorphise the other characters took much longer. Friar Tuck was going to be a pig until the producers wondered whether the church might take offence. (He was turned into a badger. No offence there.) The evil Sheriff of Nottingham started life as a goat but eventually became a wolf, possibly on the grounds that goats are about as intimidating as a gang of St John's Ambulance trainees. The

---

[1] Recycled material in *Robin Hood* is rife, from the re-use of the *Jungle Book*'s vultures and its snake's hypnotic eyes through to the church bell sound-effect originally heard in *Cinderella*. In short, with all its stolen riches, *Robin Hood* is the Robin Hood of Disney movies.

decision to base the story in England even came up for debate, with a Deep South setting a real possibility.[1]

The strangest edit of all was the removal of the Merry Men. Disney's Robin Hood has just the one: Little John.[2] The reason being that they wanted to make a buddy movie in the mould of the then-popular *Butch Cassidy & The Sundance Kid*.

I'm not making this up.

On the last day of term before the summer holidays, most primary schools of the latter half of the 20th century would have a day where you could wear your 'home clothes' and bring in games and toys. This was, and, I should hope, still is, a proud English tradition, up there with other proud English traditions such as Bonfire Night and not giving a toss about St George's Day.

Our own primary school had another end of term tradition.[3] It came at the end of the winter term, at some point in that rattlingly chaotic glory of the last week before the Christmas holidays. This tradition was likely given the codename 'Operation: Morning Off' by the teachers. It involved

---

[1] Which is why the film has lots of American voices and exotic creatures of a kind seldom found in and around Nottinghamshire.

[2] Voiced by Phil Harris, best known as Baloo in the *Jungle Book* (and Thomas O'Malley in *The Aristocats*). Despite there being only one merry man, the movie's official promotional poster said: *'Join The MERRIEST MENagerie in the world's best-loved legend'*.

[3] The school term system in England is a shambles. The winter term ends just as winter begins. Thus, kids crawl their way back into schools in early January, their joints locked stiff by hoar frost, for what is optimistically called the spring term. The spring term ends in late March, just as spring is getting its eye in.

cramming every child in the school into the assembly hall and wheeling out a projector so old it once showed footage of how best to act in a zeppelin attack. Usually, when we were unexpectedly called into the school hall, it was because something awful had happened or because one of us - and I always thought it was going to be me - was going to be publicly lambasted for their involvement in a dastardly scheme. But, at Christmas time, we knew such cruel behaviour would be off limits and that any meting out of punishment was likely to be put on hold until the grey misery of the next term. Instead, we'd sit on the cold floor, hands in laps, knowing something good was coming our way. The sight of the projector all but confirmed it. Hushed rumours would rush back and forth, up and down, diagonally, about what we were going to watch. Would it be something corny and confusing, some Christian cartoon about learning the true meaning of friendship? Or would it be something dazzling and bright? Would it be, could it be, as the rumour suggested one memorable December morning in the late 1980s, a Disney film?

The lights were switched off. Everyone cheered. Then, as all children do when dropped into darkness en masse, we did ghost impressions, shouting 'woooo' and 'I'm a ghoooost' with such mania that the teacher slammed the lights back on and said if we couldn't behave ourselves we'd go back to the classrooms to do some maths.

'Would you prefer to do that?' the teacher asked. 'No? Well, then,' he said, and, to the relief of all staff, turned the lights off again.[1]

Operation: Morning Off was back *on*.

---

[1] I loved threats like this as they confirmed what we knew all along: that, despite their claims throughout the rest of the year, deep down, teachers knew that maths was pure bum-juice and that having to do it was tantamount to punishment.

The projector wheeled into life. Four hundred heads looked up in unison. Four hundred mouths slowly opened. There, shining on the screen, were the words we'd been dreaming of. In full technicolour. We mouthed them in silence:

'*Walt Disney Pictures Presents...*'

It didn't matter what came next. We'd seen the Disney seal of quality. It's like if Nigella Lawson invited you round for dinner. You wouldn't ask what you were eating; you'd know you'd be in for a culinary treat either way (and some very strained conversation to boot). The word 'Disney' was loaded with magic. Rare magic. I almost never saw Disney films as a child. Television offered only Warner Brothers shorts or, if you were really lucky, *Tom & Jerry*.[1] So when the school - the place where maths lived! - actually showed us a Disney feature, it was comparable to a sojourn around the Haribo factory. I physically shook with excitement as the film started.

Robin Hood and Little John
Walking through the the forest
Laughing back and forth
At what the other'un has to say

Memory is unreliable, as a rule, but I've convinced myself that my memories of that winter's morning in the school hall are picture perfect. I can close my eyes and see it all. The darkness overhead. The big Christmas tree to my left, with its red, green, yellow and blue lights (in their floral glass casings) projecting a lazy glow onto the wall behind it. Rows and rows of silhouetted heads in front of me. And up high, a hanging screen, lit with the most beautiful colours and shapes: a bold, dashing fox dressed in green, living the high life in the forests of England, firing

---

[1] Younger readers may find it hard to believe that a channel as stately as BBC One used to randomly bung five-minute cartoons into its schedule, between, say horse racing and the national news. It's hard to imagine today's sedate news output preceded by a quick *Porky Pig*.

wooden arrows at enemies and saving Maid Marian. I remember, too, howls and screams of laughter - little shoes stamping on the varnished floor - as Maid Marian's burly nanny charged her way through the villainous rhinos and looked to all concerned as though she were going to smash through the screen and land in our laps. Lastly, I recall repeatedly glancing at the creaky projector in case it broke, as though, aged six, I were sufficiently versed in projector maintenance to spot a defect from ten yards.

In my childish way, not only did I want to be Robin Hood, I was also wholly in love with Maid Marian. Her voice. Her innocent motherliness. Unaware that she would one day appear to me as a patriarchal trope, I was smitten by her damsel-like distress. Were it not for her being a vixen who'd been hurriedly painted onto celluloid in a Californian workshop, we could have been very happy together. There's a song in the middle of the film which isn't sung by its famous narrating rooster,[1] but, instead, by a mystical female voice:

Love, it seemed like only yesterday
You were just a child at play[2]

As the song proceeds, Robin leads Marian by the hand through a moonlit woodland as fireflies dance around them.[3] After the film finished, the playground consensus was that this particular sequence had been '*Well* rubbish' and I agreed. Except, inwardly, I didn't think it was *well* rubbish. It was possibly the first time

---

[1] Voiced by country legend, Roger Miller, of *King Of The Road* fame (further evidence of the original idea of a deep south setting for the film).

[2] The song's called *Love* and is sung by Nancy Adams (the wife of its composer).

[3] Along with many of the film's other animals - rhinos, turtles, lions - we don't have fireflies in England, either.

in my life I'd ever been alerted to the concept of love. I kept it to myself.

'Oh, Robin, what a beautiful night. I wish it would never end.'

 For all its cross-legged discussions about photocopier toner, and for all its value digestives dunked into instant coffee, Operation: Morning Off would prove educational. That distant December assembly saw the beginning of my schooling in the most confusing subject of all. A subject that would become all the more troublesome when I veered away from cartoon damsels and onto the real thing.

#8

The Simpsons - 'Marge Be Not Proud'

'Christmas is a time when people of all religions come together to worship Jesus Christ.'

Bart Simpson

The Simpsons and Christmas have what's known in East London soap opera lingo as 'previous'. Its first ever episode was a Christmas special and it now regularly has festive editions. However, so strong and well-loved was that 1989 debut episode,[1] the producers were wary of making another. It wasn't until deep into *The Simpsons'* seventh season - when cracks were beginning to appear in the masterpiece - that they tried again.

---

[1] An absolute peach, in which the family get their dog, the aptly-named greyhound, Santa's Little Helper. (1989, though... Where has that time gone? To youngsters today, *The Simpsons* is as old as *Sgt Bilko* was in 1989.)

It was called *Marge Be Not Proud* and ranks among the finest half-hours (or, to be precise, 22 minutes) of television ever created.

What made *The Simpsons* so great in its 1990s heyday was how it toyed with gushing TV sentimentality, using it as a set-up for jokes:

Marge: *Homer, is this the way you pictured married life?*

Homer: *Pretty much. Except we drove around in a van solving mysteries.*

And:

Homer: *I think the saddest day of my life was when I realised I could beat my dad at most things, and Bart experienced that at the age of four.*

In spite of this, many classic *Simpsons* episodes[1] still focused on familiar, vital issues - death, birth and almost everything in between - and did so with more dexterity than could reasonably be expected of a TV cartoon that spent the rest of its time being hilarious. You can see the eyes of *Simpsons* fans water at mere mention of some of its more tender episodes, for example, *Lisa On Ice*, *Bart The Mother*, *And Maggie Makes Three* and the flawless *Lisa's Substitute*. The 1995 Christmas episode, *Marge Be Not Proud*, is every bit as liable to moisten the iris and focuses on one of art's oft-avoided relationships: that between son and mother.

The plot revolves around Bart's desperation for a violent new video game, *Bonestorm*. His mother, Marge, refuses to buy it. Like any other helpless ten-year-old, Bart concocts a plan - a plan that *I* also made in my own days of dependent youth:

---

[1] A 'classic Simpsons episode' constitutes anything made before 1997. It's been mostly appalling since, like comparing Shakespeare with *Shakespeare's Way With Words*.

'Maybe if I stand next to the game, looking sad,' muses Bart, outside the Try-N-Save[1] supermarket, 'somebody will feel sorry for me and buy me one.'

He gets into position, but has to watch on as a ponytailed delinquent barges past with his wealthy young mother:

'Gavin, don't you already have this game?' the mum asks.

The boy barks back that he doesn't. 'And get two copies,' he adds. 'I'm not sharing with Caitlyn.'

The mum follows his orders.

'That must be the happiest kid in the world,' Bart sighs, as they walk away, two copies of *Bonestorm* in hand.

Bart then does the only thing a desperate kid can. He turns to crime,[2] slipping *Bonestorm* inside his rarely-seen hooded top.[3] Caught by a tattooed security guard, he's then forced to watch a short film about shoplifting (starring Troy McClure). Bart is released on the condition that he never returns to the Try-N-Save. The next day, Marge tells Bart that they're having a family photo taken. Guess where.

Whilst at the Try-N-Save, despite his best efforts at hiding, Bart is seen by the tattooed security guard, who grabs him. Marge leaps to her son's defence, saying her son may be naughty but he'd never steal. The security guard shows the CCTV

---

[1] *The Simpsons* has always been a hotbed of great shop names: the 'Toothless Elephant' piano store being a favourite of mine.

[2] 'Four-finger discount,' says one of his friends, inadvertently bringing to mind Postman Pat's Yakuza initiation.

[3] The Simpson family, and all members of their fictional town of Springfield, nearly always wear the same items of clothing. They seldom age, too. Homer's date of birth was once revealed as May 12th, 1956, making him 63 at the time of writing. Bart and Lisa should now be in their late thirties, at least. Not that it matters, except when trying to keep characters fresh after three decades...

footage of Bart in the act. Sure, stealing a game isn't a big crime *now*, the guard moralises, but, pretty soon, Bart will be 'stealing stadiums and, er, quarries'. Bart's lucky, he adds, not to be thrown into Juvenal Hall.[1]

Back home, Homer tries his best at disciplining his shoplifting son, but, of course, goes off-piste:

'Stealing? How could you? Haven't you learned anything from that guy who gives those sermons at church? Captain What's-his-name? We live in a society of laws. Why do you think I took you to all those *Police Academy* movies? For fun? Well, I didn't hear anybody laughing, did you? Except at that guy who made sound effects. *[Homer makes sound effects and titters]* Where was I? Oh, yeah - stay out of my booze!'

The episode features very little of Homer but his genius dominates. Every moment he's in is riotous,[2] from his obsession with eggnog (refusing to drink anything else until the new year) to his gentle hint to Marge that he's going to buy her an expensive watch for Christmas ('Now she'll really be surprised when she opens that ironing board cover!' he tells himself). If the above rant at Bart wasn't glorious enough, his more considered methods of discipline are just as wayward:

---

[1] We're then treated to Bart's haunted daydream of what Juvenal [sic] Hall is like. Inside, he visits a gaunt, ill-looking Santa sitting behind a protective perspex screen. He wishes Bart a barely audible 'Merry Christmas' before giving him his gift: a book of carpet samples. A sign on the wall says, 'Juvenal Hall: Proud Home of the Soap Bar Beating'.

[2] It's also a great episode for hidden jokes, including the sign outside the Try-N-Save that reads: 'In honour of the birth of our saviour, Try-N-Save is open all day Christmas'. Also, Krusty the Clown's Christmas TV special called *Krusty's Kinda Kristmas* - or *KKK*. (This joke was repeated in later years with *Krusty's Kharity Klassic* tennis match.)

'I've figured out the boy's punishment,' he tells his wife. 'First, he's grounded. No leaving the house, not even for school. Second, no eggnog. In fact, no nog, period. And third, absolutely no stealing for three months.'

Marge Be Not Proud was drawn from experience. Its writer, Mike Scully, based the story on a chapter from his own childhood where he was goaded into shoplifting by his peers.[1] Like Bart's relationship with his trusting mother, Scully's act created a divide. After the *Bonestorm* incident, Marge treats her son like an adult. She no longer tucks him in and she excludes him from family activities, not out of cruelty, but through thinking Bart has grown too old for such things.

An easy-to-forget facet of *The Simpsons* is just how brilliant the drawings are. Acting comedy is hard enough. Animating it must be hellish. The attention to detail in this episode – one of twenty-four made that year[2] – is stunning: any given scene is a masterpiece in how to use colour and light to tell a story. And that's without mentioning the thousands of perfectly economical facial expressions, the minor twitches here and there, that tell the audience precisely how the characters are feeling.

Somewhat out of keeping with the overall flavour of this book, there *is* a happy ending here. Bart goes back to the store and

---

[1] Mike Scully wrote some of the show's finest episodes but is generally credited as the reason for its demise when he took over as executive producer in 1997, overseeing the shift towards wacky storylines, zany jokes and the transformation of Homer from a lovable goof to a certifiably insane moron.

[2] Totalling around nine hours for just *one* year's output: the equivalent of about six full-length Disney features.

pays for a framed photograph of himself as a gift to his mother.[1] All's well that ends well and so on. But, at its core, *Marge Be Not Proud* offers a perfect representation of a real Christmas dilemma, managing to fit as much drama and laughter into twenty minutes as some of the best films manage in two hours. There are well over a hundred other *Simpsons* episodes that do likewise. If you've forgotten how wonderful this programme was, or, indeed, if you've never properly given it your full attention, maybe treat yourself to a boxset or two this Christmas. My only advice is to stick to the first seven seasons.

Oh, yeah - and stay out of my booze.

---

[1] Marge initially thinks Bart has stolen *this*, too, and, whilst chasing him for answers, delivers the stunning line, 'You can't hide from me in this house, Bart. I spend twenty-three hours a day here.'

The Christmas Alphabet

M is for...

Milk, A Glass Of

In simpler times, the children of England used to leave sherry out for Father Christmas. That was until letters arrived at the North Pole Complaints Department from irate parents, telling how the old fella had left the wrong presents, woken children up with his burping, knocked over vases and urinated in the laundry basket.

Something had to give.

The tradition of leaving milk out for Santa took off in 1930s America, when families of a Walton ilk left him a treat as a reminder of the importance of sharing during the Great Depression.[1] The tradition crossed the Atlantic soon after. Predictably, no two of our continental cousins do exactly the same thing when it comes to leaving Father Christmas a treat. The French give him wine, the Swedish leave porridge out and the Irish give him Guinness. Rudolph gets in on the act, too, often being left a carrot or handful of hay. Or Guinness, if he's in Ireland.

It's one of the most enchanting sights of childhood, to wake in the darkness of Christmas morning and see that the rim of the empty glass is milk-stained and that the saucer has a sprinkling

---

[1] This actually sounds like a plot of a *Waltons* Christmas special, doesn't it? It's not, though. Believe me, I checked.

of mince pie crumbs on it. Or splodges of Guinness, if you're in Ireland.

On the subject of mince pies…

Mince Pies

'The beef? Yeah, that was weird to me, too. But then I thought, "Well, there's mincemeat pie". I mean, that's an English dessert. These people just put very strange things in their food.'
Friends, 'The One Where Ross Got High', 1999

The sight of mince pies in the supermarket commits people to do foolish things, such as buying seven box-loads when history has proven that one box is *always* more than enough. The problem is, mince pies are stacked high in aisle one, so you see them first, loading them into the trolley in the spirit of the season. But, as your yuletide shopping spree progresses, and the aisles offer ever-enticing seasonal treats, the mince pies get forgotten, bundled into the bottom of the 'bag for life'[1] then tucked away in the cupboard, behind more exciting festive fayre. Come January, when the good stuff has gone, there they sit in bleak midwinter mode, box on box.

I annually delude myself into thinking mince pies are nicer than they are. The truth is, I don't much like them. No amount of cream can save the day. Each year, I kid myself that perhaps they'll taste better warmed up. I don't know if it's just my microwave, but I can never get the temperature of a mince pie right. They either come out with their casing having meekly imploded or at a temperature so hot and furious that the interior black lava bends my spoon on impact.

---

[1] These definitely warrant a quotation mark around them. Most of my 'bags for life' are stuffed inside other 'bags for life' at the bottom of my pantry. For life, most likely.

I'm not the only one whose mince pies (eyes) are bigger than their stomach. To satiate public demand, the Mr Kipling factory make *three million* 'exceedingly good' mince pies a day during the business-end of their Christmas timetable. The ingredients, all those spices and flavourings, make a combined journey of approximately 62,000 miles before being locked up in their pastry prison.[1]

The story behind the mince pie is as long and as dull as you might expect. They started life as real mincemeat pies - 'tartes of flesh' as one 14th century cookbook grimly called them - containing ground beef or lamb. The pastry casing was designed to keep the interior from going stale, meaning that the pies could be stored for up to a year.[2] Alarmingly, the fleshy mincemeat was accompanied by the majority of other flavourings with which we associate non-fleshy mince pies today: cloves, orange peel, currants, raisons, mace etc. It must have tasted like a sausage roll stuffed with Jelly Tots. It was the Victorians, with their swaggering accumulation of luxury resources, namely sugar, which dictated the pies become wholly sweet.

An olde Englishe maxim claimed that eating one mince pie a day, from Christmas through to Epiphany, meant you'd have twelve months of happiness. After the initial week of vomiting.

❆❅❆❅❆

---

[1] For all the pies' dourness, their ingredients come from a range of glamorous, jet-setting locations: Brazil, America, Asia, Greece, Turkey and across Africa. All for a measly little pie.

[2] In Georgian times, lavishly decorated mince pie casings were something of a status symbol. The more outlandish the better. If they'd had Instagram back then (and, by God, I wish they did), Christmas timelines would be little more than sequences of sepia-tinged photos of artistic pastry patterns.

Mistletoe

Kissing under the mistletoe. A tradition that only really exists as a plot device in *Holby City*. Never have I, in real life, seen two people kiss under mistletoe. Nor have I ever *heard* anyone talk about having kissed someone under mistletoe. Watch a soap opera, however, and the stuff is setting affairs going left, right and centre.

Something of a myth surrounds the festive origins of mistletoe. The rumour is that it was used in some sort of sordid sexual initiation ceremony involving druids and wicker men. Alas, the truth is nowhere near as racy, other than the fact mistletoe was known as 'oak sperm' to the Ancient Greeks. Much more likely (and there's a lot of academic guesswork when it comes to this particular tradition), is that mistletoe was brought into homes as a largely innocent - i.e. sans sexy druids - beacon of peace and (non-saucy) love. By the late 18th century, the men of Britain had sneakily created a tradition whereby it was considered unlucky for a woman to refuse a kiss under it.[1] It worked, for a while. But all things come to an end, with Cliff Richard's 1988 hit *Mistletoe & Wine* generally credited with draining away any remaining semblance of sexuality the plant may have hitherto been associated with.

If you do have mistletoe in the house, whatever you do, don't kiss the stuff itself, for goodness sake. The toxins within are strong enough to give you a fortnight's worth of the two-bob-

---

[1] This is despite the grim reality that kissing men back then would in itself constitute bad luck, what with their brown stumpy teeth and battered gums. It's like claiming it would be unlucky not to kiss a damp patch on the carpet behind the sofa.

bits.[1] Not very romantic. Nor is the sequence of events which allows mistletoe to grow in the first place. Its seed spreads after being eaten by birds, duly digested, then fired from their behinds. All being well, it will then stick to a tree and mutate.
Giz a kiss, dahlin'.

Morecambe & Wise

You can't escape Morecambe & Wise at this time of year. If you look at your current *Christmas Radio Times*, I guarantee that BBC Two will be airing at least one new documentary about them. Or a biopic. Or a recently unearthed episode found in the video vault of a Senegalese public library, now restored and remastered for broadcast, in full, for the first time since 1971.

The Morecambe & Wise Show was festive by association only. The duo were quick to realise that they ought to keep Christmas material to a minimum. Too many jokes about 'Father Christmas, holly or cotton-wool beards' (to quote Mr Morecambe) and the shows wouldn't be repeated throughout the year. Hence why, for all of the famous *Morecambe & Wise Show* Christmas moments - *Singin' In The Rain*, Angela Rippon's legs, *Anthony & Cleopatra* etc. - few are Christmas-themed.

The pressure of penning the Christmas extravaganzas told on the show's sole writer, Eddie Braben, who, after 1971's magnificent festive episode,[2] suffered a nervous breakdown and

---

[1] One of its many poisons is called 'moronic compound'. An apt name for anyone dumb enough to attempt using mistletoe as a way to pull.

[2] After the recording of which Eric Morecambe somewhat unhelpfully proclaimed to Braben, 'We'll never top that!' Poor Eddie Braben didn't just write the extra-long Christmas specials, he single-handedly penned around thirteen *other* episodes a year.

handed the writing reins over to Barry Cryer and John Junkin. Braben was eventually sweet-talked back into action with the lure of, among other things, more musical set pieces (which required less typewritten dialogue). The duo's popularity grew each year. The Christmas show was the jewel in their crown. Such was the popularity of the festive specials, and with her family's inherent hankering for the jewels in other people's crowns, even the Queen was a fan (it's said she based her Christmas Day routine around the programme).

By 1976, the pressure of single-handedly creating the nation's favourite Christmas Day treat had again got to Braben and he made for the exit.[1] As before, he was coaxed back to write what was promised to be one last show: the 1977 Christmas Special. The episode exceeded all expectations and, with its host of star guests, drew an almighty audience of around 21 million, with some estimates suggesting the number was closer to 28 million.[2]

The pair moved to Thames (ITV) in '78 for a final big bucks contract. They continued to make Christmas specials. Sadly, with both of them ageing and Eric Morecambe suffering from the dickiest of hearts, the shows lost something of their sparkle and fell back on tired material.[3]

---

[1] He wasn't the only one feeling the festive heat. 'Eric always said their happiest days were those when they weren't top of the bill,' said Barry Cryer in a 2013 interview. 'After reaching the pinnacle, the responsibility became so great. Before going on stage, Eric would pace up and down, plucking away at his pocket handkerchief, muttering to himself.'

[2] TV viewing figures are notoriously flakey, especially from the last century.

[3] Contrary to popular (ish) belief, with the exception of the first few specials, all four Thames series and all subsequent specials were written by Eddie Braben.

The death knell for the duo came in 1981, when, for the first time since the 1960s, their Christmas special wasn't broadcast on Christmas Day and was tucked away on ITV two nights earlier.[1] Eric Morecambe died not long after. Almost four decades on, the gap he and his comedy partner left in the festive TV schedules remains wide open.

N is for...

Nativity, The

And is it true
This most tremendous tale of all
Seen in a stained-glass window's hue
A baby in an ox's stall?
The maker of the stars and sea
Become a child on earth for me?

So ponders Sir John Betjeman in his poem, *Christmas*. It's a question many people will ask themselves at some point, most likely at Christmas. Even the stoniest of hearts may shimmer in December's Christian glow, with its quick feed of happy memories and religious iconography. For all the church's faults, it undeniably ups its game come December, with carol services, Christingles, festive markets and alike. Of all the yearly events, it is the nativity service, however, which may best excite a dormant heart and, in the words of Anne Brontë, 'kindle

---

[1] This was actually due to Thames TV not having the contract to broadcast on Christmas Day that year (an honour belonging to LWT). Even so, no Morecambe & Wise on Christmas Day felt like a paradigm shift.

raptures so divine'. Personally, I find it impossible to enter an English church at *any* time in the year and not feel a gentle tug on my spiritual sleeve. But there you go, that's me. I also find it impossible to enter an English church at *any* time in the year and *not* peek at that little backstage kitchen area (always thinking I'm going to get caught and told off by the vicar in the process).

How accurate are nativity plays in relation to the New Testament version of events? Well, if one goes to any *other* church service over the period, they'll no doubt be on the receiving end of a vicar's sermon dealing with precisely that question.[1] But for those who are otherwise engaged throughout the holiday period and will miss their church leader's annual sermon on the theme,[2] let me tell you the following:

* As discussed elsewhere in this weighty publication, Mary didn't necessarily ride into Bethlehem on a donkey, it could have been any animal and was most likely a camel

* Jesus may not have been born in a stable (and the word 'inn', as used in the Bible, meant a guest room, rather than a hotel)

---

[1] The first thing to bear in mind is that the virgin birth is only mentioned in the gospels of Matthew and Luke. Neither Mark nor John discuss it. Nor does Paul in any of his letters, written (it's thought) closer to Jesus' death than Matthew and Luke's gospels. In fact, Paul doesn't even state Mary's name (he says Jesus was 'born of a woman').

[2] I don't know if it's demanded of them by scripture, but vicars have something of an obsession with talking about how nativities bear little resemblance to the version of the birth story as dished out in the gospels. Yet they're the ones who stage the bloody things in the first place.

* Forget the three kings. No one knows exactly how many wise men/kings/magi there were (although there were *three* gifts[1])

* The kings didn't follow a star, but, instead, *saw* one and read meaning into it. When they found the baby, it was at an *oikos* (a house, not a stable/barn)

* There are unlikely to have been any animals watching the birth. More unlikely still is that they would've formed a neat semi-circle around the crib. To be honest, there probably wasn't even a crib

* The shepherds and kings didn't all arrive at once. The kings travelled separately and would have taken months to get there

* It's doubtful that the birth took place on December 25th. There are no such dates in the Bible. The 25th of March was first claimed to be Jesus' birthday by a shadowy historical figure who worked it all out - using little discernible logic - in a pulsating 245AD book called *On The Computation Of Easter*. At this point, Christianity was still an illegal sect. Until 313AD, when the Roman emperor Constantine declared that Christians (and those of all faiths) should no longer be persecuted by the empire.[2] Exactly one hundred years after

---

[1] Gold, frankincense (an oil) and myrrh (a resin). Or, as we see in the classic *Bottom* episode, *Holy*: 'Gold [Terry's All], Frankenstein [a rubber mask] and Grrr [aftershave].'

[2] Constantine had won a battle the previous year after dreaming of the Christian cross the night before. His soldiers were told to inscribe Christ's name on their shields the following morning (over tea and toast). Later that day, the battle was won. Christianity had a powerful new ally. Within a matter of years, Roman Catholicism was fully operational.

the unknown mathematician had deduced that Jesus was born on March 25th, Pope Julius I decreed that this was actually when Jesus was *conceived*, meaning the boy king was *born* nine months later on December 25th (because, as everybody knows, pregnancies always last nine months to the day). Subsequently, based on that chap's Popish whim, we have celebrated Christmas on this date ever since. All this other talk about Christmas deliberately merging with, or replacing, sun-related festivals is largely unverified. Roman and secular calendars were chock-full of hooplas back then. Wherever Christmas wound up, it would have coincided with any number of festivals. The *real* reason for a December 25th Christmas is far sillier than people give credit

* None of the biblical nativity story was filmed on the onlookers' mobile phones. And there was no glitter. Nor any flushed teachers smiling in the wings, inwardly counting down the minutes til the end of term

Right. That's nativities ruined. What next?

New Year

Ah, New Year: Great Britain's annual drink-driving festival and general death knell for Christmas. It's also the one time of the year when the greatest number of people evaluate (drunkenly, possibly in a bathroom mirror behind a locked door) their life choices, with an innate tendency to adopt a negative spin.

In truth, the extent to which you enjoy New Year's Eve is usually down to where you spend it and with whom it is spent. If your plans for the evening involve sipping champagne on the banks of the Seine with Audrey Tautou, then you're apt to surmise that things are going reasonably well, on the whole.

Conversely, it's easy to feel the year's fallen somewhat shy of a raging success when the night is spent alone indoors, sipping the watery dregs of a can of Fosters and contemplating renewing your subscription to eHarmony. Even those married couples who proudly tell you they 'went to bed at half ten' can only be kidding themselves when they say that's how they truly wanted to see the new year in. And as for those broken souls who purposefully stay up to watch *Jools Holland's Hootenanny*, well...[1]

Whereas the English view New Year's as a conclusion to Christmas, things are just getting started around the world. The French, for instance, celebrate New Year with more gusto than they do Christmas.[2] Likewise, in Catholic countries such as Spain and Italy, the countdown to Epiphany truly ramps up once the clock strikes midnight. The Scots, too, feel a stronger ancestral link to Hogmanay than they do Christmas, largely because it gives them an opportunity to ad-lib a few new verses

---

[1] I only recently discovered that the *Hootenanny* is pre-recorded. Just about its only saving grace, I thought, was that it offered viewers a chance to feel as though they were just as sad and pathetic as the glitzy showbiz stars who appeared on the show (and clearly had nothing better to do with themselves on NYE). In a recent statement, the BBC defended the programme by saying it offered 'an idealised New Year's Eve party with a line-up that would surely be impossible to deliver on December 31st'. In short, those glitzy showbiz stars *do* have better things to be doing with themselves on NYE - and don't you forget it.

[2] And are more likely to send one another Happy New Year cards than Christmas ones.

of *Auld Lang Syne*.[1] When Robbie Burns produced his reworking of this auld folk song in 1788, could he ever have imagined it would be sung boisterously every New Year's Eve until well into the next millennium? More surprising still is that, despite its feat of endurance, not one human being has ever bothered learning the words beyond the opening lines:

Should auld acquaintance be forgot
And never brought to mind

Which is reliably followed by:

Ha tay de-die, ly ly de pie
For auld lang syne

A pattern which then repeats itself for eight or nine verses.

One of the strangest things about New Year's Eve is how, during the day, the media tell us how celebrations are already in full swing around the world, showing clips of Sydney Opera House looking like it's being bombed by Messerschmitts. It makes the head spin to think of other countries living in different years.

Talking of fireworks, the world famous London celebrations come at a whopping cost. 2018's bash set the tax-payer back around £2.6 million.

'It never gets boring!' beamed one of the show's organisers.

Each to their own.

It may surprise you to learn that the capital's celebrations are strictly ticketed. Officially, the show should only be seen by around 100,000 paying attendees. Millions more hover around the periphery, though, getting just as juicy a view of the fiery whizz-bangers as those who have forked out £10 for the honour. In fairness, these periphery-dwellers could argue that

---

[1] A loose translation of which is 'Old Time's Sake'. (Not sure why I'm telling you that. Add it to the long list of things you don't need to know.)

they've already *forked out £10 for the honour* with their council tax contributions.

Other than Christmas, New Year's Day is the only date in the calendar that has an unmistakable feel. To paraphrase Bono, all is disarmingly quiet. Depending on your excesses the night before, there *is* something satisfying in changing the wall calendar and inviting the promise of a fresh new start. Whether these fresh new starts yield any notable return is debatable. Only around 8% of new year's resolutions are followed through, so to speak. (A sturdier 25% of resolutions make it beyond January, before collapsing in a sweaty heap of resignation.) Oh, well. There's always next year. If you're lucky.

On that note:

Should resolutions peter out
In about a fortnight's time
Ha tay de-die, ly ly de pie
For auuuld laaaang syyyyn

O is for...

Oh, You Shouldn't Have

'The great charm about me (concluded Reginald) is that I am so easily pleased. But I draw the line at a "Prince of Wales" prayer-book.'
Saki, *Reginald On Christmas Presents*, 1901

For every cherished present we receive, there are at least five which we would never have bought ourselves if both our resources and our time on earth were limitless.

The worst type of present is 'something for the home'. Because the rule is, it has to go on display. You can't receive a clock or a fireguard or a furry tiger-print rug and *not* put them out at least *somewhere*. Putting such items where they genuinely belong - i.e. in a sealed box, underneath several other sealed boxes - is not the done thing. We all know the rule about gift horses. Politeness must prevail. Thus, terrible gifts for the home become, rather than a gift that keeps on giving, a gift that daily drains the spirit away from your favourite place.

The worst home-wrecking present I know of was from a father who paid an artist - whose talents possibly lied elsewhere - to knock up a handful of framed portraits of dear pater to go above the fireplaces of his beloved heirs. To this day, the poor sods have to glance up at the oily old duffer, with his nose slightly too long and eyes slightly too far apart, whenever they sit down to dinner.[1]

It's equally galling to give bad presents away. There are just some years where inspiration refuses to acquiesce and we're reduced to buying a loved one something so far left-field it almost belongs in the next field along. The best you can hope for in such circumstances is that you manage to pass the gift on to them without having to watch them open it. Otherwise, you're lumbered with the scenario of not only seeing their faces flush but also having to defend the gift yourself as they redden:

'I didn't know if you'd like it,' you stammer, 'but you never can tell when you're going to need a *really* reliable toilet seat. And I know you've always loved purple...'

---

[1] I couldn't resist looking online for other Christmas present horror stories. The two standouts are a bag of grated cheese and a book called *Coping With Being Adopted*, given to a boy who, until that very moment, had always wondered why he didn't look like his parents.

The 12 Songs Of Christmas

#10

Stop The Cavalry - Jona Lewie

Then from each black, accursed mouth
The cannon thundered in the South
And with the sound
The carols drowned
Of peace on earth, good-will to men!
Henry Wadsworth Longfellow, Christmas Bells, 1863

Jona Lewie: owner of the most difficult-to-remember spelling in pop music and author of the comeliest of all Christmas smash hits.[1]

Whatever compilation it appears on, whichever hits its sandwiched between - be it *Feliz Navidad* or *All I Want For Christmas Is You* - it always sounds out of place. The lyrics operate in a timeless dwelling space. On the face of it, *Stop The Cavalry* is a song about the Great War, but its narrator tells us how he's had to fight '*almost every night, down throughout the centuries*', making the song a peon to the eternal roll-call of soldiers produced by our sorry species.

---

[1] And not to be confused with retail giant, John Lewis (which is actually Jona Lewie's real name).

When I first heard *Stop The Cavalry*, it reminded me so much of the *Only Fools & Horses* outro tune - '*TVs, deep freeze and David Bowie LPs*' - that, in my childish dopiness, I thought it was sung by Rodney Trotter.[1] The singer sounded so fed up, so downbeat. So, well, *Rodney*. Most Christmas songs were about snowmen and presents. I'd never heard one about a sad soldier.

Bang goes another bomb on another town...

Wish I was at home for Christmas...

What elevates *Stop The Cavalry* above its rivals is the brass. Instantly evocative of the British Armed Forces, it also brings to mind Christmas' unsung heroes: the Salvation Army. No self-respecting market town should be without a December visit from the world's least belligerent fighting force. Their sometimes flawless, sometimes cock-eyed trumpeting (and tuba-ing) of the Christmas cause can make merry even the most mundane visit to the shops. In fact, it was the inclusion of the brass band which made Jona Lewie's record label, Stiff, put the track out as a Christmas single, suggesting he add some bells and whatnot.[2]

'There is one line,' Lewie said, 'about him [the narrator] being on the front and missing his girlfriend. The record company picked up on that from a marketing perspective and added a tubular bell.'

Stop The Cavalry (originally called *Stop The Gallantry*) was held off the 1980 Christmas top spot by both the recently shot John Lennon's *(Just Like) Starting Over* and the mercifully very much

---

[1] As I did the *Only Fools* tune in question, which was actually sung by the show's scriptwriter, John Sullivan.

[2] The label weren't interested in the song at all, at first, dismissing it as 'just another anti-war song'. Lewie rewrote it and went back to the office, playing the potential brass parts on a kazoo. Remarkably, at this point, Stiff became interested. Never underestimate the power of the kazoo.

alive St Winifred's School Choir's record about their gran (a song one can make all the more enjoyable by pretending the children are all singing to the *same* grandmother, and that the lady in question was seldom vertical). My how the pop charts staged some remarkable duels back then. With the record-buying public representing a much wider spectrum of society than today, punks and rockers would find themselves slugging it out for chart dominance with the likes of Worzel Gummidge and Roland Rat. Despite missing out on number 1 (and 2), Lewie's record still shifted around a million copies (an amount of physical sales that in today's market would warrant a Jona Lewie statue).

'I earn more from *Stop the Cavalry*,' said Lewie in 2016, 'than from the rest of my songs put together.'

Only he is surprised by this fact.

Sales of *Stop The Cavalry* were aided by a legendary performance on *Top Of The Pops*. Introduced by presenter Peter Powell as 'a band called Jona Lewie', the song was impeccably mimed by Lewie in full World War I regalia (with a yellow neckerchief), marching on the spot, with a rifle over his shoulder. Behind him stood a vast brass ensemble - also decked out in early-20th century combat chic - pretending to toot along.

Stop The Cavalry was Lewie's second big hit of 1980, after the still-cool *You'll Always Find Me In The Kitchen At Parties*. He was a known kook within the record industry, but a known talent. Having crashed the charts in his earlier years with Terry Dactyl & The Dinosaurs' *Sea Side Shuffle*, he knocked music on the head, becoming, of all things, a sociology lecturer. But a life of tweed and pipe-smoke in academic upper rooms couldn't compare to that of a rock star. He soon ditched the cardigans and got back on the music scene, only occasionally stopping to tell people off for whispering, or to recommend textbooks on Jurgen Habermas' theory of the Public Sphere. After his roaring

1980 comeback success, a career of smash hits seemed inevitable. As it was, *Stop The Cavalry* would be his last ever *Top Of The Pops* appearance.

Christmas hits may put turkey on the table every year, but they play merry hell with your street cred.

There is an honesty to the lyrics which keeps *Stop The Cavalry's* head below the trench line. Maybe this is due to it being about *all* soldiers, rather than those fighting in one specific war.[1] There is a sense of helplessness from the song's lowly footman, being patronised by Mr Churchill (*'who says we're doing splendidly'*) and having to march *'to and from'* the enemy. My favourite line involves the mysterious Mary Bradley. It's such a perfectly chosen name, leading one to think of a white-laced, rosy cheeked innocent sat alone by her coal fire:

Mary Bradley waits at home

Followed by a crushingly modern threat to her own life:

In the nuclear fallout zone

The song may sound safe and homely now, but it was released in a time of frightening global tension, as America rushed to elect cowboy impersonator Ronald Reagan on the strength of his pro-war rhetoric.[2] The US maintained preparation for war by continued use of nuclear missile sites in and around the United Kingdom, making the homeland of all Mary Bradleys a close target for the Soviet Union.[3] *Stop The Cavalry's* message of

---

[1] Although Lewie wore World War One gear on *TOTP*, the inspiration for the song was the doomed Charge of the Light Brigade in the Crimea.

[2] As the years went by, Reagan realised that the Lord God Almighty - that eternal tinker - actually wanted him to be the man who saved the world with *peace*, rather than the man who saved the world with nuclear bombs. Good job, really.

[3] The American bombs were only removed from the UK in 2008.

peace was perfectly timed. The soldier, speaking for all soldiers throughout history, vows to end war if he ever has the power:

If I get home, live to tell the tale
I'll run for all presidencies
If I get elected, I'll stop
I will stop the cavalries

'The solitary soldier,' said Lewie, 'daydreams to himself that if there were ever an office for all the presidencies of the entire world, he would stand for that office and if he won the election he would make sure that he himself would end the gallantry and stop all the guys in the cavalry in all future wars from ever charging to their deaths again.'

That's what they all say.

The Yule Log

NOVEMBER - Part Two

Fri 16th -

The town lights were switched on tonight. A mini-carnival. I bumped into an old friend who said she likes 'How often Sheringham gets together to celebrate nothing much'. And you have to give it that. No town in Britain has more merry shindigs. 'Merry Shindig' is almost an anagram of Sheringham.

 The light switch-on is exactly the same every year. The same street vendors standing in the same places selling the same balloons and the same drinks and the same food. The same raised platform hosts the same members of the Salvation Army brass band playing the same carols in the same order. Children from the same school sing the same carols. The same shops stay open beyond their same usual trading hours. I meet the same people in the same spots. The same clutch of teenagers zip up and down the same side-streets on the same mini-scooters, pulling the same wheelies and wearing the same clothes. The same mums and same dads push the same buggies (containing children who never grow up), and pull the same dogs on the same leads. The same crush of people congregate and shiver near the same town clock, counting down at the same time. Then, as the same lights flicker on overhead, against the same black sky, the same people, myself included, all look up. And the same cheer goes out.

You can't knock it.

Sat 17th -

Went to a rugby match. Saracens vs Sale. I'd never been to a professional game of 'rugger' before. The difference to a football crowd was immeasurable. There was no swearing and very little shouting. The enthusiasm was obvious but manifested itself in gentle applause. The game was terrific, ending in a knife-edged decision from the ref to award the home team a vital, last-minute winning try. The crowd clapped more politely than ever. Just last week, Norwich City beat Millwall in similar circumstances, winning 4-3 in remarkable fashion (the score was 1-1 after 80 mins). The fans went wild, hugging each other and jumping, screaming, as their beloved City players wildly bundled themselves into a heap of delirium by the corner flag. Each sport has its place, but I don't think you can beat football, with its pantomime villains and dumb, dashing heroes and for its unspoken agreement amongst fans that we should pretend it's all very, very important.

At the end of the rugby match, as the claps died down, the players walked off the pitch, taking their gum shields out and running their hands through their costly haircuts. Then, wonderful carnage. Everybody in the ground was invited onto the 4G pitch to mess around and kick rugby balls. It looked like a cross between 'Where's Wally' and a pastoral snow scene sketched by Phiz.

Sun 18th -

Finally saw the Coke ad. Well, heard it. I was in the bath at the time, with the door wide open, as befits a playboy such as I. Then, from down the corridor, came that unmistakable chant: 'holidays are coming, holidays are coming...' A tune I shall never tire of.

Mon 19th -

Saw the Coke ad again.
And again.
And again.
Hmm.

Tues 20th -

Bed at half-eight for the second time in a week. I wanted to read. I'm nearing the end of the first novel in 'The Forsyte Saga'. You can measure your enjoyment of a book by how you treat those last fifty pages. Ideally, you want to be desperate to read it and sad when it's over. The worst thing is to keep checking how long you've got until you can tick it off as another book you can tell people you've read. I raced through. I want to see the 60s TV version. It was a global sensation at the time of broadcast. Something like 100 million people watched it worldwide (it was particularly popular in Russia, bizarrely). I imagine it to have shaky walls and lots of accidental glances at the camera. I love that kind of thing.

Weds 21st -

Woke at 5am, slowly suffocating with an unblockable nose. I've had a light cold/cough for about two weeks now. I tried the trusted technique of rolling over in bed to face the other way, but even that failed me. Then I went for the ultimate sleep inducer: puffing the pillow up and flipping it onto the cold side. Nothing. (I've got much better at admitting defeat when it comes to sleep. I used to just lay there for hours and think about imaginary conversations and scenarios. Now, more often than not, I just sit up and read.) I couldn't blow my nose. It felt like somebody had inflated a balloon inside my head, pushing everything outwards. I switched the kitchen light on (always a queer thing to do at 5.37am) and, wearing just my pants, found a tub of Vicks Vapor Rub from a former illness. It was two years past its use-by date, which meant I definitely couldn't eat it. I tried sniffing it instead. It had no kick whatsoever; it was like a Tesco Value Ginger Nut. It smelt like Vicks but there was something missing. With frozen skin, I skipped back into bed and read my phone from back to front. Then, out of nowhere, beautiful, blissful sleep visited me, and all was well. Three minutes later, the alarm went off.

Went to the chemist's after work. One of their medicines featured a photo of a man in bed, lost to slumber's throes. It was called SleepyBreathe or words to that effect. Thinking this was the thing for me, I read the back:

'Clears nasal passages by up to 32%!'

It was about 68% shy of my target. I wouldn't go bragging about those stats if I were them. I don't imagine a 32% improvement would yield the kind of results that I was seeing in the comatose victim on the box cover. Bought some Vicks instead.

Thurs 22nd -

Awful night's sleep. Woke at 5am again. Really could've done with my nasal passages being up to 32% clearer.
 Arrived home to find a 'Sorry We Missed You' card from the Royal Mail. In order to collect my things, I now need to get to the post office before 10am on my day off. I don't believe they're sorry they missed me at all.

Fri 23rd -

Went for a drink after work. Played pool. Most people get better at pool the longer the session goes on, but I always find that my first few shots are beauties then I go to pot (forgive the pun). I over-think the angles. The same thing happened when we played darts. We had a mini tournament. I went for treble fourteen and got it. Ten minutes later, I'd hit a wall (forgive the pun). There was a Christmas tree in the clubhouse, fully lit, in the corner near the bar. It reminded me that I needed to get my new one, ASAP.
 My cold is much better but my voice sounds like that nerdy teenager in 'The Simpsons', breaking halfway through words. Really embarrassed myself on the way out of the Indian takeaway:
 'Goodbye, sir,' they said.
 'Chiiiuhhszh,' I whimpered, my throat too pathetically fragile to say the word 'cheers' properly.
 Now I can never go in there again.
 The football starts again tomorrow, after the dreaded 'international break'. There won't be another such

pause until March 2019: a distant, alien time - although, by the time you read this, it will be long gone. Odd.

Sat 24th -

Bought a Christmas tree from Homebase. Before that, I went to a Christmas fayre at a village hall. It was the same hall I used to go to nursery in. It had been repainted and revamped in the intervening years, but the aura lingered. I'd once ran screaming around it, climbed its climbing frames and got told off for using my fingers as a pretend gun. Today, I don't think you'd fit two of me lengthways across its floor. The ceiling, once an unfathomable godly dwelling, was now a step-ladder away. Where once we'd sat in circles and read stories, drinking whole milk from spotty plastic cups, there was, today, five or six tables laid out, adorned with festive bric a brac.

My mother had parked round the back of the hall into such a nifty space that she couldn't reverse out of it. We'd been penned in by a 1980s Mazda covered in animal welfare stickers. She had to find the owner. I overheard an old Norfolk boy giving another old Norfolk boy the scoop on how best to spend his morning:

'Oi shink you orta go up the road to the Shoyre Horse Senter,' he said. ''Parrently Father Chrismuss is there. Hass free ter get in today!'

The Shire Horse Centre. I hadn't heard that name in a while.

It stirred another nursery memory. Perhaps the sweetest in my Christmas canon... On that very driveway, outside that very village hall, aged four, wrapped in twelve coats, being loaded onto the back of a trailer with a host of equally coat-heavy children. It was darkening, but not nighttime. Horses pulled us away. Bells jingled. I had to hold on tight. I can still feel the juddering of the cart shaking my little liver. We went slowly over the bridge across the train track, closer to the moon, overlooking the faraway black woodlands and the cottages around the common with their yellowed windows. We went to the Shire Horse Centre to feed the animals, then back over the bridge into the village hall to meet the man himself: Father Christmas. He sat waiting for us in the corner on a wooden chair, next to a gas radiator protected by a copper cage. 'Ho ho ho,' he said and I couldn't believe it was happening. This was the universe's centre, its focal point: this warm, golden corner of a church hall under a dark blue sky. I touched his leg, the red hem of his garment. He gave me a present. I remember asking if I was allowed to open it, what with it not being Christmas Day yet. He must have acquiesced because I did open it. It was a colouring book with a dog on the front. No other present I ever received released the same perfect happiness than that colouring book from Father Christmas himself. For with it came the knowledge that Father Christmas was real, everything was possible - from monsters to flying cars - and that the stars above were pinned to a finite navy sky for no other reason than for us to gaze up at and count.

Inspired by the old Norfolk boy, we went to the Shire Horse Centre again (now an animal sanctuary). I hadn't been since that horse-drawn nursery group trip circa 1987. It unlocked all the memories. The stables and barns. The smell of hay and manure.

They had a wider range of creatures than in years gone by - alpacas, llamas, turkeys - as well as heart-tuggingly cute things like donkeys and bunnies. From every

vantage point I saw the village from a new angle.
Children and families flocked in. It was all very serene
and goodly. The sky was grey and cold and Christmas
was in the air.

Then, like I said, we went to Homebase.

Sun 25th -

A story from yesterday that I didn't want to include for
fear of bringing the mood down. It haunted me all last
night so I can't let it pass without comment today.

At the animal sanctuary, as we'd queued to get in, my
mum saw a man she half-knew. He had a wild haircut
and was dressed like he was expecting to be drafted into
the army any second. I performed a shameful character
assassination, privately slotting him into the category,
'person who probably steals things from unlocked
sheds'. He was with his partner - herself on-guard
should the opportunity for an Appalachian hike
suddenly present itself - and their young daughter. As
they queued, the daughter jumped up, grabbing at her
father's belt for attention. He ignored her, chewing his
gum.

As you may recall, on account of the Christmas-themed
morning and the presence of good ol' Father Christmas,
entry to the sanctuary was free. Unless, said a sign by
the entrance, you intended to meet FC. That particular
honour had a tariff attached. There's no such thing as a
free Christmas dinner, and all that. Five pounds was all
they wanted. A fair price. Not much. But to the two
parents mentioned above, it was everything. My mum
spoke to them. They hadn't known about the fee; they
couldn't take their little girl to see Father Christmas

after all, despite, I should expect, having promised her all week that that was what they would be doing.

'They're going to walk into town instead,' Mum said.

Town was three miles away. And I had to wonder what precisely they'd be doing there without £5 to spend.

Mum, far from a dollar-waving Housewife of New Jersey herself, had contemplated giving them the money but didn't want to come across as patronising. I wondered how we could make it look natural, maybe placing a fiver on the ground next to them and hoping they 'found' it. We had to give it a go. But we couldn't find them. They'd gone. Their walk into town had started.

I now can't help but think of how I'd swooned last night over my cherished horse-drawn trip to see Father Christmas way back when I was a toddler. The thought of being blocked off at the hall door that night and told that, yes, Father Christmas was in there, and, yes, all the other children will see him but that, no, I couldn't, is more depressing than I know how to deal with. Because that is precisely what happened to the little girl yesterday.

If this were a film, someone would've given them the money, or they'd have found it or won it or whatever. Or, worst case scenario, the little girl would use the moment as inspiration to work hard and live her life to the full, going back to the grotto in her wealthier carnation and paying for all the children to see Santa for free. Wouldn't that be nice? I suspect the reality won't play out like that. As long as there are gits like me in the world, to judge and critique on first sight, nothing will be easy.

Of all the money I'll fritter away this Christmas and every other, that £5 I couldn't spend will be the most costly.

241

Tues 27th -

Walked past a real Christmas tree today. It smelt divine. Literally. A gift from a better realm. I do love the smell of artificial trees but have to admit, it had been a long time since I'd had a good waft of a real one up close. I can still smell it. It made my nose feel warm.

Weds 28th -

The BBC monthly weather outlook has been released, leading up to the 23rd Dec. No surprises. Wet, overcast, with 'above average' temperatures. I don't understand how December temperatures are above average every year. The people working out these stats need to get their calculations checked: if it's always above average, the average ought to change.

Red sky tonight. Shepherd's delight. I'm tempted to dress up as a shepherd one evening, when the sky is glowing rouge, and walk around chirpily saying to passers-by, 'Quite frankly, I'm delighted'.

Thurs 29th -

Haven't started my present shopping yet. Need to get my rear into gear. It's the wrapping that's the killer. I've often held off buying extra gifts because the thought of wrapping them has been more of a deterrent than the cost. So lazy.

As far as the local supermarket is concerned, every day is Christmas Eve from here on in (until Christmas Eve). The songs are on a loop - 'Are ya hanging up yer stocking on yer waaalll' - and the aisle of refrigerated perishables is now loaded with party food, most of which goes out of date long before Christmas. Just who is buying mini Cornish pasties with a Dec 7th use-by date? Don't tell me they take them home and freeze them.

Bought an advent calendar. If I'm doing a Christmas diary I need to do all the Christmas things. Arrived home to find another advent calendar left on my doorstep. I live in a nice town.

Fri 30th -

And just like that, it's December tomorrow. Advent calendars. Christmas music. Everything. December! For a whole month!

Went to a nativity this afternoon. A family member was in action; a debut cracking of the boards. It was swell. Dimmed lights in the hall, standing room only at the back. A spotlight on a five-year-old dressed as a sheep. Wonderful. The carols had changed, though. I was hoping to hear the classics - 'Come & Join The Celebration', 'Little Donkey', 'It Was On A Starry Night' - but the directors went for a more modern selection of bangers. Initially, I said the classic 'Christmas ain't what it used to be' line to myself, then realised that the songs I've listed above were relatively modern when I sang them way back in the 80s, and that there were probably grandparents in the audience saying 'Christmas ain't what it used to be' back then, too. What will happen is today's children will grow up thinking their songs are the best and have to mute their disappointment as their own little munchkins sing the new Christmas favourites of the year 2040.

The 12 Things To Watch Of Christmas

#9

The Muppet Christmas Carol

Does any other children's film contain a phrase as striking as, 'The years performed their terrible dance'? I can't think of one. Not even in more refined classics like *Whistle Down The Wind* and 1992's *The Secret Garden*.[1] What makes the line additionally striking is that it comes from the mouth of a Muppet: a two-foot tall assemblage of fuzzy felt having its innards manipulated by a human arm.[2] The quote is one of many from *The Muppet Christmas Carol* to have been directly lifted from Charles Dickens' novel. Look at some of the others:

'He was a tight-fisted hand to the grindstone!'

'Scrooge slipped into the empty silence of a dreamless sleep.'

'He was conscious of a thousand odours, each one connected with a thousand thoughts and hopes and joys and cares long, long forgotten.'

---

[1] Two worthy entrants, along with *The Muppet Christmas Carol*, on any list of greatest films ever made.

[2] The name Muppet is a cross between marionette and puppet, not, as many believe, man and puppet. (Just saying.)

These lines could easily have been simplified for a younger audience or omitted completely. They aren't essential to the plot. But there they are, centre-stage, in all their Dickensian glory. Perhaps the reason behind the film's faithfulness to the text is that the Muppets always treated children with respect. They never patronised. 'Assisting the audience to understand,' was how their creator once described their duty.

Although Jim Henson trademarked his creations in 1958, it wasn't until they appeared on *Sesame Street* in 1969 that they became household names.[1] Henson's creations taught numbers and letters in a way that made learning feel rebellious. Although *The Muppet Show*, which followed *Sesame Street* in the mid-70s, was less educational, it reinforced its fuzzy stars' relationship with younger viewers (whilst gaining the affection of older ones). In their wake came TV spin-offs and numerous Hollywood movies, including non-Muppet features *The Dark Crystal* and *Labyrinth*.

Jim Henson sold his company to Disney in 1989, in the hope that the House of Mouse would look after the business side of things, allowing him to focus on creative endeavours. Months later, after complaining of a sore throat one night, he was taken to hospital where he would die of toxic-shock syndrome, aged fifty-three. *The Muppet Christmas Carol* would be the first major

---

[1] The show began life as a testing tool to see how effectively television could be used to educate children (the project went by the name 'The Children's Television Workshop', which will be familiar words to many readers). Accompanying an array of Jim Henson puppets on *Sesame Street*, were a cast of human presenters from a demographic seldom seen on American television at that time. This celebration of multi-diversity triggered a banning of the show in Mississippi, Henson's home state, where one government source was quoted as saying they 'weren't ready for it yet'. This was in 1970. Three weeks later, after a national outcry, the ban was lifted.

Muppet production he didn't oversee. It was directed by his son, Brian, and written, crucially, by Jerry Juhl, whom Jim Henson had first hired in 1961 and who'd written extensively for *Sesame Street* and *The Muppet Show*. Although Jim Henson wasn't on the set of the *Christmas Carol*, his spirit was.

The Muppet Christmas Carol performed admirably at the box office by Muppet standards, but less admirably by Disney standards. Despite the studio's heavy promotional outlay on their new franchise, the film took just $27m in the US in 1992.[1] Subsequently, the Muppet films that succeeded *Christmas Carol* had a colder, authoritative hand over them.[2] They were safe and vacuous, lacking the wit and mania of the previous works. Anybody who's seen *It's A Very Muppet Christmas Movie* or *Kermit's Swamp Years* would agree (if you can find anyone who's seen them).[3]

The most gallant aspect of *The Muppet Christmas Carol* is that it actively tries to be frighten its young audience. Children love being scared. The Muppet's depiction of the Ghost of Christmas Yet To Come, for instance, is a ten-foot grim-reaper with a black chasm where his face should be. He utters not one word and is involved in no physical or visual comedy. Likewise, the opening scenes in Scrooge's creepy candle-lit townhouse are equally spooky and have, in my humble opinion, never been bettered in other adaptations.

Of all the adaptations (and there are around thirty, not including the hundreds of TV versions/parodies), I'm certain

[1] For comparison, *Home Alone 2: Lost In New York* took $174m that same year.

[2] Or *up* them.

[3] Although the latest Disney-backed Muppet movies with Amy Adams and Ricky Gervais were both great fun. So perhaps I need to eat my words.

that the Muppet's version of *A Christmas Carol* is the one Dickens would have loved the most. As far as all Dickens adaptations go, only David Lean's *Great Expectations* and the BBC's *Bleak House* (2005) compare. *The Muppet Christmas Carol* is one of the few versions of the story that fully takes into account that Scrooge's escapades are supposed to be madcap, as well as profound. It would be easy for anybody yet to read a Dickens novel to assume that everything he wrote was some sort of dry, blustering social commentary. Modern front covers of his novels nearly always use painterly depictions of Victorian suffering, which make picking up one of his books as appealing as picking up thrush. The movies are just as skilful at missing the target: gloomy, pompous affairs, stuffed with theatre hams delivering their lines as slowly as possible in the hope of nabbing a BAFTA nomination. Such grandiosity is not (entirely) the Dickens way. His books are, with the odd exception,[1] dizzying comics. That's why so many people still read his work. And why they don't read quite so much of Herman Melville's.

The Muppets embrace the tale's humour and stay faithful to the varying flavours of the prose. Not only would Dickens have loved the way the film encapsulates his thundering storytelling, he would also have been touched by how his characters are brought to life. It's as though the Muppets were created to tell this specific story. For instance, which actor would be more perfectly suited to the role of humble Bob Cratchit than Kermit the Frog?[2] And who better to play his red-blooded wife

---

[1] *Barnaby Rudge, Hard Times, A Tale of Two Cities.* (A friendly warning.)

[2] In the absence of Jim Henson, this was the first time Kermit had had a different arm up him. His new puppeteer, Steve Whitmore, claims that Henson appeared to him in a dream the night before filming began and gave him encouragement.

than Miss Piggy? Who else could play Scrooge's one time employer, the eternal joker Mr *Fezziwig*, than *Fozzy* Bear? Or Scrooge's rigid old headmaster than Sam the Eagle? The only seemingly off-centre casting is Gonzo as Charles Dickens, yet even this works perfectly.[1] He steals the show. A quick nod, too, should go towards Michael Caine, who plays Scrooge with an artless villainy befitting a Dickensian antagonist.

'I'm going to play this movie,' Caine said before filming, 'like I'm working with the Royal Shakespeare Company. I will never wink. I will never do anything Muppety. I am going to play Scrooge as if it is an utterly dramatic role and there are no puppets around me.'

His god-awful singing in the finale is both unexpected and joyous.[2]

Dickens may also have liked the way the film cheekily pokes fun at him. When Scrooge accuses the ghosts of Marley & Marley (Statler & Waldorf - yet more perfect casting) of being figments of his imagination, Scrooge says, in a direct quote, 'There is more of gravy than of grave about you!' To which the Marleys reply, 'What a terrible pun! Where do you get these jokes?'

Those who grew up watching *The Muppet Christmas Carol* on VHS, as I did, will know a different version to those who have

---

[1] Gonzo was chosen to play Dickens precisely because he was the least likely. The original plan was for the more popular Muppets to play the ghosts who visit Scrooge, until it was thought that having unfamiliar ghosts would add an air of mystique.

[2] The standard procedure in these sorts of films is to allow its stars to mime whilst a better vocalist nails the notes. But it is essential to the spirit of the story that Scrooge *really* sings, and does it abysmally.

only seen it on television or DVD. This is because the VHS version includes an exclusive, and pivotal, scene.

The scene in question features the song *When Love Is Gone*, sung by Scrooge's one-time fiancé, Belle. In it, she explains her reasons for leaving the miserable git. It's one of the many flashbacks that the dainty young Ghost Of Christmas Past shows Scrooge, and by far the most affecting:

Yes, some dreams come true
And yes, some dreams fall through
But now the time has come for us to say 'Goodbye'

It's the moment when we see our lead character become vulnerable. The young Scrooge sits and listens as the old Scrooge looks on, unseen, unheard, faintly singing along to a song he's heard once before.

'Spirit, show me no more,' he begs, as Belle's song fades. 'Why do you delight in torturing me?'

'I told you,' replies the ghostly child, 'these are the shadows of the things that have been. That they are what they are, do not blame me.'

A vital moment, you'd think.[1] The years have performed their terrible dance, however, and it's been axed. Cut from every version. None of the countless re-releases and double disc 'Special Editions' include the scene, not even as an extra. Disney's official view is that the song is too complex to be understood by children. A standpoint sadly out of keeping with the spirit of their own glory days.[2]

---

[1] And worth watching for the scenery alone: a sweet and cleverly concise recreation of a snowy Victorian morning.

[2] We should be thankful that Pixar have the freedom to make decisions independently of their parent company. Imagine the cuts and edits Disney would have made in order to protect children from things simply too 'complex to be understood'. *Inside Out* would have been over in twenty minutes.

＊

For a film so bold in scope, it's miraculous that only a couple of the special effects look dated, especially when you bear in mind that it was released the same year as *Honey I Blew Up The Kid* (and nine years before *The Mummy Returns*). The rest of the film looks glorious, relying on models, puppetry and camera tricks instead of crude computer graphics.

For faithfulness, originality, wit, warmth and spirit, *The Muppet Christmas Carol* is unrivalled. For a film to be both faithful and original is quite some achievement, but then it *is* quite some film. It is richly referential in a non-knowing way. What other children's film has cameos for Molière and Dante? What other children's film deals with homelessness and poverty so adroitly? Hell, even the songs are great (mostly),[1] all tinkly and toe-tappy.

Like Scrooge at the end of the story, *The Muppet Christmas Carol* has 'become all things to all men'.

Well, some of them. Me, mostly.

#10

Only Fools & Horses

The breakthrough came in 1985. *To Hull & Back*: the first full-length episode and the first to be scheduled in BBC One's Christmas Day primetime slot, airing at 7.30pm, directly

---

[1] Written by long-time Muppet songwriter, Paul Williams (by which I mean, he wrote *for* the Muppets, not that he is one). His most famous song being Kermit's *Rainbow Connection*, he also wrote *Fill Your Heart*, which David Bowie covered on *Hunky Dory*.

against ITV's *Minder* in an act of wilful aggression from the BBC's new controller, Michael Grade.[1] Of the two shows, time has been far less kind to *Minder*, but it was just as popular in its heyday (and it featured similar characters and similar, for want of a better word, shenanigans). *Only Fools* writer John Sullivan said that when he first saw *Minder* in 1979, he thought of his own new sitcom script, *Readies*,[2] and said, 'Shit. That's that idea gone.'

Luckily for Sullivan, the success of *Minder* on ITV only made the BBC keener to develop his script. By 1985, the two shows were established favourites. In the days when VCRs could set even high-flying young stockbrokers back a month's pay, the decision to pit the behemoths up against one another on Christmas night was a cause of frustration so rabid that the national press campaigned to get the two channels to at least agree to repeat the episodes on New Year's Day. On Christmas night, though, the *Only Fools & Horses* big-budget special[3] handsomely beat *Minder* by several million viewers, leaving the BBC with something on which to annually hang its (paper) hat.

---

[1] Grade, unlike his predecessor, was a huge *Only Fools & Horses* fan and sought to give it pride of place in the schedules. As a vaguely interesting aside, another of his moves as Controller was to schedule programmes to start on the hour or on the half hour, rather than at odd times like 7.20 and 8.45. This is still largely implemented to this day.

[2] *Only Fools & Horses'* working title.

[3] *To Hull & Back*'s budget was around the £800,000 mark. An amount comparable with the era's British cinema releases. (The budget for the *Rising Damp* movie, for instance, was £125,000.) It was a figure at which some BBC bigwigs winced. After all, it was enough to buy four video recorders.

Which is precisely what they did, broadcasting a new *Only Fools* special on Christmas Day for the next eight years.[1]

In all, eighteen *Only Fools & Horses* Christmas specials were made. A remarkable number considering how few episodes there are in total of other much-loved series: *The Young Ones* (12), *Fawlty Towers* (12), *The Office* (14), *I'm Alan Partridge* (12) and so on. More remarkable still is that nearly all *Only Fools* Christmas specials were among their respective year's most watched television programmes.[2] The peak came with the 1996 special, *Time On Our Hands*, which drew an audience of 24.3m. It was supposed to be the last ever episode, a neat rounding off of the Trotter's quest for fortune. The show came back, though. And as with so many other comedies - *Arrested Development*, *Community* and *Porridge* - it ought not to have done. Between 2001 and 2003, a new episode was produced each Christmas. The first, attracted 21m. The second, 17m. The third, 16m. It was clear within minutes of the 2001 special that the comeback was dead in the water. The following two episodes were equally painful; whereas once *Only Fools* captured the authentic tenor of London, the comeback episodes were contrived and out of touch. The lines were hammier, the delivery slower. The plots

---

[1] At admittedly odd times. Although some episodes went out in the evening, others went out much earlier, at around 4 or 5pm. 1991's terrible *Miami Twice* (filmed in Florida and involving Del Boy being mistaken for a mafia don, also played by David Jason...) went out after the Queen's speech at ten-past-three.

[2] By the 1990s, *Only Fools & Horses* stood alone as the BBC's festive box office guarantee; even at the time of *To Hull & Back*'s success in '85, however, shows like *Last Of The Summer Wine* and *Open All Hours* (also starring David Jason) were pipping it in the Christmas ratings. But then, *they* weren't going up against *Minder*.

stretched the realms of possibility.[1] Added to this, the studio audience, glad to have the hottest ticket in town, bawled and hollered at every line for fear of under-reacting to a potentially legendary moment (of which these three new episodes would prove to offer none).[2]

The *Only Fools & Horses* Christmas specials offer the very best and very worst of the series. Egged on by the larger budgets, John Sullivan often went big with his plots. Some of his grand ideas worked, others fell flat. The high points were 1988's *Dates* (in which Del Boy first meets Raquel) and 1989's *Jolly Boys' Outing* (a 'beano' to Margate); both specials sandwiched the show's immaculate sixth series and both scored high on the plausibility front. The low points include the three comeback specials (2001-3), *Miami Twice*, *Fatal Extraction*[3] and, well, just about all the other feature-length episodes.

Sitcoms offer us a home from home. Few popular comedies are set in unpleasant situations. Even things like *Fleabag*, *Bottom* and *Father Ted* have something oddly snug about them. For all its damp patches and clutter, the Trotter's high-rise flat has an appealing domesticity, particularly when decorated with a Christmas tree and foil streamers. The problem with the show's yuletide specials was they often took the characters away from this setting and had them boating off to Holland or hunting

---

[1] The Trotters inadvertently harbouring an Iranian business-man as an illegal immigrant, for example.

[2] For another example of this 'over-eager' audience phenomena, watch the second series of *I'm Alan Partridge*. Nearly every moment of physical comedy gets an unwarranted round of applause.

[3] The weirdest of the lot: Del attracts the attention of a stalker. I could watch that episode a thousand times and still not understand it.

hidden treasures in far flung places i.e. beyond Peckham. The archetypal *Only Fools* episode, a typical crowd-pleaser, ought to always start in the flat, end in the flat, and feature little but the café and the pub in-between.

Lennard Pearce (who played Grandad) once told Nicholas Lyndhurst that he was glad these new-fangled video recorders were invented because it meant he would live forever. Even if the show was cancelled, he said, someone, somewhere, was sure to like it and keep it recorded. As it was, *Only Fools & Horses'* popularity held on regardless,[1] immortalised by regular repeats on the BBC (as well as thirty times a day on GOLD).[2] Despite now being on YouTube, Netflix, DVD and, as Grandad Trotter predicted, VHS, millions *still* tune in to the programme whenever it airs on BBC One. In terms of an enduring mass popularity, nothing compares. No other British show can possibly claim to have so many long-lasting, instantly identifiable catchphrases. Just look at this lot:

You plonker
You dipstick

---

[1] Certainly when compared to other big hitters from the 80s and 90s e.g. *Fresh Fields*, *Men Behaving Badly*, *Terry & June*, *Sorry*, *Bread*.

[2] Its popularity is even more impressive considering the episodes have been butchered by edits and musical copyright issues. The shows get especially grim treatment by the BBC, who hack them to pieces for fear of offending. Jim Sullivan said this of how extreme the edits of his father's masterpiece have become: 'For example, Del saying "Monchengladbach" to Anna in the episode *From Prussia with Love* had been removed – our only conclusion being that some bright spark at the BBC, unsure of what this actually means, but gripped by the sheer terror of possibly, perhaps, just maybe, offending somebody, decided it best to be safe than sorry.' From music to dialogue, not *one* of its many DVD boxset releases contains complete and unedited content.

You wally-brain
He who dares wins
Knock 'em bandy
As they say in [insert random French district]
This time next year, we'll be millionaires
Alright, Dave?
Pukka
Cushty
Cosmic
You know it makes sense
During the war
Mange tout, mange tout
No way, Pedro
Don't be a [insert timid expletive] *all your life*
Lovely jubbly

It has even spawned a genuine modern proverb with the line 'It's a bit like Trigger's broom'. A saying which has all the hallmarks of a common Shakespearean misquote and which may well be around long after the show itself has *vanished into thin air*.

Rather than condemning it, the faithfulness of the 1980s London tongue and the attention to detail with sets and costumes has given the programme the added allure of a timepiece. It continues to find new fans. But for those of a certain age, *Only Fools & Horses* has an extra ace tucked up its sheepskin sleeve: it stepped in on Christmas Day and, even when not at full strength, drew families together, from great grandmother to great grandson via middle-aged parent and grouchy student, and played to that eternally difficult crowd with a dexterity not matched since. The one constant of highly successful Christmas television shows is not that they make everybody roar with laughter, but that they are just about good enough for the whole family to put up with. It sounds like such an easy thing to achieve, doesn't it, a show that most people *won't mind* watching. Simple. Can you think of the last programme to achieve this feat, though? A programme that could air in the late afternoon on December 25th and appease about a third of the population? If you can, I expect the name on your lips might well be *Only Fools & Horses*: a show on the cusp of its fortieth anniversary.

Buy shares in the GOLD channel.

You know it makes sense.

The Christmas Alphabet

P is for...

Pantomime

'He who says he does not like pantomime either says what he does not think, or is not so wise as he fancies himself.'
James Henry Leigh Hunt, *Pantomimes*, 1828

Initially a form of 16th century Italian street theatre,[1] panto was later brought to England by theatre impresario, John Rich. During lulls in dramatic performances, a member of the cast would come out and wave a 'magic bat' to signify that the show was about to take a comedic turn. The 'magic bat' was also known as a 'slapstick'.

 However, it was early 19th century performer, Joseph Grimaldi, who took pantomime's popularity to the next level. A star of the stage from an age when most people are still busy teething, Grimaldi's lifelong clowning in numerous Drury Lane and Sadler's Wells pantos became legendary. It is he who's thought to have started the trend of audience participation - oh, *yes* he is - and it is he who's thought to have been the first British clown to whiten his face, something which remains deeply hilarious - oh, *no* it doesn't - to this day. One of those who saw the great Grimaldi perform was a young boy by the name of Charles

---

[1] Known as 'commedia dell'arte': the comedy of art. A very fancy name for what is effectively a combination of funny wigs and thinly-veiled nob gags.

Dickens. A lifelong fan of the stage, Dickens would one day edit Grimaldi's memoirs, securing the clown's place in the popular imagination.[1] By the time of the book's publication, deep into the 1800s, the majority of classic lines and tropes which we associate with pantomime were fixed. They were, if you'll permit me the opportunity, *behind* us.

Today, pantomime defies all the odds and endures as a - generally quite expensive - family treat, generating around £60m annually for British theatres, as well as providing former soap stars, punch-drunk boxers, and members of 90s boybands with a vital festive revenue stream. Although associated with Christmas, panto was formerly a year-round affair, with its key season being Easter, which goes some way to explaining why their stories are seldom Christmas-themed.

Plonk

What would Christmas be without copious amounts of alcohol? Easter, I guess.

For some people, every night of the year provides an opportunity to neck claret in remembrance of the blood spilt by our Lord. For most, though, only Christmas offers the chance to enter this world of daily excess. December 25th is the big one, naturally, but those days *around* Christmas are just as dangerous, all rolling into one giddy mess of cheese boards and nightly sessions on the plonk, leaving one in a merry carefree swill.

---

[1] Dickens decision to work on the panto star's book surprised many. In modern terms, it would be like Hilary Mantel putting the sweeping historical epics to one side and thrashing out a biography of Christopher Biggins.

The numbers are startling. A poll conducted in 2018 revealed that Brits intended to consume up to twenty-six units per day over Christmas.[1] Our first drink would, the survey revealed, be supped at around the 11.54am mark. The nation combined expected to knock back a whopping six billion units in a proud show of spirited unity not seen since the evacuation of Dunkirk. Those polled were asked *why* they planned to drink so much. What do you think the answer was?

Because it's Christmas.

Pudding, Christmas

'Wilson and I couldn't finish our share of the plum pudding. We have all slept splendidly and feel thoroughly warm - such is the effect of full feeding.'

Robert F. Scott, *Dec 25th*, 1911

Another important player on the *'because it's Christmas'* front, it's difficult to conceive that Christmas pudding could survive under any other circumstances than tradition. Originally known as 'plum pudding' because of its abundance of prunes (maybe it ought to have been called *prune* pudding), Christmas pudding would traditionally be made in the run up to December 25th, with each Sunday in advent being known as 'stir-up Sunday'. The day was so-named not because the families of olde Englande were Bob Marley fans, but because they would *stir* the pudding mix on that day. The mix was stirred from east to west, clockwise, in honour of the Magi who themselves travelled from east to west (allegedly). Secret treats were hidden in the

---

[1] For context, the average amount consumed on a night out is around sixteen units, which is also the approximate amount the NHS recommend as a *weekly* allowance.

pudding, such as silver coins, wishbones, mini-anchors and countless other things that could choke the merriment out of an innocent child.

One unverified claim is that the non-English-speaking[1] king, George I, began the tradition on Christmas Day, 1714. Apparently, his majesty demanded plum pudding with his dinner.[2] What the king wanted, the king got. Even when it came to prune-based desserts. George I was subsequently known by some as the 'Pudding King', although the engraver of his headstone opted to neglect this fact. Shame.[3]

Q is for...

Quality Street

'It's Quality Street. Choose your personal favourite.'
Saddam Hussein, 2002

I could have spoken about tinned sweets in general here. All the classics. Roses. Heroes. Celebrations. The problem is, you see those the whole year round. You might receive them any time,

---

[1] Yes, OK, fine, he was *German*. Sigh. I'd gone *so* long without writing that word...

[2] 'At six o'clock' precisely, according to one unerringly well-informed source.

[3] George was buried in his native Germany in 1727, having died there on a state visit. He was the last British monarch to be buried overseas (at the time of writing). He spoke many different languages: German, French, Latin, Italian, Dutch, but *not* English. This made him somewhat unpopular with those who did i.e. everyone in England.

say if you were leaving a job or had looked after someone's budgie. Quality Street, on the other hand, have an unshakeable affiliation to Christmas. Seldom, if ever, will you see a Quality Street tin in May and even if you do, it'll probably be full of sewing equipment and plasters.

Plus, Quality Street begins with a Q.

I bet if I asked you to close your eyes and imagine the smell of a newly opened Quality Street tin, you could do it. And I bet the most pronounced scent would be that of the Strawberry Cream. Probably because, regardless of their modest popularity, they outnumber every other sweet. Each year, Quality Street makes the news for one reason or other, whether it's the ever-shrinking tin sizes[1] or the ever-changing contents. In 2018, QSHQ (Quality Street Headquarters) publicly addressed the controversy of the proliferation of Strawberry Creams compared to fan favourites The Green Triangle and The Purple One:

'The assortment,' said a Quality Street spokesperson,[2] 'is made of up of three different types of sweet: fruit creams, chocolates, and toffees and fudge.[3] Each tub is broadly split into thirds along these lines, which is why you will get more sweets like the Strawberry Cream, one of only two fruit creams. [You get]

---

[1] Or, to be more accurate, *plastic tub* sizes. This is all rather scandalous, in truth. The size of the average Quality Street tub has fallen by 40% since 2009. To bring about meaningful change, might I suggest writing to your MP on the subject? Assuming Parliament will be fully operational by the time this book goes to print.

[Hot off the press: Quality Street sizes have dropped again for 2019 - from 720g to 650g - and parliament *isn't* fully operational. RP Oct '19]

[2] What a job!

[3] I'd call that *four* different types, personally.

fewer of The Purple One and Green Triangle, [as they] are just two of the five mainly chocolate-based sweets.'

So, now we know.

I think.

What we definitely don't know, though, is *why* they are split evenly into 'three different types of sweet' in the first place. What a curious policy. The official Nestlé line is that the split is something or other to do with nutritional content, as though they're concerned about the width of the nation's waistlines (something that's hard to believe when you consider Nestlé's alleged misdemeanours worldwide[1]).

In an attempt to quell the debate over the selection of sweets, Quality Street teamed up with John Lewis[2] in 2018 to offer a pic 'n mix option. For just £12 (!), customers could select precisely which sweets they stuffed into their tins. Whether Nestlé were concerned about the 'nutritional value' of people's choices in this particular instance remains unclear.

'Everybody's got a favourite Quality Street sweet,' said their senior brand manager,[3] 'so providing a pick 'n mix option could spell the end of that particular Christmas debate.'

The only debate that remains is whether it's worth £12 for the privilege of choice.

------

[1] Too plentiful and depressing to go into here. Should you choose to look into it, though, the list of Nestlé products to boycott doesn't stop at chocolate and cereals. They own, or have a hand in: Nescafé, Vittel water, Perrier water, Purina and Felix cat food, Bakers and Winalot dog food, L'oreal, Maybelline, Garnier, The Body Shop, Ralph Lauren, YSL, Diesel, and Häagen-Dazs ice cream. Luckily, they sold their rights to Branston Pickle in 2002.

[2] Not to be confused with Jona Lewie...

[3] Again - what a job! I hope there's a sassy young *junior* brand manager, too, awaiting promotion to the big chair.

It wasn't always big business and senior brand managers, though. Quality Street were formerly made by the Halifax company, Mackintosh. A family business, Mackintosh began making tinned assortments of sweets in 1936 as a way of offering working class families a chance to afford what was, at the time, a costly treat. Until Quality Street[1] arrived, boxes of sweets were largely a novelty reserved for the well-to-do (with the exception of the relatively cheap All Gold and Black Magic). By keeping down production costs – mainly by individually wrapping the sweets and not laying them out seductively in costly plastic trays[2] – the Mackintosh family achieved their goal of producing a popular, affordable sweet selection. There were eighteen original varieties of which five survive to this day: Toffee Penny, Toffee Finger, Green Triangle, Caramel Swirl and The Purple One. As their first newspaper advert proudly proclaimed in 1936, Quality Street was 'absolutely the biggest and best in quality and value'.

For decades, the tins had a picture of a sergeant major and his young wife (known, reputedly, as Miss Sweetly and Major Quality[3]). This was an attempt to give the tins a touch of Regency class. The couple were removed in 2000, possibly as a result of Miss Sweetly's affair with General E. Tasty. Whatever the reason for the couple's divorce, the popularity of the sweets remained; Nestlé – who acquired Mackintosh in 1988 – churn out millions of tins per year. No wonder QSHQ can afford so many spokespeople and brand managers.

---

[1] Which took its name from a J.M. Barry play. (My goodness this book contains some bizarre facts.)

[2] The Mackintosh factory was the first to have a machine which twisted sweet wrappers automatically.

[3] Yet more trivia!

To end, a quick word about that Saddam quote. It was taken from an interview with George Galloway in which, sensing the noose around his neck, Mr Hussein made a concerted attempt to appear an anglophile. The type of anglophile who has tins of Quality Street around his house in August. MI6 were too shrewd to fall for the ruse, though. Nobody has Quality Street when it isn't Christmas.

The 12 Songs of Christmas

#11

December Song - George Michael

George Michael's other Christmas song. Unlike the multi-million selling party favourite, *Last Christmas*, which rolled in on the crest of the Wham! wave, this one came from nowhere.[1]

Four years on from his last studio album, *Patience*, which itself had been five years in the making, George Michael had become something of an outsider by the time of his 2008 download-only single, *December Song*. The only station to give the new track any airtime was Radio 2. *I stumbled upon it by chance. The composition - a slow hymn to a lonely childhood Christmas - seemed so un-George-Michael-like that it was only the vocals that gave him away.*[2]

Everything about *December Song* was surprising. In particular, that it was bookended by a sampled choir from an old Sinatra

---

[1] *Last Christmas* remains the biggest selling song to not reach UK number 1, kept off the top by Band Aid's *Do They Know It's Christmas?* (which also featured George Michael). Fans tried to make the song a posthumous chart topper in 2017. It stalled at number 2. In 2018, of its own free will, it reached number 3. Seemingly destined to never reach the top, it's still done decent business for a song written by George in his bedroom as a schoolboy.

[2] *'This year, to save him from tears...'*

song, *The Christmas Waltz*. The lyrics went places I never expected a George Michael song to go. It was a peon to finding positivity in even the darkest of domestic Christmases:

Sweet December song
The melody that saved me
On those less than silent nights

Even writing the words now, they don't seem in keeping with somebody who used to be in Wham!:

There was always Christmas time
To wipe the year away
I guess that Mum and Dad decided
That the war would have to wait

It's a rare thing to remember first hearing a song. I can recall that Saturday night vividly. I thought George Michael was back. It turned out he wasn't. Instead, this would be one of his rare resurfacings. The next year,[1] even deeper into his enigma phase, he stunned everyone by appearing on the 2009 *X-Factor* grand final. This, bear in mind, was a time when *X-Factor* was a Saturday night colossus, dominating tabloid front pages.[2] With an audience of over ten million, it wasn't the most likely of places for a hermit to emerge. The producers treated their star guest to the obligatory VT montage of his hits and sales statistics:

OVER 100 MILLION WORLDWIDE RECORD SALES!

12 UK NUMBER 1 SINGLES!

10 US NUMBER 1 SINGLES!

When the camera cut back to the live studio, the man himself walked out from the dry ice, like a *Stars In The Eyes* contestant

---

[1] *'To save him from tears...'*

[2] These days, ITV have to carefully schedule the show around *Countryfile*, so that a feature on Cumbrian sheep-shearing techniques doesn't pilfer even more of their viewers away.

deigning to be George Michael. He was instantly recognisable. But different. Instead of *Freedom*, *Faith* or *Fastlove*, he sang, of all things, the previous year's free download, *December Song*, which was being tentatively re-released as a CD single.

I could believe in peace on earth
And I could watch TV all day

Hiding behind shaded glasses and a television smile, he sang the song impeccably. When it was over, during his standing ovation, he said nothing. He hurried off stage, head down, as though he felt he'd outstayed his welcome.

By the following Monday, the few available CD versions of the single had sold out. There was no time to print new copies before the Sunday Top 40. Thus, like so many songs from the late noughties, its ultimate chart position was grossly askew due to much of the artist's audience not knowing how or where to download songs.[1] *December Song* slipped in at number 14 and didn't hang around for long. It is yet to re-enter the Top 40. It may do eventually.

As 80s popstars go, George Michael was a cut above. Nurturing a borderline obsession with making new music, his early years as a songwriter were prolific. Between 1983 and '86 - the Wham! years - he wrote three albums. In the following thirty years, however, he wrote just four. Although his output decreased, he is undoubtedly one of the great British songwriters, a distinction for which he gets insufficient credit. Aside from penning numerous outstanding hits - *Praying For Time*, *One More*

---

[1] This is a phenomenon yet to correct itself. The pop singles charts used to be truly representative of the nation's eclectic/mental tastes. Now it's representative of the tastes of the free-streaming under-30s. This is why the album chart, where the majority of units are sold in supermarkets, are a little less alienating.

Try, *Spinning The Wheel*, *Fastlove*, *Kissing A Fool* - he was the first British artist to write, produce and perform a number 1 record (*A Different Corner*).[1] And he was far from an apolitical celebrity droid. When all the hip-and-happening, devil-may-care pop-punk acts of the early noughties were too scared to voice disproval of the invasion of Iraq, George Michael was one of a handful of older musicians (Bruce Springsteen, Dixie Chicks) brave enough to do so with his song and video, *Shoot The Dog*. It was a move which near enough killed his career in the US.

Improbably, 2008's *December Song* was written with a Spice Girls reunion in mind. It was then going to be offered to Michael Bublé, until its composer decided to keep it for himself. I can't imagine the song would feature in this book if either of those artists had performed it. I doubt I would ever have heard it. If ever a voice gave a lyric meaning, it's George Michael's on *December Song*.

After years of making headlines for all the wrong reasons, it was only when George Michael died that many of his good deeds came to light. He'd secretly given away millions and millions. Regular recipients included Childline and Macmillan Cancer Support. All of his profits from *Last Christmas* were donated to the same Ethiopian famine appeal championed by Band Aid. Like Elvis Presley, Michael Jackson and many other poverty-born superstars, he could be moved into the most open-handed acts of charity at short notice. Having watched an episode of *Deal Or No Deal*, for instance, he privately paid £15,000 for a contestant to have IVF treatment. He kept his act of kindness so secret that the lady herself didn't know who'd

---

[1] He also played every instrument on *Last Christmas*. Not one session musician was used. He even shook the sleigh bells, whilst Andrew Ridgeley made the tea. (*Last Christmas* was a double a-side with the outstanding *Everything She Wants*, also written and performed entirely by George, with Andrew again on tea duties.)

paid for the treatment until after her benefactor had passed away. He paid off a woman's £25,000 debt after overhearing her crying about it in a restaurant and tipped a student nurse £5,000 for the same reason. He later gave a free Christmas concert for thousands of NHS staff as a way of thanking them for how they had looked after his terminally ill mother.

George Michael was found dead in bed on Christmas morning, 2016. After a complicated post-mortem, heart failure was the considered verdict. His boyfriend believes it was suicide and claimed that George had already tried to end his life four times. The date was all the more significant as the 25th of December was also his mother's birthday. Talking of her death, George had once said, 'I was in a black hole. I think I might have been one of those cowards who chose a nasty way out.'

Maybe since you've gone
I went a little crazy

So starts the second verse of *December Song*, before returning to its chorus telling of warring parents and lonely television watching.

Right. That's it. No more. The next Christmas song I talk about *will* be full of sparkly joy.

The Yule Log

DECEMBER - Part One

Sat 1st -

Opened my advent calendars. The one I'd found on my doorstep had Homer Simpson on. The one I'd bought was a supposedly upmarket Thornton's effort. The chocolate tasted exactly the same in both. What a mug I am.

Made a concerted effort to do most of my Christmas shopping in my hometown this year. After a three-hour trek around the shops, I'd bought just three things. All of them confectionary. I spent £14 on a box of liquorice and a box of mints. The lady who served me, who I took to be the shop owner, was so truculent towards another member of staff that I wished I'd been more chivalrous and said that, on account of her unpleasant nature, I'd be buying my liquorice and mint elsewhere, thank-you. (I'd be £8 richer, too.)

A few weeks ago, as I was walking around town, I overheard an elderly holidaymaker in a flat cap saying to his wife, 'Enjoy t' shops, duckie. Giy'it twenty years and they won't be here'. I thought he was a complete prick at the time. Yet, as I sat in the comfort of my lounge and smashed through the remainder of my Christmas shopping in about half an hour on Amazon, I couldn't help but think he might have been onto something.

Trees are going up on Facebook. I'm fighting the temptation to get my new one out of the shed. The commonly accepted rule with Christmas trees is that you don't put them up until December. But if social media has taught us nothing else - and it arguably hasn't - it's that plenty of people put theirs up much earlier, sometimes doing it when 'Strictly Come Dancing' still has ten contestants left.

Listened to '2000 Miles'. Always the first song I choose to hear in December.

Sun 2nd -

Inspired by the ads I'd seen a few weeks back, I bought a special moisture-collecting contraption that you plonk on your windowsill. It'd arrived in the post yesterday. The moisture gets soaked into a circular cake of chemicals then drips into a little pot. 'One drop in the first 12 hours!' the box promised. By this morning, there were enough drops in the pot to hand-wash a minibus. I must do some serious breathing in my sleep - probably all those pulsating dreams I have about drowning. There are few greater feelings than buying a gadget and discovering that the gadget works. Too often do these little gizmos fail to do the thing they promised. I felt like taking the moisture-laden pot out into the street this morning and showing people what I'd done in the night, like a proud toddler pointing at his warm potty.

Three football matches in a row today. A wife would never put up with that. This is such a gorgeous time in the football calendar, though. I love that the 4pm

Sunday kick offs need to be fully floodlit. As little as twelve weeks ago, we could look at our clocks at 8pm and say, 'Tell you what - the nights are drawing in a bit now'. Now they draw in at half-three.

Tonight is the night of the 'X Factor' final. I've been true to my word and watched none of the series.

Mon 3rd -

Remembered something my nanny used to say which used to make me shake with excitement. In the run up to Christmas, instead of asking what day of the week Christmas fell on, she'd ask, 'What night does he come?'

Tues 4th -

I used to put my tree up on December 1st. I wait that bit longer now. Get the decs up too early and the novelty wears off. And the tree lights normally break by the 25th, leaving you in a situation where you have to make a last-minute dash to Argos or keep the duds up, experiencing a non-lit Christmas tree in keeping with Lutheran tradition.

I keep seeing other people's trees flickering in their windows. It happened last night on the way to the quiz. Reds, blues, yellows, pinks. All flashing serenely in the bay windows.

That's it. Mine are going up tomorrow.

(We came joint third in the quiz, if you're interested. For the fiftieth time in my life, I got the answer wrong about the codename for the Allied invasion of Normandy. The answer is Overlord, and not, as I always confidently proclaim, Dynamo.)

The news is swamped with Brexit. The BBC website have their scary 'Breaking News' banner headline on every page, babbling on about some incalculable disaster or other. There's another story about how the televised debate between May and Corbyn (a debate for what end, I couldn't possibly tell you) isn't going to be broadcast on the BBC. The internet is on fire. People talk about footballers being obsessed with social media, but MPs are the real online prima donnas. Life in Westminster would be a lot less reactionary and wild if they could reign their Twitter time in a little bit.

Still not one person has mentioned Brexit to me in real life since this diary started. Jeremy Corbyn has requested that the televised debate not be broadcast at the same time as the 'I'm A Celebrity Get Me Out Of Here!' grand final. If this doesn't serve as a pointer towards how much of a fig the general public now give about the subject, I don't know what does. That they'd prefer to watch Shane Ritchie, or whoever, munching on a kangaroo's knacker is telling.

Elsewhere on the BBC website, there was a story about a man being released from prison who impaled three children on spikes in his garden in 1973. Also, an article about Tumblr's decision to close all pornographic accounts. The headline, on the BBC remember, was 'Tumblr's porn ban abandons the marginalised'. It's got to be one of the worst sob stories of the year. Besides, there's probably some loon out there with a fetish about having their fetish marginalised and abandoned by social media. For this happy chap, tonight is his lucky night.

Weds 5th -

No mention of last night's terrifying, alarming, godawful Brexit news (whatever it was) in the real world. Not one word.

Put the new tree up this afternoon. I don't think I've ever put the tree up and done all the decorations so smoothly. Still took about two hours, though. I don't know how. Possibly because I stopped for a cup of tea every fifteen minutes and stood there drinking it whilst staring at all the boxes that required unpacking. I managed to get through the operation without putting my back out, too. Some years, I've stretched myself out of action to the point where I've required painkilling suppositories. It's no way to start the season, nightly cradling yourself into the foetal position and fingering a prescription Crayola up your back-passage.

My only concern with the new tree is that it is leaning slightly to the left. This is known in the artificial tree manufacturers' game as 'doing a Daily Mirror' (if it leans slightly to the right, it's known as a 'disappointing family member'). I can't get it to stand straight. It's got until January the 5th to resist toppling.

Decorating the tree is a delight. To make the occasion extra festive, I switched the TV to one of those music channels buried deep in the listings. These channels - and there are plenty of them - all have similar shows rolling round the clock from November to December. They feature former popstars presenting videos of Christmas hits whilst sat in front a green-screen snowstorm. There's one which stars a very old and ruddy Noddy Holder basically shouting in between songs for three hours:

'Y'ALROIGHT POP PICKERS? 'OW THE DEVIL AM YER? 'ERE'S A CRIMBO CLASSIC FROM DAVID ISSIX FROM NOYNTEEN AYTY FREE!...'

The one I watched today featured someone from Atomic Kitten and, I think, a member of Blue. They were laying on a bed, offering scripted flirtations and pulling faces of disdain at the camera whenever the other said something wacky. Like all these things, it was shot and broadcast in full LD (Low Definition). The picture was shockingly bad. At times it looked like an illegal stream of a game of kabaddi from the early 80s. The poor pixellation suited the two presenters as their own careers had burnt out before HD arrived, in the days of The Box and its once-high-tech scrolling text messages ('whoos on here 2nite den?'; 'got 2 play new gerri halowill song next so good to here'). I'd love to know how much the two presenters got paid for their appearance. I bet they're not on the Noddy Holder scale.

Thurs 6th -

Even though I've only had it a few days, the little condensation contraption in my bedroom is already swishing with absorbed water. The air in my flat must be mostly H2O. It's a wonder I don't wake up with a wet head most mornings.

The tree is still 'doing a Daily Mirror'.

Wonder if I ought to change my plans for the book and do a chapter on 'Fairytale Of New York'. It's played to submission by the radio but it really is special. Like Lennon's 'War Is Over', you can hear it fifty times in December and think nothing of it, then, for whatever reason, it will randomly knock you for six. It's one of the few pop songs where the lyrics look good on paper. A real work of art. The line that gets me, as it got me today, was this:

'Can't make it all alone - I built my dreams around you'

Incredible.

Fri 7th -

It was on this date sixteen years ago, that I first came home from uni for Christmas. I couldn't wait to get back to Norfolk for a prolonged period. My uni was in High Wycombe (famous alumni: n/a), a forgotten market town with genuinely shocking areas of deprivation and a bus station that belonged in 'Children Of Men'. On the eve of my escape, I was too excited to sleep so got up at about 6am. I walked down from Halls to the 24-hour Tesco and bought my flatmates a box of mince pies out of the last of my autumn semester funds. I wrote them a cheery note and left it on the sticky kitchen worktop with the pies. For all my worrying about not fitting in, my first semester had been quite good. I'd taken too much stuff with me, though, so loaded the car with things to take home. At the halfway point, we stopped at a Little Chef and I ate a parentally-bankrolled Olympic Breakfast (with its little oval chips) that I could never have afforded myself.

The whole journey back was tinged with fear for the lunchtime kick-off between my virtuous, godly Manchester United and the evil poseurs, Arsenal. Those were the days when the two teams battled it out alone for the league title and their duels went a long way to determining who was going to come up trumps in May. I'd spent the last part of the journey looking out in awe of the Norfolk countryside and its dead, wintry charm. I couldn't bear to think about the match, nor could I bear not to. It was a race to get back in time for kick-off. Running into the house, I dumped my bags in the hall and got down on my knees in front of the TV. It took ages to come to life. The sound came first. A black screen. Then the game was there. The big, green pitch. The crackly sound of a cold, impassioned crowd. The score in the top lefthand corner. Nil-nil. Nineteen minutes played. But United were on the attack. A ball flashed across the penalty area. A red shirt, late to arrive, caught it sweetly.

Euphoria.

My memory won't let go of that day.

Sat 8th -

Bought the Christmas 'Radio Times' this morning. If it weren't for the date on the front, it could have been last year's edition; the cover looked so similar. Then I remembered how I'd thought the same thing last year. I went online to look at previous issues. Five covers out of the last eight Christmas editions have featured Raymond Briggs' characters. Six out of eight have included the phrase, 'It's the legendary double issue!'. And seven out of eight have said 'Merry Christmas & a Happy New Year!' in the same font. Having had a cursory glance at the listings for Christmas Day, most of the programmes are the same, too. The only evolution is the price. The 2012 edition - with The Snowman on the front and a 'free Snowman book' - was £2.80. This year's edition - also with The Snowman on the front and a 'free Snowman book' - is £4.90. I guess they know schmucks like me will buy it regardless. Only in real financial dire straits (Financial Dire Straits would be such a good name for a tribute band) would I go downmarket and buy 'TV Choice' (whose own less-legendary double issue is priced at a more-than competitive £1.20. It must have cost about 16p in 2012).

Haven't bought a single Christmas card yet. WHSmith were asking for £6.99 for ten. Almost every pack had only one design in each. I hate that. Mix it up a bit. I'm not going to give everybody I know the same card. You want a bit of variety, especially for £6.99. (It's all the more galling as you know that, in about two weeks' time, they'll be covered in discount stickers.) There should be a Christmas card pick 'n mix, where you buy any ten designs for £3, any twenty for a fiver and so on. If only. Instead, I left empty-handed. There was added dilemma in that not only will I need a job-lot for friends and colleagues etc., I also have to adhere to the unwritten rule of not giving your nearest and dearest cards from a multipack box. I needed to buy eight or nine individual cards for them, too. Avoiding the thrill of being fleeced like a shepherd's prized lamb, I went to the market. A chap there sold individual cards for 50p a pop. They were a bit naff (pictures of rabbits in scarves reaching up to put letters into postboxes, or of badgers sitting in an armchair by the fire), but when you've just spent £5 on a TV guide that's already built into your Sky box for free, you need to make all the savings you can.

Oh, I do love Christmas. Except for the bits that rile me so.

Sun 9th -

I've taken to drinking sherry at the quiz of a Sunday night. It is dangerously tasty. The only thing is, it comes in one of those ridiculous glasses that looks like it should be on a mantlepiece filled with daffodils. I look a complete prick drinking it in a social club where the Carling comes at £2.90 a pint.

We lost by a point. It was my fault. I dropped a ridiculous one. Here it is:

'Who released a book of poetry called "Songs of Innocence & Experience"?'

Like a shot, I said Leonard Cohen, and patted myself on the back for my bookishness.

The answer, obviously, was William Blake. I couldn't have been more wrong. I might as well have said Gazza.

Although slow to dish them out, I <u>received</u> my first cards of the season. Three of them. From fellow quizzers. Dizzy with sherry, I stood them on my bookshelf in the hall when I got back. Very nice.

Mon 10th -

Another quiz tonight. We had the following question:

'Which 18th century poet wrote the words to the hymn "Jerusalem"?'

I was in there like a shot.

'Leonard Cohen!'

(Kidding. This time I <u>did</u> put William Blake.)

Every year, this particular quiz has a Christmas raffle. Every year, it goes on too long. Tonight's didn't wrap up until nearly eleven. Nobody else seemed bothered, but then they're mostly retired and don't have to be awoken by their phone at 6.45am. Although, knowing old people, they've probably already been awake for three hours by that point, having washed the conservatory windows, de-iced the Viva and read several newspapers.

Once I'd bought my strip of raffle numbers, I noticed that the prizes (all neatly lined up in the pub's bay window) already had their winning numbers attached. I checked each one from a distance and was certain I saw one of my numbers - 433 - stuck to a box of orange Matchmakers. It was better than nothing. However, when the quiz was finished (we came sixtieth, or thereabouts), and the lucky numbers were being read out, I spotted someone walking off with my Matchmakers. The announcer kept calling numbers into the mic:

 'White 198?... Blue 275?... Blue 274?... Blue 273?... White 433...'

433! My number!

'Me!' I shouted, excited, confused and ashamed in equal measure. Maybe a prized-selection of orange Matchmakers was coming my way, after all.

A lady leaned into my orbit to hand me my winnings: a box onto which was written, 'The Art of Glass Painting'.

We're told not to look gift horses in their mouths, but I'm pretty sure that the rule is made void if the gift in question is a box onto which is written, 'The Art of Glass Painting'. I don't know what the devil to do with it. It almost certainly began life as an unwanted gift, before being donated to the raffle out of the goodness of the owner's heart. Now it's unwanted again. A team-mate suggested wrapping it up and giving it to someone else. No chance. I'd hate to be responsible for creating the look on their face as they opened it. There's enough hurt in the world.

There's always one table who win disproportionately big in raffles. They sit and laugh out loud each time they win something new, rubbing their newly acquired bath salt into the wound. Our table, with a grand total of twenty tickets, had 'The Art of Glass Painting' to show for its generous ticket-buying spirit.

I love watching people during a raffle. Even if they've only got one ticket and have memorised it, they'll still glance at it every time a number is read out, just to check that they haven't misread it. People sit there, smiling angrily and performing pantomime tuts, wondering aloud why they even bother when they 'never have been lucky at raffles'. The relief of the win, whatever the prize, must be rooted so deeply in the human psyche that the study of it would make a half decent proposal for a PHD. Even though I didn't want the bloody thing, I held 'The Art of Glass Painting' proudly under my arm as I exited.

Tues 11th -

No glass painted as yet.

- To Be Continued -

The 12 Things To Watch Of Christmas

#11

Home Alone

This holiday contender from John Hughes is too crass, too loud and too violent to be added blithely to Christmas viewing traditions.
Jeanne Cooper, *The Washington Post*, 1990

Before I knew of stage schools and pushy parents, I used to think child stars were plucked at random on their way to the sweet shop. I pictured limousines pulling up outside a Spar, and cigar-smoking backseat passengers leaning out of tinted windows, telling children they'd 'got what it takes' to 'make it' in movies. To which, the children would ignore the *Charlie Says* commercials and hop into the limo to follow their hitherto unmentioned Hollywood dreams.

No such limousine picked up Macauley Culkin. He took the traditional method of aspirational transport: stage school and pushy parents. By the time *Home Alone* began shooting, Culkin[1]

---

[1] Who, on Christmas Day 2018, vowed to change his middle name to Macauley Culkin after conducting a fan vote. He is now called Macauley 'Macauley Culkin' Culkin. Could've been worse. *I* voted for 'Macauley McMauleylauley McCulkin Jnr/Snr PhD', in the hope of giving copywriters a stroke just by typing his name. My suggestion garnered one vote, alas. Mine. My other suggestion was Attention Seeking Oddball, which, again, yielded disappointing returns.

was a haggard old pro with years of experience behind him.[1] A starlet from the same New York stage school that would produce the likes of Uma Thurman and Sarah Jessica Parker (and, for some reason, Anastasia), Culkin had been doing films and TV since the age of four. It was his role in 1989's *Uncle Buck* which would introduce him to *Home Alone*'s writer and producer, John Hughes. Hughes set about penning a script with Macauley Culkin in mind. *Home Alone*'s director, Chris Columbus, was happy with Hughes' choice:

'He doesn't look like one of these Hollywood-perfect kids,' Columbus said. 'His ear is bent a little bit. He had a great voice that was not annoying, it was just charming.'

If you haven't seen it, *Home Alone* is about a large Chicago family who go to Paris for Christmas and accidentally leave their son, Kevin, behind. Rather than knocking on his neighbour's door or calling the police from the nearest phonebox[2] - thereby ending the film after about twenty minutes - little Kevin McAllister goes it alone (at *home*). Thus begins what *The Sun* TV pullout might class as a 'knockabout romp' in which a ten-year-old boy sets about pretending to be an adult.

To add a touch of menace to the tale, the adult-free McAllister family property is targeted by two serial crooks. When little Kevin gets wind of the burglars' intentions, he once more

---

[1] Although he was still too young to be allowed to work later than 10pm. A legal requirement which created havoc for the number of night shoots *Home Alone* required.

[2] The family phone lines are destroyed in a snowstorm at the start of the movie, meaning Kevin can't make calls from home. He does, however, somehow manage to order lots of takeaway pizzas...

neglects the possibility of making a 911 call from a nearby phonebox and, instead, sets traps around the house.[1]

The crooks are played by Joe Pesci and Daniel Stern who perform the roles with a adroit measure of threat and vulnerability.[2] Pesci was so fond of using the f-word during filming that the production team had to teach him to use the word 'fridge' instead, on account of the children. Pesci took the role so fridging seriously that he made a point of not being seen by Culkin on set, so that whenever they met on camera, Culkin would retain a sincere sense of intimidation. The plan worked. Pesci scared the little fridger fridgeless.[3]

Back in the early 90s, I was close to Kevin's age. Our similarities ended there. Kevin's lifestyle was a dream, an unreachable Elysian field hidden a million Hollywood miles beyond the thick curved glass of the television screen. We had precious little, whereas the McAllister family had everything, exercising an off-the-hip wealth that made me drool: the cable television; the big bottles of milk and even bigger bottles of Coke; the $100 pizza deliveries (the only thing *we* had delivered were water rates). The McAllister's huge house and the array of cars didn't register with me. Nor did Mr McCallister's ability to

---

[1] The plot was later accused of plagiarism by the makers of a French movie with the simple-to-remember title, *3615 Code Père Noël*. The film is about a young boy who violently protects his grandfather from a dangerous Christmas invader.

[2] Robert De Niro reputedly turned the role of a burglar down.

[3] In one scene, Pesci bites Culkin's finger. 'During one of the rehearsals,' Culkin later revealed, 'he bit me, and it broke the skin.'

pay for about twenty people to spend Christmas in Paris.[1] It was the small stuff that got me. I suspect I may not have been the only scraggy child drawn to such aspirational luxuries under the concrete grey skies of Britain's forgettable, and largely forgotten, 1990-92 recession.

(If the McAllister household looks familiar to first-time viewers, by the way, it's because they may have seen it in any one of John Hughes' many 80s movies, among them, the impeccable *Planes, Trains & Automobiles*, *Ferris Bueller's Day Off*, *Sixteen Candles*, *Breakfast Club* and the aforementioned *Uncle Buck*. Many of the *Home Alone* interiors were shot in the actual house.[2])

What I was most jealous of, though, was Kevin's confidence. The way he microwaved his own macaroni cheese, tipped pizza deliverers and asked shopkeepers whether their toothbrushes were approved by the American Dental Association. And, of course, the way he defended his family's keep.

'I'm the man of the house,' he says, with Hollywood swagger.

Hollywood Swagger could've been the name of Culkin's autobiography, such was the impression he made on set. One young cast member said that the children all felt the pressure of

---

[1] Something that, in later years, has made me wonder long and hard precisely what it was Kevin's dad did for a living. The film is silent on the matter, but the novelisation claims he was a 'prominent businessman'. His mum, the book says, was a fashion designer. I hope she didn't design the clothes she wore on screen. She dresses like a curtain.

[2] You'd think the house - situated in a wealthy village way north of Chicago - would be a sought-after property. It was last sold in 2012 and went for just $1.5m. A million less than expected. In an age where a one-bed converted cinema toilet sells for £7.4m in Hackney, the building represents something of a bargain. Not least for its potential as a museum similar to that of the *A Christmas Story* house.

being in such a huge movie series. But, she argued, 'Imagine the pressure Macaulay had as a ten-year-old. He's the whole movie. He talks to himself in half of it. I can understand why he stepped away from the spotlight.'

Director Chris Columbus was equally in awe of Culkin, especially when he found out how messy the boy's home life was:

'We didn't know that much about the family at the beginning. As we were shooting, we learned a little more. The stories are hair-raising. I was casting a kid who truly had a troubled family life.'[1]

Home Alone proved to be a financial juggernaut, making around twenty-seven times its $18m budget at the box-office alone. For all its Christmassy sentiment, it was *still* the number 1 movie in America in February 1991, and was making the top 10 as late as June that year. By then, it was the third highest grossing movie of all time, behind only *E.T.* and *Stars Wars*. It should go without saying that the grouchy, quasi-intellectual mass of cinema reviewers were lukewarm to it on release. The public thought otherwise, deeming *Home Alone* an instant classic.[2] To this day, when screened on freeview, the movie will almost certainly become a trending topic on Twitter.[3] Aliens could be probing

---

[1] Nutshell: his dad was his agent and reportedly something of an unpleasant one. Macauley was one of seven children. They grew up in a two-bedroom apartment. The father is now said to live 'in exile', like Napoleon.

[2] A friend told me that people were being mugged for copies outside his local Blockbuster in Slough the night it was released on rental VHS. This might say more about Slough than it does about the film, though.

[3] Indie band, The Staves, even released a song in 2018 which featured the chorus, *'Are you watching Home Alone, too?'*

Boris Johnson on the doorstep of 10 Downing Street and *Home Alone* would *still* force its way to the top of the national discourse:

'OMG - Home Alone is on E4!!!! #xmas #prayforboris'

Home Alone has spawned four sequels. The second, featuring Macauley Culkin, is a watchable, near-enough joke-for-joke remake of the first. The other three are straight to DVD non-entities. None get close to the charm of the original, with its snappy one-liners and heavily festive colour-coding.[1]

A multi-millionaire - a literal *Richie Rich* - by the time he was ten, Macauley Culkin was so desperate for a normal life that he retired from acting, aged fifteen, and voluntarily enrolled in high school. He has only occasionally emerged from his shell, usually with TV cameos (such as in *Will & Grace*) and minor movie roles. Aged eighteen, the millions he accrued for his childhood performances went into his bank account in one lump sum:

'I felt like some kid worked really, really hard and I inherited all of his money,' he said in 2018. Despite recent stories about his relative paucity, he remains wealthy enough to never need work again and, in his own words, can treat everything he does 'as a hobby'.

Recent 'hobbies' have included TV wrestling appearances and forming his own rock band, The Pizza Undergrounds, who specialise in covers of Velvet Underground songs with key

---

[1] From the wallpaper to the clothes, almost everything in *Home Alone* is either red, white or green. Check it out for yourself. It does sort of ruin the film, though.

words changed to make pizza-related puns.[1] Culkin's more noteworthy moments in the public eye include appearing in court to defend Michael Jackson[2] and being arrested - and briefly imprisoned - for possession of marijuana. Now living in Paris (like a true McAllister), he is understandably keen to distance himself from his *Home Alone* persona, making his 2018 appearance in an advert for Google an unexpected treat. The ad featured Culkin as a fully grown Kevin McCallister, using Google's voice-activated commands to do all of the neat little tricks from the movie on his behalf (turning the lights on and off, activating the furnace etc.).

Appearing in the *Home Alone* franchise was a largely positive experience for the children involved. However, some were scarred by the experience. Diana Rein, who played Kevin's sister, Sondra (a cross between Sonia and Sandra?), suffered from a sense of anti-climax:

'It created an addict out of me, in the sense that I was always looking for my next "fix" to book something. It sent me on a twenty-year journey that I gave everything to, without getting much in return. It messed with my sense of self-worth. I was always looking outside of myself for validation.'

---

[1] The band started when, according to their drummer, 'We realised you can replace most any word with "slice" or "cheese"!' Some of their songs include: *Take a Bite of the Wild Slice* and *Pizza Gal*, which, believe it or not, is supposed to be a play on *Femme Fatale*. The band cancelled their UK tour around eight seconds into their first gig, after being subjected to a not wholly undeserving barrage of beer and swear words (although I don't exactly know what the audience were expecting when they bought tickets).

[2] The young Culkin had slept in Jackson's bed but claimed there was nothing untoward going on, other than the fact he was sleeping with an adult man.

Imagine how much more trying it was for Macauley 'Macauley Culkin' Culkin, getting pushed into movie roles by his father, appearing in Michael Jackson videos (and beds) and hosting Saturday Night Live, aged eleven. Fame. Fortune. The stuff of dreams. Until they come true.

We shouldn't pity him, of course. He'll be idling about in Paris with his 'hobbies' for the rest of his young life, whereas you and I will have our dreams coldly awoken by an alarm clock most days. Including first-thing tomorrow morning.

John Hughes' run of hit movies have come to define 1980s America. He was on top of the world by the time the 90s rolled around. As well as some of the films already mentioned, Hughes also had a hand in the majority of the *National Lampoon* movies, as well as *Weird Science* and *Pretty In Pink*. Then, out of nowhere, he stopped making movies. He retreated to the north country and lived on a farm, meticulously keeping notebooks of ideas and jokes, with little obvious goal in mind. He occasionally emerged to write a handful of scripts (*Baby's Day Out*, *Flubber* and *Maid In Manhattan* among them) but was otherwise a recluse, by Hollywood standards. Many believe that the shock death of John Candy, whom Hughes had cast in so many of his films, including *Home Alone*, had ended his love affair with the industry.

'He talked a lot about how much he loved Candy,' said his friend, Vince Vaughn. 'If Candy had lived longer, I think John would have made more films as a director.'[1]

---

[1] Candy's performance in Hughes' *Planes, Trains & Automobiles* is up there with any other lead comedy performance you could care to mention.

As an example of John Candy's talent, take the following improvised speech, included in the final edit of *Home Alone* after a long day's shooting:[1]

Mum: But tell me, have you ever gone on vacation and left your child at home?

Gus: I did leave one at a funeral parlour once. Yeah, it was terrible, too. I was all distraught and everything. The wife and I, we left the little tyke there in the funeral parlour all day. All day. You know, we went back at night, when we came to our senses, there he was. Apparently he was there all day with a corpse. Now, he was OK. You know, after six, seven weeks, he came around and started talking again. But he's OK. They get over it. Kids are resilient like that...

Whereas most John Hughes films serve as quirky timepieces, *Home Alone* still feels fresh. Why, I can't quite say. The jokes are still funny. The set-pieces are still clever. The violence is still shocking.[2] Most importantly, little Kevin McCallister is still completely charming.

John Hughes died of a heart attack whilst out taking pictures for his notebooks in New York in 2009. What projects he had in mind are unknown. Whether they would have ever seen the light of day is another matter. His career blossomed and wilted in synchronisation with many of his leading stars, including Macauley 'Macauley Culkin' Culkin. Hughes was happy with things being that way. An easier approach to take, I guess, if you'd created *Home Alone*.

---

[1] All of John Candy's *Home Alone* scenes were filmed within a gruelling twenty-four hour period.

[2] I can still *hear* the steam-iron falling.

The Christmas Alphabet

R is for...

Radio Times

As you may have gathered, I grew up in front of the television. I was photosynthesised by its light. I'm not ashamed of this. Television lives in my bones and breathes through my skin. All items of furniture in my lounge face it; humble wooden primitives praying to their Sun God. And if television *is* Lord of the lounge, then the *Christmas Radio Times* is its bible: words written by man but whispered by the Spirit.

Just like God, the *Radio Times* has a dwindling fanbase. First released in 1923, the magazine[1] was classed at the time, somewhat oddly, as the 'official organ of the BBC' (whether there were any bootleg organs knocking about, it's hard to say). When television schedules were added in 1936, it became the world's first TV guide. Television listings took priority over radio listings for the first time in 1953, and it was suggested that the magazine's name be changed to the *TV Times*. The idea was rejected from up-top on the basis that television was merely a fad. Two years later, ITV joined the broadcasting game. They had their own magazine. They called it *TV Times*. This did nothing to dent the *Radio Times'* popularity. It remained

---

[1] To be strictly accurate, it wasn't a magazine in 1923. It was printed on one sheet of paper. Newspapers were initially reluctant to provide radio schedules because they saw the new medium as a threat, so the BBC had to print their own.

Europe's biggest selling magazine for many years. Modern circulation figures, alas, are down drastically.[1] Yet, in another Christian parallel, it is Christmas which draws the congregation back to its church and offers renewed hope. The Christmas *RT* sells around two million copies[2] and generates profits of £7million. Once Christmas passes, though, the churchgoers lose their zeal, allowing the voice of the non-Christmas *Radio Times* editions to echo around a hollow church, into the large ears of its faithful, elderly minority.

Ah, the feel of it in my hands. That sweet, grainy *Christmas Radio Times* paper. That extra weighty festive bulk, like a big, fat, happy grandfather who's eaten too much raspberry trifle. It's crammed with page upon page of my two favourite things: Christmas and television. Each year upon purchasing, I pore over the schedules, circling potential highlights in biro. It's tragic and glorious.

Jerry Seinfeld once called the TV guide, 'The world's most thrown reading material - always thrown, never handed, to another person.' By the end of the week, a regular TV guide is usually in such a state that it can only be identified by its dental records. It gets thrown, kicked, sat on and used as a coaster. My *Christmas Radio Times*, on the other hand, never receives such shoddy treatment. The closest it comes to being violated is

---

[1] It shifts about 500,000 copies a week, which is still good going by today's standards. However, at the start of this decade it had a million sales a week. In the 1950s, it sold about nine million. A week.

[2] Albeit down from its all-time high of 11,220,000 sales in Christmas 1988. This wasn't just a high for *Radio Times*. It was an historic high for print media. It remains the biggest selling issue of *any* British magazine ever.

when I carefully remove the '*RT Summer Holiday Guide*' from the middle.[1]

The *Christmas Radio Times* goes into a charming amount of detail about each programme. Surely no other publication would tell you that, among the show's other stars, the December 28th episode of *Coronation Street* features a receptionist played by Christina Biscuit. Or that the BBC's major seasonal Agatha Christie adaptation, *Largely Pointless Murder At The Vicarage*, has minor characters called 'Aloof Man' played by Jonny Ballbag and 'Concerned Woman In Vestry' played by Jenny Haddock. It's all totally unnecessary information, exclusively of interest to the actors in question. Their involvement is of zero artistic merit, but how sweet it is that the *Radio Times* slips them a mention. It makes me want to stand and sing the national anthem.

The covers of regular TV guides are a sloppy concoction of spoilers and photo-shopped images of soap stars in which the heads are too big for the bodies. They use colour schemes so bright they make blind people squint. And their pages have a horrible fragrance. They smell of boredom. A mixture of Sundays, ink, vinegar and rat urine. The *Christmas Radio Times*, alternatively, smells like yesteryear and powdered kittens.

Despite being bought from the BBC by the vaguely dystopian-sounding Immediate Media Company, the *Radio Times* remains a Christmas tradition. When I last wrote about the magazine in 2012, the changeover had yet to fully take hold. My concerns, at the time, were that the magazine would have more adverts and

---

[1] The *Holiday Guide* is the only flaw in the Christmas *Radio Times'* evolution, an untimely reminder of the transitory nature of Christmas. I hate seeing it. Removing this appendix is a dangerous operation. One false move and the staples could fall out and spill the guts of the TV listings. If you try and yank it out in one quick go, like a magician with a tablecloth, you risk tearing the inner scripture.

flyers and lose its sparkle. It seems as though there are indeed more adverts now and, when you open the magazine, one does get rained by on promotional leaflets for hearing aids and Madagascan cruises, but, generally, not too much has changed. Other than the price. Since 2012, the cost has increased by around 40p each year. 2019's Christmas issue, should the trend continue, will cost £5.30, compared to £2.80 in 2012. With so demanding a collection plate, it's no wonder the church is gradually emptying. Even Jenny Haddock and Johnny Ballbag must think twice before buying a copy.

Reindeer, Rudolph The Red-Nosed

When Chicagoan copywriter Robert L. May was contacted by big city retailer Montgomery Ward[1] to write something for inclusion in their 1939 Christmas' colouring book,[2] he struggled for inspiration. The brief was brief. Montgomery Ward wanted something family-friendly and, ideally, featuring an animal. Desperately looking out of his Chicago office window for inspiration, out across mighty Lake Michigan, May could see only thick, grisly fog.

'Suddenly I had it,' he recalled. 'A nose. A bright red nose that would shine through fog like a spotlight.'

But what creature to use? May had an idea for that, too. Inspired, he claimed, by his daughter's love of the reindeer at Chicago zoo (and most definitely *not* by the fact that everybody associated reindeer with Christmas already), he set to work on

---

[1] Sort of an American Argos.

[2] The company gave their young customers a free Christmas gift each year. Usually a book, until they realised it was cheaper to make their own instead of buying brand new ones.

his narrative poem. Torn between the names Rollo, Reginald and Rudolph, he opted for the latter. At each stage of the writing process, he would read the latest parts of the story to his daughter and cancer-stricken wife to get their feedback.[1] Yet, their positive response did nothing to subdue a swelling sense of gloom in the young writer.

The stress of the terrible illness affecting the love of his life was taking its toll. Walking along icy cold Chicago streets on his way to work each day did little for morale.

'Here I was,' May reflected many years later, 'heavily in debt at thirty-five, still grinding out catalogue copy instead of writing the great American novel.'

As befitting the tone of practically every other chapter in this book, May's wife died later that year. Montgomery Ward suggested the job of writing their Christmas book went to someone else. May disagreed and set to work finishing the story.

'I needed Rudolph now more than ever,' the author recalled. 'Gratefully, I buried myself in the writing.'

Robert L. May came from a hardworking family. His parents had had their fortune wiped by the Great Depression. Their son - 'a sad guy', as his own daughter would later describe him - had lofty, silent dreams of restoring the family fortune. He could never have foreseen how his Christmas creation would serve as a light for his own cerebral fog.

After wariness from Montgomery Ward about a children's character having a red nose - an affliction associated with alcoholism and a life well-lived - the company published May's story of the red-nosed reindeer at Christmas 1939, giving it away to over two million children. Held up in the early 1940s by paper restrictions as the result of some international conflict or other, Rudolph's tale didn't appear again until 1946, when

---

[1] Yeah, I know. Obviously, there had to be *some* tragedy involved.

Montgomery Ward gave a further four million copies away. Soon, Rudolph became so popular that the story was published as a bona fide children's book (after Montgomery Ward *very* generously gave Robert L. May the Rudolph copyright). Many people in publishing thought it something of a risk to sell a book that had previously been given away for free, but the re-release was a smash hit, too, and was followed by a 1949 song, written by May's brother-in-law.

Performed by the singing cowboy, Gene Autry,[1] the melodic *Rudolph The Red-Nosed Reindeer* raced to the top of the charts[2] and has since sold, with its many cover versions included, somewhere in the region of 150 million records.[3] Until the 1980s, it was the second biggest selling single of all-time, behind *White Christmas*. In its path came Rudolph cartoons, Rudolph TV specials[4] and Rudolph merchandise. Robert L. May's simple underdog story - 'a story of acceptance,' as he called it - about an outcast reindeer with an alcohol problem, guiding Santa through the fog, ensured the May family were led out of their own Great Depression and had turkey on their festive table evermore.

And if the above tale isn't made into a Hollywood movie sometime, then I don't know what the world's coming to.

❄

---

[1] Whose wife convinced the reluctant star to record it.

[2] And raced straight back *out* again as soon as Christmas was over. It remains the only song to go from number 1 to nowhere in the space of a week.

[3] Surprisingly, the Destiny's Child version is the best.

[4] Including a 1964 claymation movie which is as legendary in the US as *The Snowman* is over here.

As we're clearly in no rush, permit me to pump you with some less inspiring Christmas trivia regarding flying festive creatures. The idea is thought to originate from the Norse god Odin, who rode around on an eight-legged horse whilst a raven perched on each of his shoulders. Children would leave food out for the horse at Christmas to convince Odin to fly down to ground level and leave presents. The tradition continues today in Denmark, Belgium and the Netherlands, where many children still believe that horses pull Santa's sleigh instead of reindeer.

That *we* have reindeer, not horses, in our British Christmas narrative is largely down to the popular American poem *A Visit From St Nicholas* - better known as *'Twas The Night Before Christmas* - which features the lines:

When, what to my wondering eyes should appear
But a miniature sleigh, and eight tiny rein-deer
With a little old driver, so lively and quick
I knew in a moment it must be St. Nick

More rapid than eagles his coursers they came
And he whistled, and shouted, and call'd them by name:
'Now, Dasher! Now, Dancer! Now, Prancer, and Vixen!
On, Comet! On, Cupid! On, Dunder and Blixem!'

Now, I don't know about you, but I much prefer these simple little lines:

Then one foggy Christmas Eve
Santa came to say
'Rudolph, with your nose so bright
Won't you guide my sleigh tonight?'

❄❄❄❄

Richard, Cliff

It's a time for giving, a time for getting
A time for forgiving and for forgetting

Cliff Richard, *Mistletoe & Wine*, 1989

Cliff Richard: a name as entwined with a British yuletide as Father Christmas. Yet, for all the furore, Cliff's only had three Christmas number 1s, and one of those was the non-festive ballad, *I Love You*, in 1960. For all who bemoan the modern paucity of Christmas-themed songs, it's worth pointing out that from the chart's beginnings in 1952, right through to Slade's 1973 superhit, *Merry Christmas Everybody*, there were only *two* festive-themed number 1 singles in the UK.[1] The rest of the Christmas number 1s were the usual blend of novelties, ballads and beat music.

Cliff's other Christmas chart-toppers - *Mistletoe & Wine* and *Saviour's Day* - were released in 1988 and 1990 respectively. As much as it pains me to say it, both singles were released a *long* time ago. So, why does Sir Cliff have such an affiliation with Christmas? His turkey-like neck aside, it is most likely because he outdoes everybody when it comes to *attempting* to get to Christmas number 1.

Sir Cliff didn't start releasing Christmas-themed records until 1982, when he was already twenty-four years deep into his career.[2] It was a pop reworking of *O Little Town of Bethlehem* and it reached number 11. His next Christmas song was *Mistletoe &*

---

[1] Harry Belafonte's saccharine *Mary's Boy Child* and Dickie Valentine's completely forgotten *Christmas Alphabet*. I can only hope my own Christmas alphabet ages better.

[2] Although you could argue, if you gave a hoot, that his hideously sentimental 1981 smash hit, *Daddy's Home*, was the first.

Wine, six years later.[1] Then he charted in an unlikely 1989 duet with Van Morrison (*Whenever God Shines His Light*) which got to number 20. 1990 gave us the number 1, *Saviour's Day*. Since then, we've had *We Should Be Together*, *I Still Believe In You*, *The Millennium Prayer*,[2] *Santa's List* and *21st Century Christmas*.[3] Even though these songs didn't necessarily all hit the high spots, they would be an annual reminder of Cliff's existence. He has also put out a number of Christmas albums, one of which contains an electro version of *Walking In The Air* deserving of a listen for its kookiness alone.

For a man who strives to be associated with Christmas, you can't help but think of Sir Cliff spending his Christmas Day by a cheery fireside, sipping sherry, eating sprouts, singing carols and waiting for the Queen's Speech. Not a bit of it. The old hound slinks off to his villa in Barbados each year and sees hide nor hair of mistletoe, but, I expect, does enjoy the wine.

---

[1] A song taken from a 70s musical called *Scraps* which had been broadcast on ITV in 1987. Cliff liked the song but thought the lyrics a little too risqué and rewrote them, giving them a Christian makeover. *Mistletoe & Wine* went on to sell 750,000 copies. As a neat comparison, 2018's Christmas number 1, *We Built This City On Sausage Rolls*, sold 75,000 copies.

[2] A grim combination of the Lord's Prayer set to the tune of *Auld Lang Syne*, which made number 1 before *and* after Christmas, but lost out to Westlife on the big day.

[3] *21st Century Christmas* was kept off number 1 only by the chart's recent decision to include download sales. In terms of physical sales, it was 2006's biggest festive hit. A fact that would come back to haunt Cliff as his astonishing streak of having an original number 1 single in every decade since the 1950s came to an end in the noughties.

Royal Speech

Alf: She has to have her Christmas dinner late cos of doin' that speech.
She has to go up to the BBC.
Else: They keep it warm for her, though!

Til Death Us Do Part, 'Peace & Goodwill', 1966

From Cliff to Elizabeth. One old queen to another. I was originally going to put this entry under Q for Queen's speech, then realised that maybe there wouldn't be too many Queen speeches left. Although not a royalist by any stretch, the idea made me a little sad. I'm not sure I could stomach the wattle lines on King Charles III's neck after a heavy turkey-based meal. At least Sir Cliff has the decency to hide his neck in Barbados.

The Queen's Speech now appears in TV listings under a host of different titles. Each is quite telling about its respective channel. The stately BBC One call it *The Queen's Christmas Broadcast*; ITV call it *HM The Queen*, making it sound like one of their made-for-TV thrillers starring Patrick Stewart (never trust a man with two Christian names) and Robson Green (never trust a man with two surnames); Sky One fawningly call it *The Queen's Christmas Message*; and Channel 5 call it *World's Strongest Man: Heats*. What none of the channels call it is a 'Speech'. This must be down to the heads of each station having a distinct lack of faith in the average spam-headed Great Briton to be enticed to watch something with so dour a word as 'Speech' in its title. *HM The Queen*, on the other hand...

The first royal broadcast - or whatever the devil you want to call it - was given by the Queen's grandfather, George V, on

BBC radio in 1932.[1] The speeches began as way of uniting the Commonwealth. It's for this reason that the broadcast has always aired at around 3pm, as this was considered the most satisfactory time to reach the farthest flung corners of the Empire. After his father passed away, bad-mouthing Bognor in the process, stammering George VI grabbed hold of the speech-giving reins until 1952. Then his daughter had a go and acquired something of a taste for it. She's done one every year since, with the first televised broadcast in 1957, a move which, she hoped, 'will make my Christmas message more personal and more direct.'[2] Originally screened exclusively on the BBC, the Windsors agreed to share the broadcast rights of the Christmas speech with other channels in 1997. It's believed that they did so in response to the BBC's decision to air the still-electrifying *Panorama* interview with Princess Diana that year.

Don't mess with the Queen.

---

[1] The speech was written by Rudyard Kipling and may have contained sentiments along the lines of, 'If you can write your own speech, what with all the free time one has had to potter around Sandringham estate since late autumn, you'll be a man, my son'. The Queen, out of interest, writes her own, and is such an old pro that she's famous in the biz for nailing her delivery in one take.

[2] She'd changed her tune by 1969, when she felt the family had been over-exposed due to their appearance in a TV documentary. 30.6m people watched the programme, with its clips of the family doing the simple things of life. One controversial scene showed the Queen buying an ice cream with hard cash, which, the legend goes, she supposedly never carries. The documentary was so disliked by the royal family that it is *still* unavailable for their lowly subjects to watch. In order to see it, one must do so for official scholarly reasons and be prepared to pay a small fee to the BBC for the honour (it'd be tempting to ask the cheeky buggers to deduct the sum from your TV license quarterly).

In what is, I suggest, a more telling indictment of the quality of terrestrial television's output rather than a reflection of ma'am's popularity, the Queen's 2018 speech was the most watched programme on Christmas Day. It pulled in 6.4 million viewers. Catch-up viewers increased the figure to around 7 million.[1] (By contrast, on Christmas Day in 1986, 19 million people watched *Eastenders*. By the time the repeat of *that* was aired, the viewership had grown to over 30 million.)

Charmingly – and so as not to end on a bum note – while her family gather around the Sandringham television set[2] to watch her speech, the Queen will sometimes get up and go into a different room to view the broadcast alone, away from any distraction. It's her own method of quality control.

S is for...

Salvation Army

'Soap, soup and salvation.' Those were the reasons the Salvation Army first went to war on the streets of east London in 1865. To cleanse the dirty. To feed the hungry. And to lessen congestion in and around Hades.

Originally known as the Christian Mission, their aim was to bring the word of the Lord to the east-enders, giving hope to 'society's most vulnerable and marginalised' e.g. Nick Cotton, Phil Mitchell, Dirty Den et al. The difference being that the Christian Mission wanted to offer practical help, rather than the dreaded *thoughts and prayers* of other denominations. They gave people food, places to stay, career advice and just about

---

[1] By which time, it had slipped down to fourth most-watched.

[2] On hire from Curry's. £22 a month.

anything else they could reasonably require. Soon, the good fight was fought beyond London and the name 'Christian Mission' was ditched for the more eye-opening 'Salvation Army': a name which was quickly stripped of all potency by being shortened to the painfully friendly sounding 'Sally Army'.

In keeping with their new military theme, Salvation Army members/troops were kitted out with forces-like uniforms. Discreetly, politely, their army invaded most of the western world, setting up barracks across the USA, Canada and Europe. Their weekly newspaper, *The War Cry*, still shifts around 40,000 copies per issue and is priced at a highly competitive 20p.[1]

But it is their music I want to talk about: the very sound of Christmas. What British high street would be complete without the warm, brassy toots of the local Sally Army band on a clear-blue Saturday morning in December? Seeing them there, standing in a circle, in their dark regalia, as though about to depart for Sevastopol, is one of life's true joys. So many Christmas traditions are performed for the sake of it, but the Salvation Army's gently-fudged renditions of *Hark The Herald Angel Sing*, *Deck The Halls* and alike are essential pieces of our December jigsaw. Something about a chilly morning makes the sound of their slow and steady brass piping carry across an entire town. Their music is just as sweet and warming from a distance as it is close up. It's only a soul of the stuffiest nature that could fail to be stirred by its beauty.

❄ ❄ ❄

[1] The majority of issues are sold in pubs towards closing time, when the Army's hardy soldiers visit the hot, drunken saloons of Britain in full get-up; it's a sight which can shock some particularly *merry* old timers into thinking that Operation Sea Lion has finally reached its key phase.

Selection Box

Whenever I see clips of plastic clogging up the waves on some distant utopian beach, the first thing I wonder is how much of the plastic has come from my own selection boxes. I've received at least two selection boxes per year since as long as I can remember, and each has had either a plastic backing or a plastic interior casing. If my maths is correct, that's enough non-biodegradable material to disrupt the flow of at least one tropical rivulet.

I'm not the only one donating such a shameful gift to the earth's ecosystem. Once a costly treat in the Edwardian age, by the mid-to-late 20th century, selection boxes were cheap and cheerful presents which sold by the millions.

So much plastic. And it's all still out there somewhere, floating about.

My favourite selection boxes - if you'll permit me to momentarily focus on a positive - were imitation stockings. The very thought of them takes me back to the 1980s. Sock-shaped, they had a white netted cover and a red plastic backing. I can even tell you what was in them: a Mars, a Marathon, a Topic, a blue Bounty, a red Bounty, a Twix, Opal Fruits and Skittles.[1] And there was none of this modern fun-size malarky going on. The chocolate bars were plump and the Twix had *two* fingers. Two fingers which - I'd like to think - were both raised to their modern day counterparts, but which were, more likely, both raised to the distant utopian beach mentioned above.

---

[1] You can see one such stocking hanging on the wall of Geraldine's cottage in the 1996 *Vicar Of Dibley* Christmas special. Oh, I've put some research into this bloody book.

Snow

'It was snowing. It was always snowing at Christmas. December, in my memory, is white as Lapland.'

Dylan Thomas, *A Child's Christmas In Wales*, 1952

Each year in the run-up to Christmas, I nightly check the BBC Weather Twitter feed for the link to their latest long-range forecast. It's the ultimate self-inflicted pain for a festive romantic. I don't know why I do it. The Christmas weather pattern is near-enough identical every year: a cold and frosty early December; a less cold and frosty mid-December; then, four or five days before the big one, the quick jab of the forecaster's dagger:

'Notice the change in the pressure patterns. This means the air will be coming off the Atlantic, an altogether milder direction...'

If you believe the statisticians, then we've had ten widespread white Christmases in the last fifty years. *I* haven't had one in thirty-five years, though, so there must have been a hell of a lot of snow in the 1970s. What's happening here, of course, is that white Christmases are being declared on the flimsiest of technicalities. The Met Office's official definition is for 'one snowflake to be observed falling in the 24-hours of 25th December somewhere in the UK'.

One snowflake. And we rarely manage that.

The problem is that idiots like me have been brainwashed by Christmas cards. We've seen too many Victorian landscapes with children skating on frozen lakes or sledging down hillsides under pink skies. Based on no empirical evidence, I grew up thinking Christmas was usually white and fluffy, and that *I'd* just been unlucky. I didn't figure the ruse out for a good few years. As far as I'm concerned, snow-laden Christmas cards breach the Trade Descriptions Act. To quote Greg Lake, 'They sold me a dream of Christmas'. And to quote S Club 7, sort of, 'I've never had that particular dream come true'.

By law, Christmas cards should be more realistic. Instead of cheery snowscapes, they ought to depict middle-aged men in t-shirts, walking their dogs. Instead of light-footed robins tip-toeing on icicled branches, they should show my granny turning the thermostat down. There should be less of this Santa-in-a-sleigh nonsense, too. He really doesn't need one; no child in England would be able to sleep for the sound of it screeching on the parched tarmac, scaring the shit out of the tomcats.

The movies are equally misleading. I can't think of a Christmas film that doesn't involve a glimpse of snow somewhere along the way. Even the ground around the office tower in *Die Hard* has a fresh layer - and that's a Christmas film about terrorism.

Everything about a mild Christmas makes me that bit grumpier: the taking off of jumpers; the opening of windows; the comments about the ironically named snowdrops coming through at the bottom of the garden. My mum lights a coal fire every Christmas Day. It looks jolly festive but by mid-afternoon the heat is insufferable, like Rio De Janeiro in carnival season. Our turkey voluntarily gets in the oven to cool down. The portraits on the wall drip with sweat, before mutating into something resembling a Dali.

I'm not greedy. I don't necessarily need a *white* Christmas. I'd gladly settle for a relatively cold one. Something non-mild. Just anything other than these relentless last-minute swings to unseasonable warmth. My fantasy is that one year, just one bloody year, the presenter of the long-range forecast will turn to the camera and say, *'Make the most of the mild weather because things are about to change. Beginning on Christmas Eve...'*

My ultimate yuletide nightmare would be the rest of the country getting a white Christmas but my own town missing out. It's bad enough when such injustice happens outside of the Christmas period, having to watch on as the nation slips into cosy lockdown, posting their photographs of snowmen and log-fires on Facebook whilst rain hammers against my window. But to wake on Christmas morning, with rumours of snow in the air, then open my curtains to reveal a bog-standard wet mess, oh, it would break me. Rain is at its ugliest when forecast as snow. Its cold, soppy flaws are more pronounced. I mean, have you ever tried making a rainman instead of a snowman? There's no comparison. Although, admittedly, the former is much better at remembering phone numbers.

Incredibly, there are some oddballs out there who hate snow. I can't understand it. It's not as if it's a constant blight. 'One bit of snow and the whole country grinds to a halt,' they tut. Is this a bad thing? Grinding to a halt is something we don't do enough. On Christmas morning this year, millions of us will unwrap next year's wall-calendars. Nearly every day between this Christmas and next will be dedicated to work. Employment is a thankless slog for most. Anything that offers a rare excuse to stay indoors - wearing novelty slippers and watching *The Repair Shop* - should be embraced.

For me, there's nothing more beguiling than the cloaked silence of an early morning snow, that interlocking of magic and reality, God among us, and whatnot. Snow mutes the workaday world. It commands a curious respect, whatever date it falls. But I'm not embarrassed to admit that I will forever long for it to do so on *the* big day. To hear the silence of an early Christmas morning silenced further still by a layer of snow. The quiet upon quiet. Ah. If that day should ever come...

Sprouts, Brussels

Notice the plural? Brussels not Brussel. I always call them Brussel sprouts, but they do originate from medieval Brussels. Possibly. Mysteriously, the Romans are thought to have had them, too. They boiled them all day to keep their homes warm and the scent inadvertently drove them insane. Hang on, I might be getting sprouts confused with lead piping.

Lolz aside, the Romans really *did* have sprouts. It's just the Belgians were the ones to properly corner the market in those smelly mini-cabbages.[1] It must be odd for a city to be most famous for its association with a lumpy brassica. Paris conjures up images of artisans smoking in all-night cafés. London offers up red phone-boxes, theatres, and corridors of power. Brussels makes you think of farts.

For all their goodness - more vitamin C than you'll find in an orange - sprouts are synonymous with wind. Bad wind. The sort of wind that could clear a Tokyo subway station for fear of a gas attack. The sort of wind that requires you to physically cock your leg up beforehand, lest it make your pants pop. The safest thing to do when a sprout emission brews is pretend you hear the doorbell and get yourself outside, away from society, and unleash it in cold air. That way, no one gets upset. Although the honking and quacking *can* dupe the neighbours into thinking that a skein of wild geese are flying overhead, tempting them all out into the garden, binoculars in hand.

Despite the social faux pas they create, sprouts are regular guests at our Christmas dinner tables. The sprout industry is worth somewhere in the region of £650million. Their popularity is likely due to how simple they are to grow and how kindly they respond to inclement weather. It's thought that, rather than killing them off, a good frost only serves to make them tastier. Why it is they have a specific Christmas association is harder to deduce. The Victorians certainly drew attention to them, fascinated by the technological feat these

---

[1] I'm not being loose with that term, sprouts *are* mini-cabbages and nothing more. Don't let them try and tell you differently as you toss them into the pot.

miniature cabbages represented.[1] But that's about all the info we've got. Whatever the reason for their festive prevalence, sprouts are here to stay.

Excuse me, won't you, I think I just heard the doorbell.

Stockings

Here's yet another tradition that has its earliest *recorded* roots in Clement C. Moore's poem, *'Twas The Night Before Christmas*.[2] The true origins, however, are believed to be from St Nicholas, who, Turkish legend goes, overheard the financial struggles of a family and snuck into their house, down the chimney, and slipped gold into their stockings.[3] The reason why people put oranges in their stockings in later centuries was to represent the gold once left by St Nicholas. He was one of the most popular saints long before Christmas became a commercial phenomenon. Around eight hundred churches in England are named after the Turkish do-gooder.

Today, most families use stockings as decorations only. For a start, they don't have much give; anybody who's tried to fit a snooker table into a novelty sock will know that. Much more popular now are 'Santa Sacks'; these store-bought bumper-sized plastic bags - with a picture of Father Christmas on the front -

---

[1] They often ate their sprouts on toast.

[2] A poem that Moore was less than fond of, going so far as to pretend for decades that he didn't write it. Some people still think he didn't, claiming it was stolen from a newspaper. The poem *was* suspiciously jolly by Moore's standards, a known grouch and vehement advocate of slavery.

[3] Sounds like he was up to no good to me. His name was 'Nick', after all.

have the capacity to placate even the most demanding of cherubs. In our family, we took the secret third option and used to leave empty pillow cases out on the landing for our jolly visitor to fill. Times were hard.

Stocking Fillers

A little girl called Silé Javotte
Said 'Look at the lovely presents I've got'
While a little girl in Biafra said
'Oh, what a lovely slice of bread'

Spike Milligan, Christmas, 1970

Perhaps nothing best sums up the evolution of Christmas than the term 'stocking filler'. Taken at face value, it means something which fills a stocking. In its modern guise, though, it means 'presents which aren't the *main* presents': the gift-giving equivalent of a starter. I ended the last entry by saying that times were hard because I *only* got a pillow case full of presents as a boy. Rewind a hundred years and I'd have bitten your hand off just to own a pillow, let alone a case with which to fill with presents once a year.

 Like the Christmas Eve Box, the calibre of stocking fillers has mutated in recent years. Now you'll see things like computer games (£50) and trainers (£70) advertised as stocking fillers. To me, stocking fillers ought to be genuinely cheap and cheerful. When I was kid, I knew no different. I had no idea of the gulf in value between a box of crayons and a Lego set. And, anyway, I thought they all came from the unassailable decisions made by Mr Claus. So, even if I thought my elder sisters *had* trumped me in the value stakes, I knew I was in no position to question it. I'm not saying parents should stop spending money just because I wasn't the recipient of great riches, but I do think they could cash in on children's innate angelic innocence[1] a bit more.

I remember seeing a critique of Charles Dickens which said that you knew he was being lazy when he described things in list form. Well, if it's good enough for Dickens, it's good enough for me. Here are some of the 'stocking fillers' we used to get in our house:

Selection boxes; crayons; colouring books (thick, wholesome things printed onto grey, rough paper); plastercine (not Play-Doh, but a long box of ribbed, girthy strips of different colours which would all end up in one dull coloured ball); my very own mug; pencil cases; velvet art (with four felt tips sellotaped together); a cassette single (I had *Slam Jam* by the WWF wrestlers and *Mr Blobby*); then a main present, along the lines of a personal stereo or a board game or a car with flashing lights. And, naturally, batteries. Wrapped. My car wasn't going to flash without those now, was it?

---

[1] Soft-headedness.

The Yule Log

DECEMBER - Part Two

Weds 12th -

Awoke in the middle of last night in a hot sweat. It ought to have been a cold sweat but the reason I woke so suddenly was I'd left the heating on. In that disturbed, panicky way one does in the dead of night, I ran to turn it off with the same urgency I'd employ to escape a ticking bomb. Thoughts flashed in my mind about how much money I'd wasted. In my midnight stupor, I was thinking it would be about £40. In the morning, I realised it would be closer to £4.

It was an apt start to what has been a lousy day. A succession of bad things. None of them major, but all enough to convince me that bedtime will be the highlight. That's if I remember to switch the heating off. The last act of the day will be watching Manchester United. Doesn't bode well. They're not shy of tainting even the best of days.

[Note: As soon as I finished writing this, I checked my emails. A bill from Vodafone and another from British Gas.

And United lost 2-1.]

Thurs 13th -

We're beyond the halfway point. Twelve days left. Heard Shakin' Stevens' Christmas song on the radio. What a great tune. I only wish snow <u>was</u> falling all around us. I love the lyric 'Room is swaying, records playing'. The idea of <u>records</u> playing, rather than Echo Dots, is so sweetly old fashioned.

Remembered today how a girl in my playgroup once told us about how she'd seen Father Christmas delivering presents on the landing on Christmas Eve. Awoken by the sound of sleigh bells, she slipped out of bed, tip-toed across her room, and got on all fours to peek through the tiny shaft of light under her door.

'I sawed his boots,' she told us. 'He holded all the presents in a bag.'

Fri 14th -

Last day of work. My enduring love of Christmas is likely due to my career in education; I've <u>always</u> had a long December break. Maybe I might not be so sunny about things if I worked Christmas Eve and went back on the 27th. In my current job, we get three and a half weeks off. The stuff of dreams.

What is less dreamy, is the bout of tummy shame that meant I missed the end of term staff party. My belly had been making suction noises all morning but I didn't realise how bad things were until I knocked on my mother's door - with the purpose of getting a cup of tea - and got no reply. I called her. She was shopping. My gut dropped. I held everything in, using muscles that I seldom call into play. I thought I was going to have to ignore the age old wisdom of not defecating on your own doorstep. I panicked. I was sweating. What a disaster. She arrived in the nick of time. I remembered Billy Connolly saying about how he'd once sat on the loo 'not a second too soon'. A perfect description. It's such a grim illness that it's hard to give it as an excuse. I said I had a headache. A headache that required going through several cans of Oust.

Sat 15th -

Absolutely Baltic outside. The kind of wind you can hear whistling into your house through gaps you never knew existed. Went to Sainsbury's, walking into the driving wind, and stood under their big heated fan in the doorway (what Alan Partridge calls 'the warm air curtain') for so long that a queue formed behind me. On the return leg, the cold wind blew my scarf off. I was worried it might undo my belt.

As I'm writing this now, the darkness is total. Apparently the evenings officially started getting lighter as of yesterday. This is the darkest it's been though, on account of the low cloud. It's 16.17 and I'm lit only by the light of my laptop and the Christmas tree in the corner. The wind has picked up further in the last hour, roaring against the window like Cathy desperately trying to give me the lowdown on Heathcliff. Although my fireplace has been bricked off - not my decision, might I add - I can hear the wind doing its thing behind it.

Did lots of wrapping throughout the day. With the exception of a couple of bits, I'm all done. The presents are under the tree for collection. I'm not sure what to do with myself now. Oh, actually, yes I am: I'm going to do bugger all. In style.

Watching people unwrap presents brings out a competitive side to me which I have to rail against. I sit there mentally divvying up what the presents cost in terms of both thought and money. What a thing to do. It's not that I don't want my own presents to be upstaged, rather, I don't want to be humiliated. If you buy someone a pair of slippers and the next present they open is an expensive watch, the poor old slippers - bought with just as much goodwill - are left blushing in the corner. There's a lovely bit in 'Bridesmaids' where Kristen Wiig makes the bride a CD of their favourite songs since childhood, then watches on as a new friend upstages her, handing the bride tickets to Paris to meet her dress designer. Ugh.

Sun 16th -

Church carol service tonight. I go every year. It always starts with the lights being turned off, followed by the choir walking down the darkened aisle holding candles, singing 'Away In A Manger'. There is nothing so beautiful as the accidentally-off-key opening note or two of a church organ. Tonight's didn't disappoint. Puurrr, dahhhh. The very sound of it made my heart skip.

The church was packed, as ever. On your way in they give you a handmade book with all the readings and hymns. Every year I check for 'Tomorrow Will Be My Dancing Day', a medieval banger. It was in the set tonight. Yes! Although I love the carol service above all other annual rituals, I still spend most of it measuring how long of it is left, thinking 'Oh, good' as I realise we're hurrying on. I will never know why I do this.

Late night cheese and port. Saw in a documentary that Hitler had bad breath. I knew that due to his vegan diet and drug dependency his guts produced terrible stinks for those around him to silently endure, but the bad breath was a new one on me. Just think, on top of everything else, he stunk like a wheelie bin. What a guy!

German women idolised Hitler to such an extent that, like a baby-cheeked member of a boyband, he had to keep his relationships top secret lest his fanclub feel that life was no longer worth living (which, after a few years of his spasmodic rule, it wasn't). This is the ultimate evidence that women are as attracted to power as to blue-eyed good looks. Let's face it, Hitler looked like a complete bell-end, even by the standards of 1930s German political circles, where, admittedly, the emphasis on style was on somewhat of a back-burner. If you ever need cheering up after hearing about the atrocities dear Adolf inspired his country to commit, just study that photo of him leaning against a tree in his lederhosen, with his stern expression and belt wrapped high around his belly button like the sort of bloke you'd desperately avoid talking to at a bus stop.

Talking of what women want, I reactivated my online dating account today. It's that time of year where the numbers on dating apps swell due to the realisation among thirty-somethings that not everyone goes to their parents' house for Christmas dinner. Oddly, I had an influx of messages from women I'd contacted months and months ago, generically telling me that they didn't think we were 'compatible' and wishing me 'all the best' in my 'future search'. It did little for morale. One woman messaged me saying that she 'tends to feel a bit low' on Christmas day and that her family have asked her to stop buying everyone so many presents (which she does to compensate for something). And what do you know, I feel a bit morose all of a sudden.

316

I'd better type 'Hitler lederhosen' into Google images. That's the stuff. Ha. Look at that pillock!

Mon 17th -

'My least favourite thing in the world,' I said to my sister in the car, 'is being dropped in it by other people. Life's hard enough dealing with your own problems; it drives me nuts when other people's stupidity makes my life difficult.'

The full-stop had barely settled on the above speech when a woman jumped out in the road in front of us, waving her arms madly, begging us to stop.

Behind her, a tall old man was having a heart attack or choking to death. A shorter, not-so-old man was holding onto him. My heart juddered. The car screeched to a halt. The girl waved her arms at me, pointing at the man.

'My dad, my dad,' she screamed, going down to her knees.

The tall old man wasn't dying.

He was fighting. With the shorter, not-so-old man. And it was the <u>younger</u> of the two who was the dad. And it was the <u>older</u> of the two who was the aggressor. They had each other grabbed by the lapels of their walking regalia. The older threw infrequent, misfiring fists. The younger got close to his face, swearing on tip-toe.

I called the police. Just before dialling, I looked at my homescreen and saw I had a couple of unread Facebook messages and Instagram comments from my chipper, former life of ten seconds earlier.

'Fire, police or ambulance?' asked a tired voice.

'Police,' I said, quickly.

'Thank you. One moment.'

317

The girl screamed for me to get out of the car and do something. But what the hell could I do? I wasn't going to swoop in and break it up. I didn't know who they were, why they were fighting (although instinct told me it was about something mundane - and I'd be proved right) or who to defend. Above all, despite the girl's panicked cries, the fight looked like something from 'Coronation Street'.

'Police,' came a new voice.

I told the voice what was going on, giving my best guess as to what was happening. I had to answer a host of questions, including descriptions of their clothes ('one's in a dashing green weave from the Debenham's autumn collection and the other's sporting a dazzling, lime, off-the-shoulder number') and whether either had any weapons:

'One of them's got a newspaper,' I replied, aware that I wasn't being helpful. 'I think it's "The Telegraph".'

Across the road, an elderly lady watched on. I wanted to tut at her and say, 'Old people these days', but didn't think this the ideal time for such a gag. A bloke ran from a house and, doing a much better impression of a man than me, went gung-ho into breaking up the fracas.

'The older man's walking away,' I fed back to the police operator. 'The woman's still crying. The smaller man is comforting her.'

'We're on our way, Sir. It's being treated as an emergency call. Believe you me, we'll be with you as fast as we can.'

Half an hour later, the emergency response team arrived at a pace that could be best described as loose. By this point, the old man was long gone, sat at home trying to salvage what remained of the cryptic crossword from his torn newspaper. We found out that

318

the brawl had started after the old git had shouted at the girl for no apparent reason. This caused her young (ish) dad to drive around looking for the man to give him a piece of his mind. Things escalated from there. All perfectly excusable, of course; there are few better reasons for two grown men to have an actual fight in the street, I'm sure you'll agree.

When asked if they wanted to press charges against the old man, the girl said, 'Nothing will happen.'

'We could nick him for GBH,' replied the young policeman.

We'd gone from 'Corrie' to 'The Bill' in next to no time.

We stood by the side of road for another half hour, answering questions I'd already answered over the phone, drawing glares from passing cars.

I don't know how the rest of the saga played out because we left the scene. All I know is I'm still not fond of other people hijacking my life with their hot-headed stupidity. Life has more than enough incidents and accidents without the need to manufacture them.

Tues 18th -

Bored of street violence, today I made my first ever visit to the Cromer Pier Christmas 'Seaside Special'. It was everything I expected it to be.

Two-thirds full, the audience was largely made up of the elderly and the severely elderly. The show consisted of a comedian from the Bruce Forsyth school of gag-telling, and a fire-eating magician (according to the promotional material, which I shall quote verbatim: 'The king of cool Will.i.am once described him "you are cool".') Between their skits - which involved the duo dressing up as elves, women and other ridiculous characters - we were treated to an operatic blonde and a dancing troupe working their way through a repertoire of Christmas standards and, bizarrely, a lengthy 'Jesus Christ Superstar' medley. The dancers were made up of two slick-haired guys and four leg-kicking dolls with bright red lips and ceramic teeth. One of them was heartbreakingly pretty. I spent most of the time wondering how much money they made from the show. I guess they stay in a nearby hotel for the duration of the run. I don't think they were local. Too young. Too glossy.

At one point in the show, the comedian introduced guests in the audience:

'Also here with us today are the Norwich Association for the Blind,' he said, earnestly. 'Always good to see them.'

The magician did the thing everyone hates and came down into the audience. Being sat on the end of the aisle, I was the perfect target. Why do entertainers do this? The whole reason they're on the stage is that they're comfortable up there. That's why we pay for tickets to watch them. Whenever they come off-stage and walk up the aisles, the audience should be reimbursed.

Fortunately he targeted my friend instead, on account of her being more attractive:

'What's your name, sweetheart?'

'Kerri.'

'Thanks, Carrie. Now, Carrie, please pick a card, any card, and don't tell me what it is...'

Having picked her card, any card, the magician then wandered to another aisle and asked someone else to pick a card, any card.

'Well done, Carrie,' I said. We then had a whispered chat about how she always gets called that. I said it was strange because out of Kerri and Carrie, the latter is a lot less prevalent. Then we realised that throughout our discussion, the magician had been talking to the audience, explaining carefully what it was that Carrie and the other card-pickers now needed to do in order to complete the trick. But we hadn't been listening!

Argh.

The show ended with everyone on stage belting out 'Winter Wonderland'. The snow machine pumped out white flakes from the rafters. The comedian said that Cromer's is the last end of pier show in the world and that we should be proud of it and to tell everyone to keep it alive. A sentiment worthy of an echo.

Weds 19th -

Took a trip to Norwich to buy a final flurry of additional presents. The 'high street' has its own Christmas advert this year, reminding us of its importance. By God, it can let you down, though. I was trying to buy a Norwich kit for my four-year-old nephew. Only two shops sold them. The shirt, shorts and socks combined cost £70. I asked one of the shorted-boys in Sports Direct about England kits instead.

'Hent got any, mate.'

'Oh,' I said. 'Do you know where I can get one?'

'In Norwich?' he said, with a snort.

'Yes,' I replied.

'Yurl be lucky. They're like gold-dust.'

That was my reward for a heated morning of lumbering around the city, being shoved and shunted by the crowds. (Luckily, I later found a place where England shirts weren't like gold-dust: the internet.)

I went to a toyshop. Every toy was cheaper on Amazon. I bought them from the shop but I don't really know why

I was endeavouring to help prop up something that, to me, seems unviable. There's talk of upcoming changes to the rates that online shops charge for their products. The aim is to give the high street more power again. But why should we? Why can't the rates change so that the high street becomes <u>cheaper</u> rather than the internet becoming more expensive? If shops aren't evolving sufficiently to offer a service worthy of rivalling the internet, what's the point of bailing them out?

The journey back to the coast was splendid. The sky pale blue with wintry white trails of cloud. The arms of the trees were black and spindly, bereft of leaves. It was the perfect December afternoon. The sun was already setting and so weak that you could look at it without squinting. Along the coast road, the white wind turbines, far away on the sea's horizon, looked pink. Walking through town, to my flat, the shop fronts were all alight for the coming sunset. I could see my breath. I remembered why the high street needed saving.

Thurs 20th -

Had the loveliest afternoon at my sister's. We had soup and tiger bread and watched television in front of the log fire whilst my niece and nephew played on the floor. I asked my niece (seven) what her favourite Christmas song was:

'The one where the man gives someone his heart and then that person gives it away the very next day,' she replied.

On the way home, we passed one of those madcap houses with more Christmas lights than bricks. As with all these homes, the next door neighbours <u>also</u> had outside lights, but nowhere near as many. I love this.

Look out for it yourself. Next time you see one of those over-lit houses that are visible from Mars, look at the neighbour's effort. It will almost certainly be about 70% less spectacular. It says so much about them:

'No, no, we're not party poopers, actually. Look, we've got lights, too. The difference is, we do it tastefully, unlike them next door.'

Or, even more deliciously, maybe they're the result of neighbourly oneupmanship. Perhaps the more sedate lights go up first and the neighbour twizzles his beard (no arguments here, please - it's bound to be a bloke) and thinks:

'Call that a light display? I'll show them. Honey, I'm just popping to The Range.'

Fri 21st -

What day is it? It took me about a minute to remember upon waking this morning.

Saw 'Mary Poppins Returns' at the cinema. I hadn't planned to go. Got a last minute invite. (My first question was, 'How long is it?' The answer, I discovered, was 'Very'.) It is probably the most beautiful film I have seen this year, visually. You could watch it with the sound off. Given the quality of the songs, this might not be a bad idea. The original 'Mary Poppins' had six or seven outstanding tunes. This had just the one. The others were like 'Mary Poppins' b-sides. Also, I didn't believe in Emily Blunt. She lacked the authority of Julie Andrews. (Even though, when Andrews play Mary Poppins, she was seven years younger than Blunt - and making her movie debut.) There were times when Blunt slipped into a Margaret Thatcher impression. It looked like watching an actor doing a posh voice. With Julie

323

Andrews, you believed she was the real deal, possibly doing a spot of upper-class nannying on the side of her Hollywood work.

And now, for my favourite joke of the year:

Today is the shortest day. It's flown by...

Sat 22nd -

Things are getting real now. December the twenty-second! Even the hardiest of anti-Christmas fiends must be relenting. Three more sleeps. When I was a kid, the closer Christmas got, the further away it felt. I was like Captain Scott, staggering home across the endless white tundra, to a place I knew I couldn't reach.

This is the first day of the 'Radio Times' listings from the Christmas edition. I'm adding things to my Sky planner. The fridge is full of cheeses, treats, and drinks. I'm all set.

Checked the dating website. Nearly every profile begins with 'I don't know what to write in these things'. There is something unnatural about online dating. It amazes me when people on there show off about how great they are: how they travel the world, how they are top of their professional field, how downright witty they are, how driven. Makes me want to message them and ask, if they're so cool and with-it, why, pray, have they had to come to the circus to find love. One absolute rotter had written as her profile headline:

'Wat U C is wat U get!!!'

To which I had to resist from replying:

'A terrible human?'

The best people, the dignified and friendly ones, never bloody reply to my delightfully witty messages. Perhaps I should put 'Wat U C is wat U get!!' on my wall.

Watched 'A Christmas Story' before bed. I hope all the people involved in making that film know just what a gift they've given the world. The final scenes, when Christmas morning arrives, are perfection. The whole movie feels as though someone has filmed my dreams. It already says everything I wanted to say in this book; it almost feels holy.

Watching it, I realised that I'd subliminally bought the same dressing gown as Ralphie's dad. I paid about £100 for it a few years ago, thinking it magnificent but not being able to express why. Now I know: it's been touched by the 'A Christmas Story' magic. It is easily the most cavalier item of clothing in my possession. I'd wear it outside if it was socially acceptable.

Tomorrow is Christmas Eve-Eve!

Sun 23rd - Christmas Eve-Eve

Although I've written about a host of Christmas songs for this book, I don't think I've listened to them enough this year. I might be imagining it, and I probably say it every year, but, even with keeping this diary, Christmas has crept up on me. I felt like I had all the time in the world to listen to certain songs and watch certain films but, all of a sudden, it's the day before the day before and I'm off the pace.

Rain all day. Everything is dripping wet. The day drew in at 3pm. Had an enormous roast dinner. Bit of a gamble so close to the big day. Need to make sure I keep food consumption on the easy side.

The best thing about this time is year is finding something suitable to watch on the afternoon TV schedule and planning the whole day around it. Any other time of year and the process seems like something only a hermit would do. At Christmas, such behaviour is positively encouraged. I watched 'Up' on BBC One.

Remembered how much I hate it when, in published diaries, the writer breezes over Christmas, saying something like:

'Spent the day with Fiona after all. Her parents came over. Roger was actually very lovely. Games and then port. Felt better.'

It's worse when they skip it altogether, going from Dec 21st to Jan 17th as though nothing has happened.

I spent a good five minutes just looking at my tree this afternoon. It's hard to remember a time when it wasn't up, lighting the corner of the room, half-blocking the doorway with its cumbersome yuletide revelry. I looked at all the little decorations and trinkets hanging from it. Each one has a story. I've still got more than a few Woolworths ones which have seen more glittery days, but which I'll always keep.

A touch of melancholy has swept over me. It always does when Christmas draws very close as I simply love the December build-up so much. The hustle and the bustle and all that jazz. All the memories from the run-up now seem brighter and more jovial: the bingo at Yarmouth; the town light switch-on; finding an advent calendar on my doorstep; eating tiger bread and soup in front of the fire; putting up the new tree; the animal sanctuary; the quiz raffle; haggling with Vodafone. God, even the scrap between the two walking-enthusiasts is tinged with fondness.

The twelve days are a wonderful fiesta of everything and nothing, but pre-December 25th is when the heart of the Christmas purist is at its happiest.

Mon 24th - Christmas Eve

The day has slipped away like always. Friends visited and we walked around town then went to a café overlooking the sea. The sea looks different on Christmas Eve. I used to tell myself that Father Christmas was over on the light, peachy horizon, getting ready. I love that there may be children, somewhere, today, thinking the same.

Was asked to go to a nativity. Glad I did. It was a royal mess but all the better for it. The vicar began the service with a desperate plea for more performers. He needed angels. His wish was granted before I had a chance to embarrass myself. As the characters took their turn to walk down the aisle to the mock stable at the front, their path led them over the church's heating gratings, wafting the gowns and robes of the voluntary adult angels in a kind of biblical re-imagining of 'The Seven Year Itch'. Babies bawled throughout the play and the little narrator, who was obviously chosen for her reading ability, was lost in their screams. Among the songs were two I hadn't sung since those golden primary school nativities of my childhood: 'It Was On A Starry Night' and 'Come & Join The Celebration'. I'd heard them on rare occasions but, not since the days when I couldn't tell the time, had I been required to sing them. Doing so opened the window on my past:

'And all the angels sang to him
The bells of heaven rang for him
For a boy was born, king of all the world'

It was the 'for a boy was born' line that brought this Christmas fully to life. I could remember, as a boy myself, being drawn to tune's majesty and not knowing why. This, too, from the second song:

327

'See the shepherds hurry down to Bethlehem
Gaze in wonder
At the son of God who lays before them'
It is those hidden parts of school carols that trigger the past. Notes not sung since 1987. Christmas, originally a festival of winter, has become a festival of childhood. Some people want to forget their childhood, some can barely remember it, and some, like myself, are tethered to it. 'Christmas is for the kids,' and all that. But we are all children. In bigger clothes. With gas bills and nagging doubts. With an awareness of our numbered days.

'Let the little children come to me,' said Jesus, when he himself wore bigger clothes. Only, he wasn't talking about little children.

If I could offer one bit of advice for those who feel bereft of Christmas spirit, it would be this:

Go to a nativity.

It is actually Christmas tomorrow. Tonight, technically. Midnight. The real deal. The season to be jolly. Holidays have come. Tomorrow! Tonight! Now.

After the service, I went to my mum's and, as per unspoken tradition, we watched 'TOTP2'. One thing I always like to think about is how these old 'TOTP' Christmas performances - e.g. Jona Lewie doing 'Stop The Cavalry' - were probably watched in that same house the night they were originally broadcast, when, out of my siblings, only my eldest sister had shuffled onto the mortal coil. A gateway opens up for me at my mum's on Christmas Eve night. I can smell the tangerine skins and pine needles of the years when we had square, single-glaze windows which froze on the inside; I can smell the tumble-dried empty pillow cases we'd leave on the landing; finally, as I exit the house, to walk home alone, I half-fancy I can hear my childhood footsteps creaking up the stairs to bed.

Walking back along the coast road just before midnight, my journey was lit by the milky glow of an almost full moon. The sky was dark blue, and lighter still around the stars. No noise. The kind of silence where you can hear a twig cracking under a hare's foot six miles away. I walked past the village church and saw yellow lights illuminate the windows for the approaching Midnight Mass. The organist played a flat chord or two, testing his fingers. Quite unexpectedly, out in the cold darkness, wholly alone, close to a December midnight, a couple of birds began singing in the trees. Perhaps they were on their way to mass. All the way home, past white, moonlit fields, I kept thinking about a line from a U.A. Fanthorpe poem about the nativity:

'This was the moment when nothing happened'.

The laugh is, it's almost certain that if the nativity story really did happen, it wasn't on December 24th/ 25th. Sometimes, though, it feels as though it did and it was. The walk from my mum's usually takes twenty minutes but I spent an additional twenty stopping to look up, gazing in wonder.

Tues 25th - Christmas Day

Spent the day with Fiona after all. Her parents came over. Roger was actually very lovely. Games and then port. Felt better.

[Kidding. The diary shall return for the final twelve days.]

- To Be Continued -

The 12 Songs Of Christmas

#12

Some Children See Him - Martha and Rufus Wainwright

Suddenly a great company of the heavenly host appeared with the angel, praising God and saying:

'Glory to God in the highest heaven, and on earth peace to those on whom his favour rests.'

When the angels had left them and gone into heaven, the shepherds said to one another, 'Let's go to Bethlehem and see this thing that has happened, which the Lord has told us about.'

Luke, Chapter 2, V13-15

Other songs may need to be heard at the right moment, in the right way, but this one stops me in my yuletide tracks every time. It exists so far outside the canon of festive classics that the song, in all its forms, doesn't even merit its own Wikipedia entry, which, considering *Blue (Da Ba De)* and *Pretty Fly (For A White Guy)* do, could be classed as something of a slight.

Written in 1951 by American jazz performer Alfred Burt[1] and Wihla Hutson,[2] *Some Children See Him* has been covered by a (heavenly) host of stars over the years, including Perry Como and James Taylor. But *this* is the version. Rufus and Martha Wainwright. Brother and sister.

Despite being one of the great modern songwriters, Rufus Wainwright dwells on the popular periphery. The most likely reason for this is that his songs are so lavishly produced and take such work to work-out, that he has never had, and will almost certainly never have, a career-defining radio hit. Of his ten most played tracks on Spotify currently, seven are cover versions (as is *Some Children See Him*). His best known recording is a cover of Leonard Cohen's *Hallejulah* which features on the soundtrack to *Shrek* (typically of Wainwright, though, it's *not* the version featured in the film itself; that honour belongs to John Cale). His voice splits opinion: a cross between a drunken Thom Yorke and an even drunker Broadway diva. His sister, Martha, began as a backing singer for Rufus but is now a star in her own right, with an equally loyal following and an equally sedate reputation when compared to popular music's big hitters. For the record, she has a voice like a reasonably sober Broadway diva.

This particular recording comes from a Christmas album recorded with musical Wainwright family friends called *The*

---

[1] Burt wrote a new Christmas song each year and sent them in the post to his friends. Delightful, yes? Then allow me to add that, in the grand tradition of this book, he died tragically young. Boom!

[2] Who, for my money, ought to have married ex-Manchester United midfielder, Quinton Fortune, to give herself a stonkingly funny name.

McGarrigle Christmas Hour.[1] The recording features the likes of Emmylou Harris and Beth Orton singing traditional carols, but it is Rufus and Martha's little known version of a little known song that is the standout.

Some Children See Him is about the different ways that Jesus Christ is depicted around the world. '*Some children see him*,' the song says, '*lily white*'. Others see him '*dark as they*'. Wihla (Fortune)'s lyrics are happily old-fashioned, with references to '*almond eyes*' and '*skin of yellow hue*'. Why happily? Because the song has the most gentle soul. It is a message of acceptance. A dated message of acceptance, yes, but a particularly liberal one given the time and country it was composed in.[2]

Rufus takes the lead on the first verse. Martha, the second. Both are accompanied by slow piano and woodwind. For the third verse, a choir join in and the music stops. All we are left with is the singing of different voices at different levels, as though a group of carollers are singing just for us:

O lay aside each earthly thing
And with thy heart as offering,
Come worship now the infant King.
'Tis love that's born tonight

---

[1] The siblings' father (not present on the album) is folk icon, Louden Wainwright III; their mother and auntie, respectively, were Kate and Anna McGarrigle. Louden Wainwright's absence can be explained by his always-fractious relationship with his children, particularly his son (as crystallised in Rufus' guaranteed tear-jerker *Dinner At Eight*); seeing Louden pop up on a family Christmas album would be like seeing Prince Charles 'crew deep' in a grime video. Wonderful, but very unlikely.

[2] This isn't the only Christmas song to call people 'yellow'. Lennon's *Happy Xmas (War Is Over)* refers to '*yellow and red ones*' and Johnny Mathis' vomit-inducing *When A Child Is Born* talks about '*black, white, yellow*' children as though they're snooker balls.

The beauty of it is that, just like a real choir, you can't quite hear the words they're singing. The whole song has the atmosphere of an evening church service. It sounds as though it was recorded in the 1950s and left to age in a vestry cupboard:[1]

Some children see him lily white
The baby Jesus born this night
Some children see him lily white
With tresses soft and fair

Some children see him dark as they
Sweet Mary's son to whom we pray
Some children see him dark as they
And, ah, they love him, too

There's only so much I can say about *Some Children See Him* as the likelihood is you haven't heard it yet.[2] All I can say is, do it now. Unless you're reading this in August, in which case, give it a few months. My discourse is equally limited by the fact precious little information about the recording exists. Maybe I ought to have waxed lyrical about Mariah Carey instead.
Nah.

❄ ❄ ❄

I can't help but notice we've reached the end of the list. Bar a brief mention of Christmas compilations later on in the alphabet, that's it for the music talk. Did I mention any of your favourites? Did I pique your interest in anything new? Will you

---

[1] Instead it comes from the era of canned Relentless.

[2] This isn't me trying to sound all waspish and cool, by the way. It really *is* an obscure song. I wish it weren't.

333

ever be able to hear Wizzard without thinking about poor old Miss Snob & Class 3C?

And just so you don't think I'm a coward, if push came to shove, and I *had* to pick a favourite Christmas song, I guess it would be...

Oh. I can't do it. I *am* a coward. Some of you aren't going to like my last choice of TV programme, either.

The 12 Things To Watch Of Christmas

#12

Match Of The Day (Boxing Day)

Sorry about this, but it has to be done. On the plus side, no one dies tragically young at the end of it.

In Britain, Christmas and football belong to the same family. They're so intrinsically linked that last year (2018), the Italians borrowed our idea and re-introduced football on St Stephen's Day.[1] So well-known is the British festive fixture hoopla, though, they called it 'Boxing Day Football', even though Italians don't call the day Boxing Day.[2] Possibly by way of honouring past English footballing traditions, 2018's Italian Boxing Day football was marred with shameful violence, resulting in a murder outside Inter Milan's stadium. Inside that

---

[1] After a 47-year break.

[2] They call it St Stephen's Feast Day, or, if you'll permit me the opportunity to go high-brow: *Il giorno di Santo Stefano*. Although, in truth, the Italians don't celebrate the day much, further dismantling the casual assumption that they are a country of fervent Catholics. 'Nobody in Italy reads the Gospels, really nobody,' said Pier Paolo Pasolini when asked if he thought his film about Jesus would cause a scandal in his homeland. This was in 1969.

same stadium, a black defender was booed throughout and treated to monkey chanting. The country's deputy prime minister tweeted, 'At the beginning of the year I will convene the leaders of supporters of Serie A and B clubs so that the stadiums and the surrounding area will once again become a place of fun.'

At the beginning of the year, you say? No rush, eh, pal?

One year on, the monkey chants continue. In September 2019, Inter Milan striker Romelu Lukaku voiced dismay at such chants only to be reassured by an official supporters' statement that 'this attitude of Italian fans [is] a form of respect'.

God knows what they do if they hate you.[1]

Fortunately, besides the odd gaggle of tosspots, English football is a more clean-cut affair. There's too much money involved for it not to be. Although some may claim it was better in the past - at a time when the people in question just so happened to be younger, happier, and have far less cause to visit their GP on a frequent basis - the English top division is still the fastest and toughest on the planet. The world watches. Every Premier League game is televised somewhere.[2] In America, the games are now shown on the major network NBC, rather than hidden away on obscure cable packages. As a result, soccer has leapfrogged ice hockey to become the nation's fourth most watched sport. And it's the Premier League they watch. Burnley vs Southampton. Wolves vs Everton. It's hard to believe at times, especially as the sport consists of two forty-

---

[1] Considering what the Romans allegedly did to Jesus, that statement might actually be true.

[2] Annoyingly, everywhere but here. The UK is about the only place where selected games are blocked from broadcast, which is why so many fans have to result to streaming sold-out games from abroad, watching West Ham vs Brighton with Greek commentary.

five minute chunks of uninterruptible action. For all its day-glo logos and sponsorship deals, the Premier League can actually be an advertiser's nightmare.

The appeal of English football[1] is that it has a more rough 'n tumble spirit than its overseas competitors. And Boxing Day football has an almost mythical rough 'n tumbly quality. The games are always that bit more loose, with players having spent the previous day eating caviar and watching their children unwrap Range Rovers. The fans are in a more lethargic mood, too, addled on well-wishes, Harvey's Bristol Cream and bad television. It all adds up to create an anything-goes feel to the occasion. It has always been thus. Take a look at these results from Boxing Day, 1963:

Blackpool 1-5 Chelsea
Burnley 6-1 Manchester United
Fulham 10-1 Ipswich Town
Leicester City 2-0 Everton
Liverpool 6-1 Stoke City
Nottingham Forest 3-3 Sheffield United
Sheffield Wednesday 3-0 Bolton Wanderers
West Bromwich Albion 4-4 Tottenham Hotspur
West Ham United 2-8 Blackburn Rovers
Wolverhampton Wanderers 3-3 Aston Villa

Only Leicester and Everton let the side down with their paltry two-goal affair. Imagine the editors at *Match Of The Day* having to sort that lot out. Imagine a night where Burnley tonking Manchester United 6-1 wouldn't be the obvious opener:

---

[1] I'm not going to be polite and say 'the appeal of *British* football'; the Scottish Premiership is barely a competition. It's been won by either Rangers or Celtic every year since 1985. Yet supporters of both clubs still act as though winning it is worthy of recognition.

'But we'll start at Craven Cottage,' says host Gary Lineker, 'where Ipswich were looking to see if their new defensive strategy would pay dividends against their hosts, Fulham...'[1]

The Boxing Day *Match Of The Day* is the small black coffee of the Christmas feast. It rounds off the festivities, bringing a taste of normality to the palate. You can't fail to see the glory of an English football ground at this time of year: the floodlit grass; the orange withering sunsets above the stadiums; the well-wrapped fans; the steam coming off the players' shoulders.[2] Still too early in the season for the games to mean too much, the players adopt a more cavalier approach to defending. The referees get lost in the excitement of it all, giving penalties away for reasons as innocuous as two opponents brushing shirts or somebody forgetting to tie their bootlace. That it's broadcast on the BBC - Christmas television's standard bearer - adds an extra layer of nostalgia. When you're watching the Christmas *MOTD* by the night's fading fireside, you do so in the knowledge that millions have done so at that time, on that date, for decades;[3] the only difference is that Jimmy Hill and Des Lynham have been replaced by Gary Lineker and a host of modern greats (and, inexplicably, Jermaine Jenas).

It's not just Boxing Day, the whole festive football period is clogged with a hamstring-stretching schedule. In 2018, there

---

[1] Fulham winger Gary Leggett scored a hat-trick in three minutes that day. A record that's likely to remain undisturbed for a while yet.

[2] Another gently uplifting feature is that the fixtures themselves are arranged by the FA so as to involve as little travelling as possible for away supporters.

[3] Matches actually used to be played on the big day, up until the 1950s when public transport companies vastly reduced their Christmas Day services. (Further evidence that Christmas wasn't more lovingly observed in the past.)

was a full round of matches on Dec 22nd, 26th, 29th and Jan 2nd.[1] The yuletide schedule can have such an effect on the number of injuries a club sustains that almost every year there is a debate about whether there should be a winter break. (That's what happens on the continent, by and large; European players kick their feet up and relax for a week or two, while the English teams go hammer and tongs.) Some say the winter break is the secret of foreign teams' successes at the World Cup, a logic I've never been able to work out.[2] Regardless, the debate is now over. There *will* be a staggered winter break from the 2019-20 season onwards, meaning, naturally, that England can fully expect to win the 2022 World Cup and the majority of all other World Cups from this point on.

Something to look forward to.

As it stands, the Christmas fixture free-for-all is safe (with the winter break taking place *after* it). The only thing to worry about is the impact of the 2022 Qatar World Cup - and the ongoing celebrations in England afterwards. Due to the heat, the tournament will be played in winter for the first time in its history, plonk in the middle of Europe's major football seasons. Qatar won the bid to host the tournament by claiming they'd build air-conditioned stadiums, perfect for use in the summer. With the role of hosts in the bag, it became clear that even with these new air-conditioned stadiums, the event would have

---

[1] It was even more action-packed in 1963. Just *one day* after playing out those ridiculous scorelines, the same teams met one another *again* at the other's ground. Manchester United, West Ham, Bolton, and even the literally decimated Ipswich Town, all recorded handsome victories over their Boxing Day bullies.

[2] Perhaps the real secret to other countries' success is that they play far fewer games because they don't have four major club competitions, as we do. (And that they are generally better at football.)

to be held in winter, where the average high is around the ice-cold 30C mark. What precisely is to be done about this with regard to the European football calendar is *still* undecided. The Premier League - and Serie A, La Liga, Bundesliga etc. - might finish later or start earlier, or they may go on with clubs fielding teams depleted of their international stars. Nobody knows. It will create fixture mayhem for possibly three years, with the seasons either side of the event having negative knock-on effects. Still, it will all be worthwhile to see England bring the trophy home. And to see Qatar - with their population roughly the size of Birmingham's urban sprawl - relish hosting a tournament that means so very much to them.

As for *Match Of The Day*, it appears to be in rude health. It began in 1964 as a sort of pre-season friendly for the upcoming 1966 World Cup[1] and was so popular that BBC Two's Controller - a sprightly young go-getter by the name of David Attenborough - stuck with it. Its iconic theme tune was added in 1970. Whereas the show used to broadcast only one match a week,[2] with the advances in technology - specifically, in recent years, digital technology - it now shows extended highlights of every game, a thought that would have made football fans of the past slaver into their beef broth.

What's interesting about *Match Of The Day*'s popularity is that it comes at a time when football fans can watch nearly half of all Premier League matches live on television. If the matches aren't selected for live broadcast, then they can, totally legally, have videos of the goals and key incidents sent to their phones fifteen minutes after they occur. By 5pm of a Saturday

---

[1] A tournament which, it should be noted, England miraculously managed to win *without* the advantage of a winter break.

[2] A match picked long in advance and, as a result, often about seventh on the list of games fans wanted to watch that day.

afternoon, you could have seen every segment of action worth seeing without having to stay awake until *MOTD* starts.[1] Yet still it endures, pulling in millions of viewers. I mean, listen to *me* waxing lyrical about it. More often than not, I loathe it. I only watch it if a manager implodes or if Man City lose at home to Chipping Norton. Like many people, I find the match edits poorly representative of the story of the game, the pundits vacuous and their 'banter' laughable (in a bad way). There's no sound on earth more annoying than Martin Keown saying how 'the Arsenal are doing wonders' or listening to Phil Neville trying to position his tongue. Yet I simply adore the programme. I cling to its existence. *Match Of The Day* is football. And the Boxing Day special *is* Christmas.

---

[1] Which is no mean feat when you get to your mid-thirties. Although it usually airs at about half-ten, *MOTD* is often subject to delay, most notably from the *Last Night of the Proms*, *Eurovision*, and most unseemly of all, *The Royal Tournament*, with its peak audience of 12,000.

The Christmas Alphabet

T is for...

Television

'This is the one day of the year we all get together to watch the television and look at the shite they put on!'
    The Royle Family, 'Christmas With The Royle Family', 1999

Television was once to Christmas what candles are to birthdays (and, to be fair, Christmas). TV shows and movie premieres routinely pulled in astonishing ratings. The 1989 Christmas Day broadcast of *Crocodile Dundee*, for instance, drew almost 22 million viewers. Prince William's blessed marriage to our darling *Kate*, in 2011, by comparison, attracted around 15 million:
'And now the holy union will be sealed with the cutting of the wedding cake.'
'That's not a knife. *This* is a knife.'
The well-worn reason behind all this is that people don't 'consume' television like they used to. Today, if there happens to be something worth watching, millions will record it or 'catch-up' later. For anyone who ever tried to get their head around VideoPlus, the ease with which we can indeed catch-up on programmes today is a welcome relief. Gone is the fear of the video timer going to sleep or of having neglected to set the recording to Long-Play (an error that caused the video to stop halfway through a pivotal scene, before angrily rewinding itself at the speed of sound). Neither are we party to that soul-destroying experience of having a recording interrupted by a

sudden buzz of static before being replaced with a ten-month-old episode of *Watchdog*. Now, my friend, we have untold televisual control.

And there's nothing on.

I'm not one for thinking the past was better. Except where Christmas television is concerned. I don't know what happened. It's as though terrestrial television gave up bothering as part of the millennium celebrations. Basically, if you don't like soap operas - or long-running dramas of a standard on par with soap operas - you're bang out of luck with Christmas telly. I don't want to keep harping on about *Morecambe & Wise* and *Only Fools* but, goodness, have they ever been close to being replaced? Most surprisingly, there's barely been an attempt to fill their boots. Modern entertainment shows, what few there are, are overly glitzy and short on laughs, whereas modern sitcoms, what few there are, are nearly all po-faced and, worst of all, understated, scared of not being poignant. Just as countless popstars spent the 1980s trying to recreate *Thriller*, so most sitcom writers have spent the last fifteen years trying to recreate *The Office*. As rotten as *Mrs Brown's Boys* is, at least it has the guts to play to a studio audience. It's telling that the UK is so starved of mainstream comedy that *Mrs Brown's Boys*[1] has been BBC One's Christmas Day comedy treat for the last eight years.

Elsewhere on the seasonal box, you get an Agatha Christie adaptation starring some faded American movie star and David Walliams (doing his serious face), you get a special episode of *Dancing On Ice* or *Strictly* filmed sometime during the hosepipe ban, and, if you're lucky, a BBC Two biopic about the tragic private life of a long-dead *Carry On* regular. Everything else is a

---

[1] Three jokes. One, it's a man dressed as an old lady. Two, the old lady swears. Three, the actors pretend they forget their lines.

repeat (of older versions of the sort of programmes listed above).

The question is, why does it matter whether lots of people watch the same programme on Christmas night? The answer is, it doesn't. It's just that Christmas Day is long. Most people get up when its dark, after a disjointed night's sleep, and for all their port-addled grinning during charades, I suspect that they'd quite like to sit down in the evening and let the professionals do the leg-work. How nice it would be to know there'd be something brilliantly funny on at the day's close. Something that would flavour your conversations for the next week. Something so good you'd watch it again two days later. In a nation bursting with talent, it's mystifying how something of note can't be rustled up.

I don't much like ascribing the Christmas ratings drought to modern technology. It lets the BBC and ITV off the hook. There are 67 million people in this country. Last year's most watched Christmas Day programme was botched-labour-fest *Call The Midwife* with 8.7m viewers. Granted there were most likely scenes involving bunting, CGI snow, and stolen kisses beneath the nunnery mistletoe, but I can understand why 58.3 million people *didn't* watch it, and chose, instead, to entertain themselves.

'Wasn't the telly awful?' is the most common of Christmas laments.

It doesn't need to be.

Tradition

I'm trying to rein in the Christmas traditions. For one thing, they're dammed costly. Case in point: Twiglet tubes. It's not that I don't like Twiglets, I just don't like them enough to eat a bucket's worth. Yet *every year* I buy the big tube and look at it with contempt as the twelve days of Christmas pass.

Why?

Tradition, innit.

The same goes for the traditional tube of Mini Cheddars and the traditional box of Jacob's Cheese Biscuits which, within fifty minutes of being opened, are drier than the walkways of Old Tucson. Most of this traditional food traditionally ends up in the bin.

Not all Christmas traditions are profligate, of course. Far from it. There are the glorious things like seeing old friends and guiltlessly necking the claret at 11am. There are films and songs, too. But even these worthwhile traditions can add up, snow-on-snow, creating the feeling that Christmas is a regimented series of rituals.

It's the breaks in tradition that have served up the majority of my fondest Christmas memories. When things go too smoothly, the days slip away. Despite being aware of this, I still struggle to embrace change; I don't know about you, but I set the season up in such a way that, if all goes to plan, it locks change out, or at least limits its likelihood.

And somehow, each year *does* bring new traditions. Last Christmas, I went to a small carol service at a village church and enjoyed it. So I'll be doing that again this year. Ten years ago, I went to a carol service at Cromer church. I've been doing that ever since, too. Basically, if I'm not careful, by the time I'm sixty, I'll have so many traditions that my entire festive period will need to be meticulously timetabled to fit them all in:

Dec 23rd, 2040:
8.03am – stand near sink, looking for toothpaste
8.05am – think about the next gas quarterly
8.06am – hum Stop The Cavalry (verse only)
8.08am – eat Twiglet

A few years back, I watched an old film called *The Holly & The Ivy*. It was about dispersed family members all trying to get back home to Norfolk in time for Christmas:

'There's something about Christmas morning,' said Celia Johnson at the dinner table, as the camera closed in. 'The first moment when you wake up. Somehow, I don't why, I always *know* it's Christmas morning... And you lie there, taking it in and realising, and this is strangest of all, that it's Christmas everywhere.'

Christmas morning. Lying awake in the dark. If only for a minute. Before the first words are spoken. The best tradition of all - and the easiest to keep.

The Holly & The Ivy is a lovely film. I'll probably watch it again next year.

Train Fare, Increases To

Here's one tradition that never fails to warm the cockles. How sweet it is to hear the annual bugle call from our betters, telling us that the cost to get to and from work shall soon ever so gently swell, like a Christmas pudding in a copper sink. And how lovely, too, that the announcement comes deep into the period's twelve days, generally at that moment when you remember you might need to wear shades the next time you check the figures in your bank account. And how *extra* sweet that it comes, also, after some sort of announcement about the train company's recent surge in profits.

Their attempts to cushion the blow by telling us about the arrival of a new 'fleet' of European-class carriages by the year 2024 (at the earliest) and of their general improvement to signalling between Plumley Bottom and Fudgetown, tend to leave us feeling as though the aforementioned blow hasn't been satisfactorily cushioned.

What hell it is to have to sit, squashed, next to an irate 60-year-old on your first morning commute in January. Especially as he informs you of how, on the continent, their trains are 'spotless' and can get you from 'Prague to Dusseldorf in six minutes' for 'three bloody Euros!'

Ironically, he's that same bloke who, a few years ago, made a point of telling you that he was voting Leave.

Trees, Christmas

'I have been looking on, this evening, at a merry company of children assembled round that pretty German toy, a Christmas Tree. The tree was planted in the middle of a great round table, and towered high...'
Charles Dickens, *The Christmas Tree*, 1850

That pretty German toy.

It was around the 15th century[1] when Hilda, Helga and co. first thought about hacking off some choice cuts from the nearby woodland and sticking them in the corner of their Bavarian lounge. The idea was that the trees would remind people of the Garden of Eden (the trees were also used in 'paradise plays' which told the story of Adam & Eve.[2]) As though bringing flammable chunks of forestry into their homes wasn't enough of a fire hazard, they spiced things up by inserting lighted candles

---

[1] Don't worry don't worry. We'll come to the 19th century any minute now. On the next page, to be precise.

[2] Christmas trees were sometimes known as 'paradise trees' as a result. I'm sorry? What do you mean you don't care? Charming.

betwixt the branches. As with some of the trees themselves, the tradition speedily caught aflame.[1]

Aside from an unspeakable interlude when the puritans prohibited anything remotely festive, Britain has its own long history of Christmas trees. Their popularity truly soared, however, when Queen Victoria and Albert were sketched next to their Coburg spruce on the front cover of the *Illustrated London News* in 1848.[2] As a setter of fashions and trends - honestly - it became the in-thing to have a Christmas tree just like the royal lovebirds.[3]

It was the Yanks, with their puritan bloodline, who were surprisingly slow to spot the monetary potential of the tree, preferring instead to avoid such paganist worshipping. It wasn't until the late 1800s that they joined the fun and never looked back, pretending that they liked Christmas more than everyone else combined.

But we know the truth.

Here's a quick question for you: which area of the UK puts their Christmas decorations up first?

---

[1] The candle tradition was started, it's said, by Martin Luther after a starry walk home had inspired him to recreate the scene in potentially deadly fireball form. The very tradition of Christmas trees was kept alive by the skin of its teeth in the 16th century, as indoor trees went of fashion. Luckily, one small community, on an island in the Danube, kept performing paradise plays at a time when everybody else had tired of them, keeping the idea of festive trees on life-support until it found favour again.

[2] Told you.

[3] The upper-classes were already au fait with Christmas trees on account of Queen Charlotte (another German) having brought them to the UK. But her great grand-daughter, Victoria, made them all, like, totally mainstream.

The answer is London.

Incredibly, those Oyster-Card-flashing socialites can't contain their excitement at this most wonderful time of the year. Around 40% of Londoners have their trees up by Dec 1st. They lead the race to do so by an urban mile. The second most impatient area is the north east, where about 20% achieve an early festive erection. Other areas are more restrained. My own East Anglia, for instance, has a decidedly flaccid 9% pre-December Christmas tree uppage. Intriguingly, Londoners also spend by far and away the most per year on trees and decorations, forking out a ridiculously high average of £296 per adult.[1]

And they all act so hip, don't they, those Londoners, with their vintage bicycles, wheat intolerances and 'secret' cinemas? If you'll recall, they're also the keenest December churchgoers. Next time they give you a monologue about how cool they are, about their Arts Council grant to film butterflies trapped on buses or about the new not-for-profit pop-up restaurant they've discovered on Berwick Street (where everything's served in red 1980s school lunchboxes with *My Little Pony* on the front), don't buy into their propaganda. As the next piece testifies, propaganda-buying comes at a cost.

[1] In the West Midlands, by comparison, where times are hard and they know a bargain when they see one, they only shell out around £84 per year. I ought to remind you, though, not to lean too heavily on Christmas stats. They're often sprinkled with fairy dust.

Truce, The Christmas

Blackadder: *Both sides advanced further during one Christmas piss-up than they managed in the next two and a half years of war.*
Baldrick: *Remember the football match?*
Blackadder: *Remember it? How could I forget it? I was never offside.*
                              Blackadder Goes Forth, 'Goodbyeee', 1989

Wilfred Owen called it the *old lie*:
'How sweet and fitting it is to die for one's country.'
There are a few other *old lies* out there, too. Perhaps the strongest rival to Owen's choice would be the old lie, regarding wars, that they 'would all be over by Christmas'. It was an untruth that repeatedly haunted all involved. There's something about the phrase which must have irked the gods; the moment people claimed a war would be over by Christmas, the cogs of fate turned to ensure otherwise.[1]
Ah, but in December 1914 how tantalising a glimpse the soldiers had of the *over by Christmas* prophecy coming to fruition. Just four months deep into the war, both sides of the trenches were largely manned by professional soldiers.[2] Up and down the lines, pockets of goodwill gradually formed, with unspoken ceasefires and back-and-forthing of what the modern audience might call 'mega lolz'. By the time Christmas Day rolled around, and hardened eyes moistened at thoughts of back home, German soldiers sang carols to their enemy across

---

[1] The only thing *ever* reliably over by Christmas is the DFS 'Autumn Sale', which becomes the 'Boxing Day Madness Sale' on Christmas Eve.

[2] The massacre of the conscripted boys-next-door was still two years away.

No Man's Land and were joined by voices of a British tongue. Peace. Harmony. With a couple of lads from the Chelmsford Light Infantry dropping a beat for good measure.

Even in war, December 25th was a day of good cheer. General Haig, who would end the conflict with more blood on his hands than an apprentice butcher, made sure that there were 'no reliefs to be carried out' and that the soldiers were 'given as easy a time as possible'.[1] The soldiers were free to do whatever they wanted. Some chose to stare at the moulding wooden slats propping up their trench. Others leant against a post. It was a right laugh. The more adventurous amongst their number stuck their heads above the parapet and made the journey out across a frosty No Man's Land, over to where, the night before, the German enemy had lit candles and generally acted unlike the murderous louts they'd been depicted as in the *Daily Herald*.

When the British and Germans met on that now-legendary Christmas Day in 1914, they exchanged stories and showed one another photographs of their sweethearts back home.[2] They also helped to bury their mortally wounded and repair one another's trenches. Extraordinary acts of bonhomie, considering. Whether an organised football match took place remains a moot point. Certainly no firm evidence exists of one.[3] That said, there *are* allusions in letters to mini kickabouts and hard-fought games of Wembley. One school of thought is that

---

[1] King George V also found time in *his* busy schedule to send each soldier a Christmas card. The gits never sent him one back, though.

[2] I've never understood why men do this. How is one supposed to react when shown somebody's partner?: 'Yeah, yeah, she's well fit, mate. Nice one. Bet she's a right handful in the sack.'

[3] The famous photograph of a tangle of soldiers all leaping to head the same ball was actually taken on Armistice Day, 1918, and was an all-British affair.

any written evidence of football matches was censored by the respective governments. After all, friendly games tend to make a somewhat underwhelming case for the importance of war.

Once those at the business end of the British army found out about the Christmas camaraderie with the Hun, they quickly knocked together a law stating that anybody seen fraternising with the enemy would be subject to court martial. And with that, Germany had, for the first time, and definitely not the last, technically beaten England on penalties.[1] The court martial ruling was followed by a programme of 'atrocity propaganda' which vilified and dehumanised the Germans. And the old lie, that the war would be over by Christmas, lived up to its billing.[2]

---

[1] Robert Graves, one of the first writers to speak of the horror of the Great War, wrote, in later years, a *fictional* account of a football match. He said the Germans won 3-2 and, with shades of Edmund Blackadder, that the winning goal was 'miles offside'. In 2014, *The Daily Telegraph* reported Graves' scoreline as fact.

[2] For the record, 306 British soldiers were shot by their fellow countrymen in World War One. Usually for abandoning posts, but also for other misdemeanours, such as fraternising with the enemy. One such victim, a sixteen-year-old with shell-shock, was given so much rum before his execution that he had to be carried to the spot where he'd be shot at. (He'd just written home to his mother: 'I will try my best to get out of it, so don't worry.') None of the 306 men murdered by the British army - sentences which were nearly all given the nod by our good friend, General Haig - were included on war memorials. The treacherous swines were only officially pardoned by the UK government in 2006.

Images of soldiers from the Great War shaking hands and playing football come around every Christmas.[1] Although seldom spoken about until 1963's *Oh, What A Lovely War*, the match is now locked in folklore. That the truce was quickly broken - and that the men involved would likely go on to slaughter one another - matters little. What matters is Christmas. Hope. Friendship. If only for a day.

'It was,' wrote *The Guardian* of the truce back in January 1915, 'the simple and unexamined impulse of human souls, drawn together in face of a common and desperate plight.'

One old truth to complement Wilfred Owen's old lie is that ceasefires are bogus. The fighting never ends. To prove my point, go online and see the fierce message-board arguments about which of the two opposing armies initiated the Christmas Truce in the first place.

Isn't life a scream?

❄ ❄ ❄

---

[1] The story was told in a lavish 2014 Sainsbury's advert. In it, the British soldiers were floppy-haired, white-toothed, smiling, physical specimens in clean uniforms. As Peter Jackson's masterpiece *They Shall Not Grow Old* shows us, real soldiers were anything but. The most striking aspect of the film's colourised footage is how malnourished and gristly the men look - and how green and stubby their teeth. Of course, that kind of thing isn't going to help Sainsbury's turkey sales. (Jackson's film also gave a clue as to why footballs may have been at the front in the first place. They were used as markers, kicked across No Man's Land and followed by soldiers who daren't look up.)

Turkey

'I want you to take this and go out and buy a turkey so large you'd think its mother had been rogered by an omnibus.'
Blackadder's Christmas Carol, 1988

We all know that one smarmy git who butters a pheasant and uploads an Instagram pic of themselves slipping it into the oven on Christmas morn, but, if you want a traditional meat down your yuletide gullet, turkey is your best bet.

'Yes, Ryan,' the pheasant-butterers argue, 'but, actually, research has led us to believe that in Saxon England, the members of the parish would traditionally get together to butter a pheas...'

'Shut it, pal - I'm here to talk about turkey!'

With the body of a Laura Ashley cushion and the head of a melted dinosaur, it's amazing anyone ever thought twice about eating a turkey when 16th century traders first brought them to England.[1] The sight of their fleshy wattle and caruncles is enough to make even the most ardent creationist end their belief in intelligent design. In all honesty, it could make a few Darwinists give up the ghost, too. And it's not as if the critters sing or make any sort of pleasant bird-like noises, emitting, instead, something resembling a cross between a death prattle and a fart in a bath.

Maybe eating them was the humane thing to do.

Turkeys became a popular Christmas meat almost instantly upon arrival (mainly because they were suitably exotic and

---

[1] It's thought turkeys were introduced to England by a Yorkshireman who traded them with Native Americans (although they were originally domesticated in Mexico). What the Native Americans received in return is lost to history. A chunk of Wensleydale and a handful of boasts about how good Yorkshire is, I expect.

tasted better than a hairy boar with an apple stuffed in its gob). They bred in mid-spring and were naturally plump by the winter solstice. Unlike chickens (with their eggs) and cows (with their milk), turkeys offered little besides their meat, making them more dispensable during the harshest months of the year. December, for example.

And they were, and are, bloody enormous. One stout turkey could last a family and their guests well into the new year. Popular legend has it that Henry VIII was the first Briton to eat turkey on Christmas Day. The craze caught on, and, barring passing dalliances with geese and swans (and those pheasant-butterers of social media), turkey remains the festive meat of choice for Henry's subjects to this day, with us consuming around ten million of the monsters per annum.

Although nobody can be sure of this, turkeys are most likely to have got their name from Turkey, where they were once traded in a greater number than even Bernard Matthews would know what to do with. In Russia, they're known as 'birds of India'. Middle Eastern countries lean towards the name 'Indian rooster'. In Turkey, they're called 'Hindi'. Interesting, right? Remind yourself to bring it up this year, during that pulsating annual conversation with a member of the extended family about how you, or they, or both, find turkey 'to be a bit dry'.

Twelve Days

If the Roman Catholic dating system is to be believed, and I don't recommend it is, then Jesus Christ was born on the 25th of December, marking day one of Christmas. Then, twelve days later - during which time Mary was inundated with visitors when all she wanted to do was sleep, cry and have headaches in peace - the Magi turned up in an unspecified number i.e. not *three.*[1] In many Catholic countries, the twelfth day is the day when presents are given, by which time, most Britons are back to work, vowing not to drink as much on weeknights and enquiring about Weight Watchers memberships.

I've said it elsewhere, but I firmly believe in the twelve days of Christmas. Mainly because the 353 other days of the year are a chore. Christmas - and by 'Christmas' I mean, the staying in and putting up of feet of a winter's afternoon - ought to be stretched to full use. Sadly, the season is getting shorter. In the United States, stores re-open on Christmas afternoon. It can't be long before the same happens here, with businesses following suit, leaving us with miserly bosses called Ebenezer chastising us for wanting to take the whole day off.

Let me be clear, this isn't a rallying cry for the celebration of Epiphany,[2] rather a carrion call to slacking at the merriest time of the year. You oughtn't have to be a very wise man to see the appeal of that.

---

[1] As you'll know from my earlier skit about nativities, there are more factual inaccuracies about the Christmas story besides its date. The popular notion that there were three kings is largely due to their giving of three gifts and their appearances as a three-piece in numerous carols, such as *We Three Kings*. But were they kings? And where were they kings of? Nobody knows. Matthew's gospel tells us they came from 'the East', but that only narrows their origins down to half of the world's nations; his gospel, written in Greek, like all of the New Testament, only uses the word 'Magi'. Kings and wise men don't get a look in. Franco Zeffirelli's *Jesus of Nazareth* has them swanning in from a host of different places, which is also plausible.

[2] Epiphany is the ancient Greek word for 'revelation', which is precisely what the Magi experienced when they found Jesus and suspected he might prove to be somebody of note.

U is for....

Under The Tree

Not to be confused with the finger-clicking showstopper *Under The Sea* from Disney's *The Little Mermaid*, this entry is all about the delights of seeing presents under the tree...

Oh, alright, I confess. I couldn't think of anything else beginning with 'U'. Especially as I'd already written about being *under* the mistletoe. This was the only letter in the alphabet where I had to look online for ideas. As usual when one goes online, there was scant inspiration to be had.

Here are some of the 'U' suggestions from other Christmas alphabets:

'Unwrapped Gifts'

'Universal Love'

'U is for Us, to whom Jesus was given - to show us the way and take us to heaven!'[1]

I guess there are a few others I could have done:

'Unusually Mild'

'Unbelievably Bad Effort From ITV'

'Um Bongo, Um Bongo, They Drink It In The Congo'

❄ ❄ ❄

---

[1] That's supposed to rhyme, by the way. Tenuous, eh? The website it was taken from also suggested the following entry:

'V is for Virgin, foretold by the sage - God's revelation on prophecy's page.'

They had something of a theme going. I made my own one up:

'Z is for zorry, which we zay to the Lord - the price of our zinz, we bare could afford.'

V is for...

Very Best Christmas Album In The World Ever, The

Not every Christmas album can be as rollickingly good as Phil Spector's. In truth, precious few come close to being good at all. As much as I love Christmas music, I am completely aware that most of it, including the stuff I like, is tosh. From Boyz II Men's *Christmas Interpretations* to Celine Dion's *These Are Special Times*, via Rod Stewart's *Merry Christmas, Baby* and Daniel O'Donnell's *O' Holy Night*, the standard is such that it's a wonder Christmas albums haven't been banned.[1]

The customary take on matters is that nobody bothers making Christmas songs anymore. It is, however, early to proclaim the *commercial* death of the Christmas record as there appears to have been a resurgence in the last few years, particularly from American artists. In keeping with tradition, it has been mostly vile. Michael Bublé is the current king of the season, emerging annually with TV specials in which, between singalongs with Katy Perry and the Cookie Monster, he talks about how he spends his Christmas (on the whole, you'll be pleased to know, he likes to keep things real). Other popular Christmas album releases of recent years feature long-dead stars having their work re-recorded with a philharmonic orchestra, stripping their once exciting songs of urgency and relegating the performer in question to the role of A Musician Enjoyed By The Infirm.

As well as commercially successful releases, there have been some genuinely great additions to the canon. Gwen Stefani and

---

[1] Special mention should go to Mannheim Steamroller, whose exhaustive output of Christmas albums has found a more than appreciative audience in the US. This is despite most of his songs sounding like they're being played by him slapping his private parts onto a Casio keyboard and recording the fallout.

She & Him have produced perfectly respectable efforts. Sia's album is a stonker and features the best original seasonal single in years, *Santa's Coming For Us*. To this list we can add albums by Fiona Apple, Kate Bush and Sufjan Stevens (who seems to be on a mission to release more studio albums than the rest of the world combined).[1] I also have a shameful soft spot for Justin Bieber's plentiful Christmas output, largely because it feels so of its time and so in tune with its youthful audience that it will, I think, have a real charm about it in fifty years. Especially when re-recorded with a philharmonic orchestra.

Visiting

A hard time we had of it.
At the end we preferred to travel all night,
Sleeping in snatches,
With the voices singing in our ears, saying
That this was all folly

T.S. Eliot, The Journey of the Magi, 1927

The Magi - John Milton's 'star-led wizards' - have form when it comes to claims to fame. Not only did they meet and greet the redeemer of humankind whilst he was yet to move onto solids, but they were also, technically, the creators of Christmas traffic.[2] Ever since they camelled their way across the parched

---

[1] Perhaps the most unlikely Christmas album came from Bob Dylan, on which, aside from the barnstorming *Must Be Santa*, he generally sang, to borrow one of his own phrases, like a clown who cried in the alley (whilst dying of an illness caused by smoking).

[2] The only fly in their claim-to-fame ointment is that nobody knows who they actually were.

desert to adorn the suckling babe with holy gifts (and so on), the trend for yuletide travel has caught on. Each year in the UK, on the closest Friday to Christmas Day, around twenty million car journeys are made. No wonder *Driving Home For Christmas* strikes such a chord. An additional fifty million 'leisure' journeys, by car or train, are made over the Christmas period, leaving Chris Rea with an open goal for a follow-up single: *Driving Around With Relatively Little Purpose (For Christmas)*.

Inspired, possibly, by the aspirational playboy lifestyle of Sir Cliff Richard - and ignoring Jane Austen's advice that December is 'quite the season indeed for friendly meetings' - about four million Brits swan the nest to sunnier climes for the Christmas season. A grinch's manoeuvre if ever there was one. Really, who could leave England during the winter solstice, with its fruity afternoon skies and cosy evenings? There's an entire year of options for holidays, yet these oddballs choose to miss Britain at its finest, trading it in for a Thai shack or an air-conditioned hotel room in Dubai. Each to their own and all that, but, goodness, to sit sipping a tepid cocktail on a humid beach, swatting away mosquitos, whilst the towns and villages of Britain awake in cold, sunny thrall to the peel of church bells...

It's all folly, if you ask me.

W is for...

Wall Calendars

Few people talk about wall calendars, yet they're absolute staples of a British Christmas. In their most literal sense, they date back as far as the Egyptians. They were far more practical in those days, of course, containing celestial patterns and detailing movements of the Nile. They didn't have Zac Efron on the front or list key Scottish bank holidays. But what a get-out-of-jail card modern calendars are for Christmas shoppers; what better way to placate a fussy grandmother than a calendar of *East Anglian Gardens*?

I particularly like how calendars are almost impossible to disguise when wrapping. There can be no doubt when you've got a wrapped calendar in your hand. The only question is what will be its subject: retro sci-fi book covers or Little Mix.

Talking of Little Mix, the last few years have seen them duel with Cliff Richard for the honour of biggest selling UK calendar. In 2018, they won the battle for the first time. Other big players annually are Tom Hardy (the actor, not the novelist), Kelly Brook (the model, not the boxer), and Elvis (Presley, not Costello).

East Anglian Gardens doesn't get a look in.

Most people associate putting their calendar up with the end of Christmas, which makes calendars a somewhat bittersweet gift for the festive enthusiast. Which reminds me, we're getting close to the end of this preposterous book.

Winter Solstice

'*Now is the solstice of the year,*' sang Ian Anderson in Jethro Tull's thoroughly unappreciated *Ring Out, Solstice Bells,*[1] before going off on various tangents:
Have the lads up ready in a line...
Seven druids dance in seven time...
Praise be to the distant sister sun...
Joyful as the silver planets run...

---

[1] So thoroughly unappreciated that it didn't even make *my* list of twelve songs for this book.

361

You don't get many lines of *that* calibre in *All I Want For Christmas Is You*. Come to think of it, most of Mariah's Carey's Christmas output is low on the druid-allusion front. Come on, girl, pull your finger out.

The winter solstice delivers a double whammy: the longest night *and* the shortest day. All caused by our planet's axis tilting us away from the sun, until the orb reaches its lowest point in the sky. The date usually falls on December 21st. It used to be the 25th, creating one big festive hoopla, until the Gregorian calendar was introduced - with pictures of hunky firemen on - and the date slipped back. Here in England, we're treated to around 7 hours and 49 minutes of glorious solstice daylight. The rest is darkness. From that moment on, however, the days become longer and longer, minute by minute, until the June solstice drenches the motherland in an almost unimaginable seventeen hours of daylight.

Even though the immediate effects of the solstice are barely noticeable,[1] the drawing out of the evenings before Christmas Day can, like the wall calendars mentioned in the previous entry, be an unseasonable reminder of the transitory nature of Christmas. No such unseasonable reminders are offered in the Norwegian island of Spitsbergen, however. The sun sets for them in November and doesn't rise until March. A four-month night. Imagine how many times they have to get up for a wee.

Woolworths

I promise not to get too emotional here, but, goodness, I loved Woolworths. Any urbanites reading this will wonder what all the fuss was about, but those of us living in and around market

---

[1] Particularly in the mornings, which keep getting darker until deep into January.

towns still feel the sting of its absence. The shop may be famed for its pic 'n mix - mostly by those who never had to rely on it for anything else - but, for some people, Woolworths was their go-to for everything. Surely it was the only shop where you could leave with a hot water bottle, a toolkit, a train set (made by the company's very own 'Chad Valley'), a baby-grow, plant food, Pop-Up Pirate and a Lee Evans video. Vitally, it was *the* place to go to buy new music.[1] And new movies. And new computer games. And new books. Some branches even served up a cooked breakfast (which, to be fair, did taste a little, well, *Chad Valley*). Their Christmas selection was equally varied. From electric lights to sugar mice, Woolworths had it covered.

You could argue that Woolworths has since been replaced by supermarkets and the internet, especially with regard to music. Obviously, we can all now buy any album we wish on Amazon, but we *do* have to wait for it to be delivered, which, in the Christmas present-buying season, can take a while. Also, when the item does eventually turn up, it does so having been dropped onto your welcome mat from a great height, as well as having been tossed around a depot by an overworked Philosophy undergraduate beforehand. And the less said about supermarket music sections, the better. Choices in a supermarket range from Ed Sheeran's latest album to Ed Sheeran's previous album, with perhaps, at best, one of those

---

[1] This isn't cosy nostalgia. Woolworths was *the* leading seller of music in the UK until the late 1990s. It remained a key player until the very end. Its demise runs an interesting parallel with the demise of recorded music sales.

compilations called *Music Mum Likes*[1] or a Ministry Of Sound compilation of *Old Skool Cuts*.

With Woolworths it was all so much easier. Walk in. Buy a CD.[2] Go home. Wrap it. Done. The same rule applied for all presents, especially those desperate last-minute affairs. Woolworths offered backwater-dwellers a gift-buying lifeline, a city within a shop.

Woolworths' problem was, perhaps, that it was cheap, but not cheap enough. Nor was it expensive enough. It played to neither end of the market. Whereas its city branches suffered from apathy from potential customers who were unsure of a reason to go in there, the appeal of market town Woolworths stores was clear: you went in there for everything.

Woolworths' demise was far from inevitable, merely a failure to move with the times. Their marketing was disastrous (Woolly The Sheep, for example) and it just felt as though the whole company refused to believe it was no longer 1993. The financial crash of 2008/9 sealed the fate of their 807 stores. A number of businesses tried to salvage the company[3] but had their bids turned down. When Woolworths crashed in December 2008,

---

[1] Featuring Cyndi Lauper, Take That, Sam Smith, Olly Murs, Coldplay, Whitney et al. Please believe me when I tell you this: there's a CD out there called *Now That's What I Call Mum*. It sounds more like a tagline running along the bottom of the screen on *The Jeremy Kyle Show*.

[2] And, while you're at it, maybe pick up some party balloons and a bag of compost.

[3] Most notably, the foodstore, Iceland, and *Dragon's Den* lounger, Theo Pathitis. After Woolworths closed, Iceland bought lots of their properties instead, which is why you're likely to have an Iceland where your local Woolworths used to be.

they were £385m in debt. Small fry in big business terms.[1] Such was the positive feeling towards the brand, the government considered stepping in to help. Alas, no such move was made and their last store shut on January 6th, 2009: the day after twelfth night.

Christmas shopping has been that extra bit difficult ever since.

Wrapping

'Everything was so nicely done up, and there were pictures stuck on the different parcels.'
Anne Frank, Diary, Dec 27th, 1943

As lovely as the end result can look, I struggle to believe people when they tell me they enjoy wrapping presents. It's one of the most cumbersome chores. There's just no comfortable position to do it in. Even at a table it requires bending and stretching in unnatural positions. And there's nothing more irksome than dealing with Sellotape. You can lose half a morning just trying to locate the hairline from when you last used it; at your most desperate, you might resort to making your own hairline by cutting across the tape with the blade of a scissor (a technique that almost never yields positive results). There are other clangers, too, such as forgetting what you've wrapped (and having to unwrap and re-wrap the offending item) and accidentally catching an already-wrapped present with a flailing wisp of Sellotape and ripping it open.

Wrapping is no friend to the environment, either. About 50,000 trees are felled each year just to supply the UK with paper. Around 227,000 miles' worth of it is then thrown away. Most is so cheaply made that it can't be recycled.

---

[1] For instance, the company took £27m in one day that very month.

The history of wrapping presents goes back just about as far as recorded history. Initially, gifts were wrapped in mammoth fur and velociraptor skin but, by the early 20th century, we had evolved to coloured paper. Tradition tells us that two brothers from Kansas City first had the idea to upgrade to *patterned* paper in 1917, charging ten cents a sheet. Within a matter of years, they'd started a trend and cornered the wrapping paper market. Their company is going strong to this day. Hallmark, it's called. They also muscled in on the Christmas card game, as you'll recall. Come on, don't tell me you've forgotten everything *already*.

X is for...

Xmas

With Xylophones and X-rays out of the question, I plumped for the spelling of Christmas as 'Xmas' to fill this difficult section. I wasn't sure if I could find anything interesting out about it, but, try this for size: the X is taken from the Greek word, Χριστός, meaning Christ. The X symbol was used in early Christian circles as a secret codeword for Jesus Christ. So there.

Generally, books of English usage recommend 'Christmas' instead of 'Xmas'.

And so do I.

❄ ❄ ❄

Y is for...

Yule Logs

Source of many a punchline come Christmas night when the stomach twists and bubbles with foreboding, the yule log has suitably murky origins. The Scandinavian solstice-time Feast of Juul is one suggested source. It should go without saying that the word might have Germanic roots, too.[1]

The original yule log was, and is, an especially girthy log put on a fire at Christmas. Tradition dictated that the burning of the yule log would prevent the house in question from catching fire or being struck by lightning. The idea was that by lighting a large log - or Yule-clog or Christmas-block, as they were also known[2] - it would, in the words of one antiquarian, 'illuminate the house to turn night into day'. (Yep, sounds like a great way to prevent house fires. They might as well have shoved a lightning rod up their chimney for good measure.)

The more common version of a yule log is, of course, the big chocolate log that nobody particularly wants to eat. For all our modern advances, most yule logs in the UK are still factory-rolled by hand. Belittle the rise of the machines all you like, but this is one of those rare occasions when the charm of the handmade succumbs to the charm of the sterile robotic fist. In other words, I'd much rather eat a yule log flattened into shape

---

[1] Scots claim that it actually stems from their side of Hadrian's Wall. But then, they say that about most things, don't they? The thought is that 'yule' is their pronunciation the Nordic word for wheel (*hjol*). So, there you go. They're effectively claiming to have invented the wheel.

[2] Both of which also sound like alternative names for a bowel movement.

by a disinfected roller than by a factory operative called Darren whose just come back from his 'comfort' break.

In Catalan, the yule log joke has been taken to *Mrs Brown's Boys*-level extremes. To this day, their depictions of the nativity often include a figurine of a peasant boy evacuating his bowels. His name translates as 'the crapper' or the 'defecating log'. How that didn't make the *Eurotrash* Christmas special, I'll never know.

Z is for...

Zzz

'Oh, goodness, look at the time. I hope Santa hasn't had to pass up this house just because some boys weren't in bed when he came by. I thought I heard Santa's sleigh bells a little while ago, going up the other side of the street.'

The Old Man, *A Christmas Story*, 1983

There's an unspoken degree of pressure with getting a decent night's sleep on Christmas Eve, particularly for those with children.[1] Naturally, there are many people out there who spend Christmas Eve getting sloshed in an attempt to declare the following morning a write-off, but this book isn't for the likes of such weasels. For the hopeless romantic, going to bed on Christmas Eve still jingles the soul, whatever your age. It must be emotional memory, all those veiled cautions from childhood

---

[1] Who have a habit of waking up with the vivacity of a milkman at the best of times, but really up their game on the big day. According to a 2018 survey, the average Christmas wake-up time for a child is 6.44am. I suspect a number of parents might want to question that finding.

that you'd better be asleep before Father Christmas arrives else he won't leave any presents. Was there anything worse as a child than being *forced* to sleep? The only thing to rival it was being told, halfway through an unstoppable youthful rage, that you were simply 'tired'.

'I am not TIIIIRRREDD!' would come your considered response.

The thought of it, the shaking excitement as you buried yourself under the cover, that Father Christmas was going to be making a stop on *your* rooftop, sliding down *your* chimney, leaving presents on *your* landing or under *your* tree. Well now. How could we be expected to sleep through that? Yet, somehow, we did.

❄ ❄ ❄

We've come to the end of our alphabet. Zzz. Bedtime.

Have I missed anything out? I'm bound to have done. The obvious one is Christmas dinner but I left it out because I'd waffled on about various components of it elsewhere. What's that? You want *more* Christmas dinner facts? Oh, alright then. Across the day, we'll consume around 6,000 calories each (although that number will be skewed by the likes of Rachel Riley at one end of the spectrum and Eamonn Holmes at the other). The average bill for Christmas dinners across the UK comes to around £20 per diner. Considering it costs about £50 per head, at least, to eat out on December 25th, it's not too bad a deal. Some married couples make the gutter press each year with tales of how they intend to charge friends and family for the privilege of eating at their table:

'PULL THE OTHER ONE - Mum Goes Crackers Charging Kiddies To Eat Xmas Nosh!'

Etc.

Turkey is still the most popular meat, with around 76% of takers nationwide. Chicken and beef come second and third, with a surprisingly lowly 7 and 6% respectively. Only 2% will butter a pheasant (and upload a photo of it to Instagram). And, for all our backslapping at how forward thinking and progressive we are, women still do an overwhelming amount of the day's kitchen work (whilst men are more likely to help assemble toys, light fires, and use the phrase, 'You've done well this year').[1] Around four million Christmas dinners go uneaten across the United Kingdom annually: the equivalent to 263,000 turkeys, 7.5 million mince pies, 740,000 slices of Christmas pudding, 17 million Brussels sprouts, 12 million carrots and 11 million roast spuds. It's easy to believe otherwise, but we are living in an age of plenty.

Now I can't stop spouting facts: Christmas sales of train sets and fix-it kits have mysteriously doubled in the last decade; only around five couples per year get married on Christmas Day[2] (possibly because, quite remarkably, nearly 50% of all clergy take the day off); in hospitals, Christmas-born babies are much more likely to be given the names Angel, Noel and, amazingly, Merry; and almost 3,000 people a year spend Christmas Day logging their annual tax information on the HMRC website.

Oh, it's all so interesting. But I better stop. It's getting late.

Now, quick, come on. Get to sleep. Or *he* won't visit.

---

[1] 51% of women do *all* the cooking themselves, compared to 17% of men.

[2] And most of those are in *Emmerdale*.

The Yule Log

The Twelve Days Of Christmas

Tues 25th - Christmas Day

Woke up about seven. The moon was still out. I went to my window and stood hypnotised by it. Against a jet black sky you can see the whole universe whizzing off in the distance, but when the moon is bright, like this morning, you see only the well-known constellations, little chains of white dots. On mornings like this, you can understand how religions start. Were it not for promising my mum I'd be at hers by ten, I'd have followed these stars in search of a child king.

Christmas morning is one of the only times where you know what you were doing on the same date last year, and the year before, and so on, right through to your earliest memory. If churches are a place where heaven and earth are supposed to overlap, so Christmas morning is a time where the past and present do likewise. No matter how old I get, the morning elicits the same joys, drawing me into a slipstream of spirits of Christmas past; for the first few minutes, at least. Until that old head on my shoulders snaps me into now.

Spent the day at my mum's. She got her 'that's that over with for another year' line out of the way quite early, but waited until 12:27 to give her 'Christmas isn't what it used to be' speech. As ever, the day was otherwise hilarious. Thought about other people's traditions. Our family has one that is so embedded that I forget it's not universal: hot sausage rolls. You can't move for them on Christmas morning.

I have never received so much chocolate as I did today. Six selection boxes, two tubs of Quality Street, three boxes of mints and a chocolate orange. I hope for my own sake they survive the twelve days. I wonder if the people buying them for me felt a twinge when they did so, like when you knowingly buy an alcoholic a bottle of wine. Enabling, I think it's called.

Dinner was so big that my stomach hasn't recovered even at this late stage. I've had a twisted, stitch-like feeling since 2pm. Nothing is helping. Especially the plate load of cheese and biscuits I added into the equation at 7pm. Between meals, we visited my nanny. Housebound in her chair, she sits in her kitchen all year round, complaining about the repeats on television but refusing to watch any new programmes on account of them not being as good as 'the old ones'. Her kitchen is so hot she could bake potatoes on the windowsill, but due to her lack of movement she's forever complaining of the cold. She was on good form today. Both of my grandmothers are Norfolk-born and have an absolutely riotous sense of comic delivery.

The walk home from mum's was less appealing than last night. I had two heavy bags, one on either side; I was loaded up like one of those mopeds you see clogging the streets in travel features about Mumbai. Clouds had covered the sky. So quiet, though. Nobody about. Black, unlit roads. Then, empty house after empty house, until the occasional brightly lit Christmas extravaganza. My little flat felt odd on arrival. My back was soaked in sweat. Drunkenly, I put the tree lights on and drank the nicest cup of tea I'd ever made. Christmas night takes on a surreal quality, especially as the day's excesses of food and drink work their way around your system. Even seeing 'Tues 25/12' on the Sky TV guide looked odd. So, too, the empty advent calendar with every door opened and its hollow plastic casing revealed.

That's that over with for another year.

Except for the next eleven days of high quality loafing. Oh yeah! This is where Christmas really starts.

Weds 26th - Boxing Day

Always a favourite day, this year went with form. Spent the day with my sister and her family, eating cheese and opening presents. Her partner and I lowered the tone by watching Norwich City on TV. I feel bad for how I always let football intrude on Boxing Day, but am pretty sure that I actually can't help it. Norwich were behind by three goals with ten minutes left. It was as though the gods were punishing us for watching it. Then, in a finale that will go down with legendary status among City fans, the 'yellows' pulled three goals back, the last coming in the 97th minute. The commentator got so excited that he called it 'the winner', even though it was the equaliser. It felt like a winner, though. Elsewhere, my own Christmas was saved by Manchester United sweeping aside the mighty Huddersfield, 3-1.

The BBC showed the legendary 1971 'Morecambe & Wise Christmas Special' and I couldn't help but wonder why BBC and ITV have made almost no effort to produce a similar show in the last thirty years. Is the Morecambe & Wise formula - which pulled in over 20m viewers - really passé? I'm sure a genuinely funny family show with good guests, singing, dancing and sketches could be a huge hit. These things can't be too expensive to make, especially during the trial periods. Why, pre-alcoholism, didn't ITV do a huge 'Ant & Dec Christmas Show' every year? Instead, tonight's primetime ITV had 'Emmerdale', 'Coronation Street' and a decade old Bond film. It was announced that yesterday's most watched TV programme was the Queen's Speech. It got 6.4m viewers. All the other 'big' hitters - 'Mrs Brown's Boys', 'Call The Midwife' - will likely have their numbers increased as the recordings and catch-ups are taking into account. Even so, they'll do well to hit 10m. The difference with a popular variety show is that it would be event television. People would watch it on the night itself.

There is a stack of opened presents in my lounge. Books, chocolate, alcohol. The trinity. Boxing Night - if that's what tonight is called - was tinged with sadness when I was young because I knew the present opening was over with until next year (we used to go to my grandparent's house for a 'spread' consisting of cold meat, pickled onions, cheddar and white bread; there, we'd receive our last presents of the year). How great it is to be an adult and just buy things whenever you want them. On that note, saw a news report about the struggles of the 'high street' and wondered whether I should chip in and do my bit tomorrow.

That's all for now. 'Match Of The Day' is about to start.

Thurs 27th (I think) -

I got to Norwich before most of the shops were open, but M&S didn't let me down. They never do. Open and willing, they'd even gone one step further this year and lined up their goods in size order, unlike other shops which have a seek and destroy policy in the sales. I fell in glorious, momentary love with about seven members of staff. Possibly my most outdated, blinkered chauvinistic view (and I've got a few) is that I love seeing attractive women working in department stores, wearing the company uniform and soaked in perfume. It is truly terrible that so many department store workers - male and female - are likely employed because of their looks and general presentation, but I do love seeing them, dressed up to the nines for a ten-hour shift on a public holiday. In a life short of glamour, it gives one a lift to know that there are still retail outlets out there who want you to feel like you're hobnobbing with the elite, even if you're only nipping in to buy heavily reduced clearance stock because you can't justify paying the usual price.

Other than the usual shirts and jumpers, I bought a dressing gown and my first ever pair of proper old man pyjamas. I may never wear them. They're too nice. Went to HMV and wondered how it survives. Picked up a DVD but couldn't face the rigmarole of queuing and then having to pay about £5 more than I would online.

Spent the late afternoon clearing my wardrobe, consigning less-deserving garments to the charity shop bag. Went to a pub quiz afterwards. Ate in. Had Chilli Con Carne. I'd been craving something normal. There was a little side salad on the plate. Normally I'd leave most of it, but I could feel the cucumber and tomato bring cold life into my body. My digestive system is currently working overtime to sap as much leafy goodness from it as possible.

Fri 28th -

A nothing day. And a beauty. All the other traditions had been ticked off and now only the best one remains: idling.

'World Championship Darts' was on. An unexpected tradition for me in recent years. I love the atmosphere. The crowd sing a song: 'Stand up if you love the darts'. I can't think of any other sport - let's, for the moment, be polite and call darts a 'sport' - where the fans stand and applaud the very occasion, rather than cheering a team or individual. Imagine going to a football match and chanting, 'Stand up if you love football'. You'd be hounded out of the ground. Do something similar at the snooker and you'd be tutted to death, then formally banned from attending any professional snooker events in the UK from here on in.

Began reading A.N. Wilson's book about Queen Victoria. She wrote around 60 million words in her lifetime, equivalent, in Wilson's words, to around '700 volumes'. And there I am thinking that writing five volumes (around 400,000 words) in eight years represented a good workload. Tantalisingly, most of Victoria's writings were censored, edited or destroyed completely, leading people to slaver at the prospect of hidden scandal. A.N. Wilson thinks the more likely reason is that her children, who did the bulk of the editing, were keen to omit the passages where she slagged them off (which is something she was fond of doing, both in person and print). The most interesting point made so far is that for all our modern belief in an EU political puppet show, 19th century Europe - and the centuries before it - was largely dominated by royal families who all intermarried. The continent was ruled by, effectively, one big family. Our own Queen Victoria had a German mother and a German family on her paternal side (although her father happened to be born in England) and she herself married a German. Still, it was nice to 'take back control' at that Brexit vote and recreate the good old days, where we were, erm, run by Europeans.

In other news, HMV have gone into administration. I feel partly to blame.

Sat 29th -

Around me, Christmas gets thinner by the day. Now all the talk is about New Year's Eve and adverts for sofas and fitted wardrobes, things for the new year and the new you.

Got a new 'Radio Times' through the letterbox this morning. Receiving something other than junk/bills in the post is thrilling. It was only £1 for 12 issues. I'll cancel after that. Of course, I might forget to. That's how they get you. Some companies' entire business model is based on the hope that people forget to cancel their subscriptions. Regardless, the thrill of the delivery has had me looking at other magazine subscriptions online. What a little treat it would be to get a new magazine every month. Why hadn't I done this sooner? God, there are some wonderfully niche publications out there, though. 'Narrow Boat', 'Music Teacher', and 'Outdoor Swimmer' are my faves so far.

My Christmas Day chocolate haul is already looking fragile.

Sun 30th -

Chris and Kate came round in the evening. What a joy to have nice people in your house and do nothing but talk. Kate is American. She told me how many gunshots she hears on a weekly basis (we did talk about nice things, too). Chris has been living with her in the States (specifically, Missouri) for about two years and has already been indirectly involved in two shootouts. The most recent was outside a hotel. When the shooters escaped in their car, there were already two soon-to-be-dead victims being treated by paramedics on the pavement. The whole thing started when one of the gun-wielders shot into a crowd outside a restaurant as a way of making a statement against how the area had been redeveloped. Amazing. Even when you clear somewhere up, the act of doing so causes shootings by people who preferred it being a shithole. No good deed goes unpunished. A miserable little saying with much truth to it.

I drank lots of port and decided that it is the best alcohol to get drunk on. Not only is it warm and fuzzy, but it makes you feel docile and full of good humour. If I lived in America, I'd hand the stuff out for free. Until someone shot me.

Mon 31st - New Year's Eve

This was one of my least favourite days as a child. Mainly because Christmas Eve is precisely one week before and you can freely use the phrase, 'This time last week'. New Year's Eve had nothing going for it if you were a kid. No presents the next morning. No special food. Just a bunch of drunken adults and even less festive television.

Went to such a fun party with colleagues from my old teaching job. I was nervous before going. I always am. I get edgy before any night out, as though I'm an understudy about to take the lead in a West End musical. What usually happens, and what happened tonight, is that I relax as soon as I arrive and wonder why I was ever concerned. House parties are the best thing about being alive. It's like a pub but with free drinks and fewer drongos. Arrived home at about two am, a year later than when I'd left.

JANUARY

Mon 1st - New Year's Day

On the seafront they had a 'New Year's Day Dip', where hundreds of people run into the North Sea and kick their new year off with hypothermia. It's something to do with charity, although I've never heard mention of which particular one. I walked down - queasy and uneasy - to watch. The air was icy. The streets were crowded all the way to the beach. I couldn't get a good view, just about making out the masses on the sands below. What I could see, however, was that the masses were already wet and calling it a day. I'd missed it.

Saw a lovely documentary about the Mamas & Papas. They've always interested me. They were only together for two or three years. The tall guitar player, John Phillips, was their creative force (he also wrote 'San Francisco' for Scott McKenzie, a contender for my favourite song of all time). The documentary was one of those 60-minute US productions made in the mid-00s that loiter in the bowels of the Sky planner. US music documentaries always focus on the positives; in this case, the songs and the performances. Later, I read about the band online and discovered the multiple tragedies and scandals in the group. The documentary only gave them passing mention. If the band were British and the documentary likewise, the whole thing would have been about the traumas.

(Just to show that my blood is Anglo Saxon, the tragedies and scandals are as follows: gorgeous Michelle Phillips was married to guitarist John Phillips but had an affair with the other bloke; John Phillips spent the majority of his adult life, which ended in 1992, addicted to narcotics; 'Mama Cass' died in 1974, aged 32, of a heart attack in London, in the same room that Keith Moon would die, also aged 32, four years later. I'd believed the urban myth that she'd choked to death on a ham sandwich.)

Put my new wall calendars up. Before I did, I flicked through last year's. Funny how you can see a calendar every day for a whole month yet have almost no memory of it ever being up. This time next year I'll do the same with these new pictures.

Weds 2nd -

Christmas is over as far as the telly is concerned. The daytime schedules are no different to how they'd be in the middle of May, with nearly every programme on BBC One, from 9am to 5pm, being about antiques or houses, or crimes involving either. My cupboards and fridge are looking more mid-May, too. The sweets and pies and all seasonal things are withering away.

Went to Cromer for the sake of going outside. Made the mistake of going into an electrical store to look at soundbars (I don't need one; yet I want one). Was approached by a member of staff who I had to humour as he played me every soundbar in the store. My ears have never been any good at deducing the difference in quality between sound systems. I had to nod along as he played terrible music to me from his phone (connected to the soundbar by bluetooth). I followed his lead at every turn:

'As you can tell,' he said, 'the difference a'tween those two dunt bear thinking about'.

'Yeah,' I nodded.

My only other comment, and I used it aplenty, was 'It sounds a bit tinny'. Oh, how that phrase has gotten me out of some awkward conversations with techies.

After walking around the town and admiring its curious beauty, I went into a little bookshop, where I felt altogether more at home. You wouldn't find me short of opinion in a place like that. It is one of those cutesy, angular shops that you have to take a step down to enter. Their stock is always in pristine condition and they have a quick turnover. I bought books about Buddhism, status anxiety, Edwardian childhood and American comedians. No retail experience can compete with the thrills of the secondhand bookshop, the high street's pluckiest survivor.

Thurs 3rd -

Some children go back to school today. It's the third of bloody January. So early. And why bother going back on a Thursday? They should knock a week off the summer holidays and stick it on the end of Christmas. Nothing brings home the end of the season like an early return to school. Some of the children, if their parents are traditionalists like myself, will be coming home to the tree still being up. My sister told me that her daughter cried this morning when told the tree would be gone when she came home. The tree coming down is to a child what a hangover is to an adolescent: the first taste of the aftershock of over-celebrating. I'm now thinking about my own return to work. A holiday that once appeared endless is indeed coming to an end. This is why we need to soak in the season while it's upon us.

Naturally, with the festivities all but over, there's talk of snow.

Fri 4th -

Spent much of the day writing about 'Home Alone'. I've still got to do pieces on 'Narnia', 'Only Fools' and 'The Simpsons'. And that's without finishing my alphabet of Christmas. I don't know how people get writer's block. I can't bloody stop. The 'Home Alone' piece is twice as long as I intended it to be and would be four times longer if I could get away with it. This book was supposed to be 45,000 words. It's already at 65,000. How I wish this was my day job. Writing. Making enough money to survive. On my visit to the secondhand bookshop the other day, I stared at all the spines in envy. So many books published and I have to resort to publishing them myself. God, to have something fully in the public domain. Next year my novel will be released. I wonder how it will go down. Silently, I expect. What a treat if it took off and kept me sufficiently in the black to make more. Maybe this book I'm writing now will be my cash cow. My very own festive one hit wonder, pumping my bank account with royalties each December.

Lovely line from Billy Connolly in his BBC show tonight. 'It's the ultimate talent,' he said, standing in a bookshop, 'to be able to jot that down and make people laugh.'

Sat 5th - Twelfth Night

Bit of a discrepancy over this. Some people class the 5th as the day to take the decorations down, others opt for the 6th. The 6th is officially Epiphany: the day when the Magi visited Jesus and gave him gifts. But today is the twelfth day of Christmas - and it's bad luck not to take the decorations down by midnight. So, mine came down. It is undoubtedly the year's ugliest errand. All those exciting bags and boxes loaded with festive smells are now being filled rather than emptied, tucked away rather than brought out. As always, I left something out by accident: a row of Christmas cards that I'd got so used to seeing I assumed they'd always been there.

And so, the diary is over. I wonder if you are reading this as Christmas ends or just as it is beginning - or perhaps in the middle of summer. I hadn't foreseen that, by doing this diary, instead of ramping up the excitement, it would end with Christmas being over, with everything going back into the shed. But then I think back to my first entry, back in hot, sticky August; today's wintry date seemed improbable then. And yet it has rolled around and shall do again next year. And every year. There's a line in 'Toy Story 3' where Woody says that going into the attic won't be all that bad because he'll be with 'Those guys from the Christmas decorations box! They're fun, right?' I love it because we never see these characters but, with that one line of dialogue, we can imagine them, all bright and happy. That's how I feel about Christmas. That it's always waiting for you. Joy in a box, hidden in a darkened corner, waiting to be opened.

You can't force yourself to enjoy something. In fact, when you try, it usually has the opposite effect. However, if I could leave one thought in your mind it would be this: be happy every time you get your box of decorations out.

You may be reading this just as a whole new decade approaches, or, has just begun. The twenties. From now on, when people talk about 'the 20s', they'll have to clarify which 20s they mean. Personally, I'm just happy to move into a decade which doesn't have a silly name (unlike 'the noughties' and the even more stupid 'twenty-tens'.)

On one of this season's many Morecambe & Wise documentaries, Eric Morecambe's son recalled how his father, when asked what he'd do differently with his life, had replied, 'I'd do it all over again - only quicker'.

If that's not a call to action for the roaring twenties, my friends, what is?

Appendix

Despite this book's length, I've still managed to leave several thousand Christmas stones unturned. It couldn't be helped. Where I would most liked to have gone into further detail is with songs and TV/films. I could realistically only cover a few, so, for posterity's sake, here are some more favourites.

Songs:

All Alone On Christmas - Darlene Love
And Anyway It's Christmas - !!!
Christmas (Baby, Please Come Home) - Darlene Love
Christmastime Is Here - Vince Guaraldi Trio
The Christmas Song - The Raveonettes
The Christmas Waltz - She & Him
Donna & Blitzen - Badly Drawn Boy
Do You Hear What I Hear? - The Polyphonic Spree
Feliz Navidad - Jose Feliciano
Home Alone, Too - The Staves
Home For Christmas - Kate Bush
It's Clichéd To Be Cynical At Christmas - Half Man Half Biscuit
Jing-a-ling, Jing-a-ling - The Andrews Sisters
Jingle Bell Rock - The Ventures
Just Like Christmas - Low
Little Saint Nick - The Beach Boys
Merry Christmas, Mr Lawrence - Ryuichi Sakamoto
Must Be Santa - Bob Dylan
New Year's Eve - Tom Waits

One More Sleep - Leona Lewis
Ring Out, Solstice Bells - Jethro Tull
River - Joni Mitchell
Rudolph The Red-Nosed Reindeer - Destiny's Child
Santa Bring My Baby Back (To Me) - Elvis Presley
Santa Claus Is Coming To Town - Justin Bieber
Santa's Coming For Us - Sia
That Was The Worst Christmas Ever! - Sufjan Stevens
A Winter's Tale - Queen
Whispering Grass - The Ink Spots
White Christmas - The Drifters

TV:

Blue Peter

Bob's Burgers, *Christmas In The Car* (2013) & *Father Of The Bob* (2014)

Bottom, *Holy* (1992)

The Blackadder *Christmas Carol* (1988)

The Box Of Delights (1984)

Carols From Kings

A Charlie Brown Christmas (1965)

Community, *Comparative Religion* (2009), *Abed's Uncontrollable Christmas* (2010)

Darling Buds Of May, *Christmas Is Coming* (1991)

Father Ted, *A Christmassy Ted* (1996)

Friends, *The One With Phoebe's Dad* (1995)

A Ghost For Christmas (BBC 1968 - 1978)

The Honeymooners, *'Twas The Night Before Christmas* (1955)

Inside No. 9, *The 12 Days Of Christine* (2015) & *The Devil Of Christmas* (2016)

The Office, *Christmas Special* (2003)

Porridge, *No Way Out* (1975)

Rising Damp, *For The Man Who Has Everything* (1975)

The Royle Family, *Christmas With* (1999)

Seinfeld, *The Pick* (1992)

The Sopranos, *To Save Us From All Satan's Power* (2001)

Til Death Us Do Part, *Peace & Goodwill* (1966)

Tom & Jerry, *The Night Before Christmas* (1941)

Top Of The Pops 2

The Twilight Zone - *The Night Of The Meek* (1960)

The Vicar Of Dibley - *The Christmas Lunch Incident* (1996)

Walt Disney Presents *Pluto's Christmas Tree* (1952)

World Championship Darts

Films:

Arthur Christmas (2011)

Christmas Under Fire (1941)

Elf (2003)

The Holly & The Ivy (1952)

Home Alone 2 (1992)

If Winter Comes - It Has! (1923)

Meet Me In St Louis (1944)

Miracle On 34th Street (1947)

National Lampoon's Christmas Vacation (1989)

Paddington (2014) & 2 (2017)
Planes, Trains & Automobiles (1987)
Santa Claus: The Movie (1984)
Scrooge (1951)
Scrooged (1988)

Oh, dear. I could prattle on at length about everything here. I might need to write another one of these books someday.

Acknowledgements

So many thanks to all of my regular readers and followers, to those of you who share my blogs and buy my books and are generally very helpful and kind. Particular thanks to Kate Ross, who puts in such a hefty amount of work reading my proofs that, in a more just society, would have her own statue. Gratitude *in excelsis*, also, to Sarah Ann Corlett for her excellent work on the cover. This one may be our finest hour.

That's all from me for now. There's nothing more to say than to steal yet another Greg Lake's lyric and wish you a hopeful Christmas and a brave new year.

Printed in Poland
by Amazon Fulfillment
Poland Sp. z o.o., Wrocław